HTML5 Graphing and Data Visualization Cookbook

Learn how to create interactive HTML5 charts and graphs with canvas, JavaScript, and open source tools

Ben Fhala

BIRMINGHAM - MUMBAI

HTML5 Graphing and Data Visualization Cookbook

First published: November 2012

Production Reference: 1161112

Published by Packt Publishing Ltd.
Livery Place
35 Livery Street
Birmingham B3 2PB, UK.

ISBN 978-1-84969-370-7

www.packtpub.com

Cover Image by Ben Fhala (anx007@gmail.com)

Credits

Author
Ben Fhala

Reviewer
Chris Valleskey

Acquisition Editor
Joanna Finchen

Lead Technical Editor
Kedar Bhat

Technical Editors
Prasad Dalvi
Joyslita D'souza
Ankita Meshram

Copy Editors
Brandt D'Mello
Insiya Morbiwala
Aditya Nair
Alfida Paiva
Laxmi Subramanian

Project Coordinator
Michelle Quadros

Proofreader
Chris Smith

Indexer
Hemangini Bari

Graphics
Valentina Dsilva

Production Coordinator
Nilesh R. Mohite

Cover Work
Nilesh R. Mohite

About the Author

Ben Fhala discovered his passion for data visualization six years ago while he was working at Parsons in New York, in their data visualization department PIIM. He is the owner of the online video training school, 02geek.com, and an Adobe ACP. He enjoys spending most of his time learning and teaching, and has a love for visual programming and visualization in general.

Ben has had the honor of developing applications for US Congress members, Prime Ministers, and Presidents around the world. He has built many interactive experiences for companies such as Target, AT&T, Crayola, Marriott, Neutrogena, and Nokia. He has technically directed many award-winning projects and has been a part of teams that have won three Agency of the Year awards.

I want to thank my cats for supporting me mentally while I was closed down and avoiding the world as I was trying to come up with good ideas for the book. I can't thank my editors Joanna Finchen and Kedar Bhat enough for the insight and help I got from them. For their kindness, support, and mainly their patience with me when I was struggling to fit my ideas into the recipe format.

A very big thanks to my technical reviewer, Chris Valleskey, for the detailed insights and suggestions that made this book better and shaped this book to be a really great one.

Thanks to Oren Ofer, which helped inspire the last recipe. To my students, co-workers, and friends at 02geek.com. Mom, for helping me through the creation of my first book. Nature and Earth for giving me a great place to be in, and the ocean for the great view throughout the writing of this book. Thanks to God for always opening up new doors to me in the most unexpected ways.

And last but definitely not the least, thanks for buying / renting / lending / reading this book.

About the Reviewer

Chris Valleskey is a young and creative thinker who currently lives in Chicago, Illinois. He started freelancing at the age of 17 and continued this role throughout college until graduating in 2011 with a Bachelor of Arts in Graphic Design and Philosophy. Although he has a normal job in the city, he enjoys spending time with his close friends as a part owner in their co-owned company. In his free time he enjoys playing Halo, drinking Mountain Dew, and hanging out with his awesome wife.

I would like to thank my wife Krista for putting up with me, and my friends and family for supporting and encouraging me in everything I do.

www.PacktPub.com

Support files, eBooks, discount offers and more

You might want to visit www.PacktPub.com for support files and downloads related to your book.

Did you know that Packt offers eBook versions of every book published, with PDF and ePub files available? You can upgrade to the eBook version at www.PacktPub.com and as a print book customer, you are entitled to a discount on the eBook copy. Get in touch with us at service@packtpub.com for more details.

At www.PacktPub.com, you can also read a collection of free technical articles, sign up for a range of free newsletters and receive exclusive discounts and offers on Packt books and eBooks.

http://PacktLib.PacktPub.com

Do you need instant solutions to your IT questions? PacktLib is Packt's online digital book library. Here, you can access, read and search across Packt's entire library of books.

Why Subscribe?

- Fully searchable across every book published by Packt
- Copy and paste, print and bookmark content
- On demand and accessible via web browser

Free Access for Packt account holders

If you have an account with Packt at www.PacktPub.com, you can use this to access PacktLib today and view nine entirely free books. Simply use your login credentials for immediate access.

Table of Contents

Preface

Today, the Web and the world are increasingly being defined by data. With the data revolution of the Internet in the early nineties and until today, more and more data has been exposed and aggregated, from government agencies, public sector information, financial information, digital media and news, and social media to private sector information, user information, and so on. With the overload of data on the Web it's easy to overlook information, as it's much harder to read and analyze in data format. That's where we come in. Our goal in this book is to open up the door to you to data visualization. With step-by-step guides that will take you from the basic creation of visual charts all the way through to complex geographical location information driven by Google Maps and Google Docs (Drive).

HTML5 and JavaScript are leading the new paths for data visualization and are moving us away from traditional client-side graph creation in Adobe Flash or server-side generated images. With the maturing of browsers, they are becoming more capable and solid than ever before. This is a perfect time to start transitioning the creation of graphs to HTML/JavaScript. But where do you start, and what is the best way to create the specific graph/map your project needs?

With that said, our goal in this book is to run through, showcase, and teach all the critical skills needed in the HTML5/JavaScript age of data visualization. Our goal is to help you make the right choice when you need to build a custom graphic or graph/chart and to help you choose the right way between creating it on your own or using third-party, small/large tools to create the graphic your task needs.

Although this is a cookbook, I've painstakingly organized it topic by topic in a very linear way, making it a great read from start to end. As such, I personally recommend that you sit back and actually read it from start to finish, and if you do so, you will learn in the process everything you ever needed to know about the two-dimensional Canvas API, how to create shapes, interaction, and various graphs/charts, and how to create them from scratch in HTML5 Canvas. You will learn how to work with and modify third-party tools, working with the Google Visualization API, Google Maps, and Google Docs. Woven throughout the book are various data formats from basic strings, external files, XML, and Google Docs to Twitter search results. As such, you will get an extra practice in loading, modifying, and working with data in JavaScript.

By the end of this book, you will have a strong working foundation in data visualization, graphing, data strategy, and HTML5 Canvas.

What this book covers

Chapter 1, Drawing Shapes in Canvas, introduces you to working with canvas. We will spend the majority of our time working with canvas when creating our charts. In this chapter, we will focus on getting to know how canvas works and how to create custom shapes with the two-dimensional canvas API.

Chapter 2, Advanced Drawing in Canvas, continues where we left off in *Chapter 1* as we master our skills in canvas by adding to our tool belt various functions. We will be working with curves, images, text, and even pixel manipulation.

Chapter 3, Creating Cartesian-based Graphs, presents our first cluster of charts under the microscope, Cartesian-based graphs. Altogether this graph style is relatively simple; it opens the door to amazingly creative ways of exploring data. In this chapter, we will lay down the foundations to building charts, and with them, will continue and expand our overall canvas knowledge.

Chapter 4, Let's Curve Things Up, leverages the capability of creating non-linear charts to represent multidimensional data. In this chapter we will create Bubble, Pie, Doughnut, Radar, and Tree charts.

Chapter 5, Getting Out of the Box, progresses into more out-of-the-box, less commonly used charts and revisits some of our old charts to incorporate into them dynamic data or change their layout. In this chapter, we will create a funnel chart, add interactivity to our charts, create a recursive tree chart, add user interaction, and finish up with creating an interactive click meter.

Chapter 6, Bringing Static Things to Life, introduces JavaScript object oriented programming, creating from scratch an animation library, adding multiple layers of canvas, and finishing up with creating a legend that is aware of its surrounding. This chapter will break us into a few new habits by first making everything dynamic followed by creating a more object-oriented program so it's easier for us to differentiate between tasks and reduce our code footprint.

Chapter 7, Depending on the Open Source Sphere, introduces you to the various libraries. The open source data visualization community is extremely rich and detailed with so many options and some really amazing libraries. Each library has its strong points and its disadvantages. Some are standalone code, while others depend on other platforms. Our goal in this chapter is both to showcase what we think are the best, most creative options online, and with it, to also learn the new skill of customizing third-party tools and expanding their features beyond their available documentation.

Chapter 8, Playing with Google Charts, explores the Google visualization API, task by task. We will look at the steps involved to create a chart and integrate it with the charting API. In the process, we will create new graphs and explore the core capabilities of this library.

Chapter 9, Using Google Maps, explores some of the features available on Google Maps to get us ready to work with mapping in general. Mapping on its own isn't data visualization, but after we establish our base understanding of how to work with maps, we will have a very stable background that will enable us to create many cutting-edge, cool projects integrating data and data visualization.

Chapter 10, Maps in Action, ties in more deeply to our topic of data visualization and mapping. One of the most popular ways to visualize data these days is by using maps. In this chapter, we will explore a few ideas on how to integrate data into maps using the Google Maps platform.

Appendix, Picking Your Graphics Technology, will explore other alternative options not covered in this book. The goal of this appendix is to set the environment up and enable you to have a better understanding of other graphing options. The appendix is not present in the book but is available as a free download at the following link:

`http://www.packtpub.com/sites/default/files/downloads/3707OT_Appendix_Final.pdf`

What you need for this book

You will need to have some basic background knowledge of HTML and JavaScript or a comparable programming language.

Who this book is for

This is not a beginner's book but is intended for JavaScript developers who want to expand their skills into graphing, canvas, object-oriented programming in practice, third-party modification, and overall data strategy and data visualization.

Conventions

In this book, you will find a number of styles of text that distinguish between different kinds of information. Here are some examples of these styles, and an explanation of their meaning.

Code words in text are shown as follows: "Set up our `grayStyle` Styling Object to be our default style:"

A block of code is set as follows:

```
var aGray =  [
    {
      stylers: [{saturation: -100}]
    }
  ];
```

When we wish to draw your attention to a particular part of a code block, the relevant lines or items are set in bold:

```
map.mapTypes.set('grayStyle', grayStyle);
map.setMapTypeId('grayStyle');
```

New terms and **important words** are shown in bold. Words that you see on the screen, in menus or dialog boxes for example, appear in the text like this: "Select the **Services** option from the left-hand side menu:"

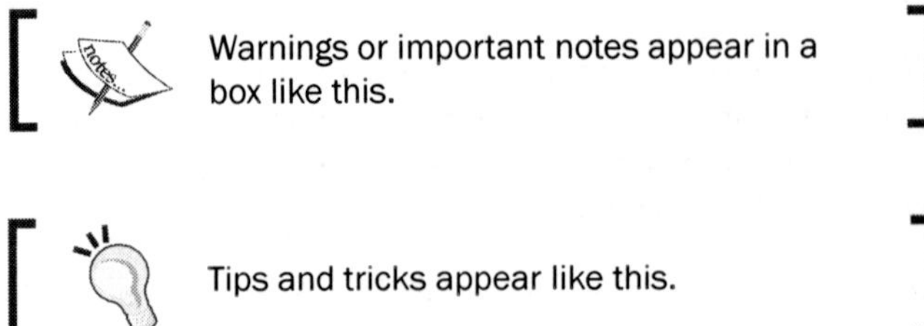

Warnings or important notes appear in a box like this.

Tips and tricks appear like this.

Reader feedback

Feedback from our readers is always welcome. Let us know what you think about this book—what you liked or may have disliked. Reader feedback is important for us to develop titles that you really get the most out of.

To send us general feedback, simply send an e-mail to `feedback@packtpub.com`, and mention the book title through the subject of your message.

If there is a topic that you have expertise in and you are interested in either writing or contributing to a book, see our author guide on `www.packtpub.com/authors`.

Customer support

Now that you are the proud owner of a Packt book, we have a number of things to help you to get the most from your purchase.

Downloading the example code

You can download the example code files for all Packt books you have purchased from your account at `http://www.packtpub.com`. If you purchased this book elsewhere, you can visit `http://www.packtpub.com/support` and register to have the files e-mailed directly to you.

The code files are also available at `http://02geek.com/books/html5-graphics-and-data-visualization-cookbook.html`.

Errata

Although we have taken every care to ensure the accuracy of our content, mistakes do happen. If you find a mistake in one of our books—maybe a mistake in the text or the code—we would be grateful if you would report this to us. By doing so, you can save other readers from frustration and help us improve subsequent versions of this book. If you find any errata, please report them by visiting `http://www.packtpub.com/support`, selecting your book, clicking on the **errata submission form** link, and entering the details of your errata. Once your errata are verified, your submission will be accepted and the errata will be uploaded to our website, or added to any list of existing errata, under the Errata section of that title.

Piracy

Piracy of copyright material on the Internet is an ongoing problem across all media. At Packt, we take the protection of our copyright and licenses very seriously. If you come across any illegal copies of our works, in any form, on the Internet, please provide us with the location address or website name immediately so that we can pursue a remedy.

Please contact us at `copyright@packtpub.com` with a link to the suspected pirated material.

We appreciate your help in protecting our authors, and our ability to bring you valuable content.

Questions

You can contact us at `questions@packtpub.com` if you are having a problem with any aspect of the book, and we will do our best to address it.

1
Drawing Shapes in Canvas

In this chapter we will cover:

- Graphics with 2D canvas
- Starting from basic shapes
- Layering rectangles to create the flag of Greece
- Creating shapes using paths
- Creating complex shapes
- Adding more vertices
- Overlapping shapes to create other shapes

Introduction

This chapter's main focus is to make a breakthrough into working in canvas. We will spend the majority of our time working with canvas when creating our charts.

In this chapter, we will master the basic shapes and styles of drawing with the canvas API. This chapter will be the graphic's backbone to the rest of the book, so if at any stage you feel you need a refresher you could come back to this chapter. Drawing lines can be... well not very thrilling. What better way to make it more dramatic than to integrate a theme into this chapter as a subtopic: creating flags!

Graphics with 2D canvas

Canvas is the primary and most thrilling addition to HTML. It's the buzz of the industry, so let's start there. We will revisit canvas again in the later chapters. In this recipe, we will learn how to draw dynamically using canvas, and create an array of colorful circles that will update once every second.

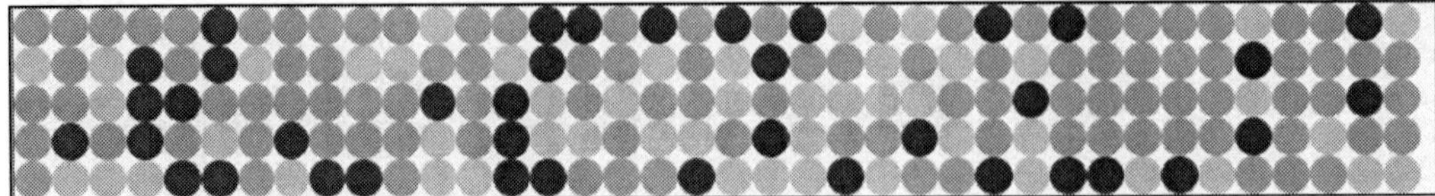

How to do it...

We will be creating two files (an HTML5 file and a JS file). Let's start by creating a new HTML5 document:

1. The first step is to create an empty HTML5 document:

```
<!DOCTYPE html>
<html>
  <head>
    <meta charset="utf-8" />
    <title>Canvas Example</title>
  </head>
  <body>
  </body>
</html>
```

> **Downloading the example code**
>
> You can download the example code files for all Packt books you have purchased from your account at `http://www.PacktPub.com`. If you purchased this book elsewhere, you can visit `http://www.PacktPub.com/support` and register to have the files e-mailed directly to you.
>
> The code files are also available at `http://02geek.com/books/html5-graphics-and-data-visualization-cookbook.html`.

2. Create a new canvas element. We give our canvas element an ID of `myCanvas`:

```
  <body>
<canvas id="myCanvas"> </canvas>
  </body>
```

3. Import the JavaScript file `01.01.canvas.js` into the HTML document (we will create this file in step 5):

```
<!DOCTYPE html>
<html>
  <head>
    <meta charset="utf-8" />
 <script src="01.01.canvas.js"></script>
    <title>Canvas Example</title>
  </head>
```

4. Add an `onLoad` listener and trigger the function `init` when the document loads:

```
<!DOCTYPE html>
<html>
  <head>
    <meta charset="utf-8" />
    <script src="01.01.canvas.js"></script>
    <title>Canvas Example</title>
  </head>
  <body onLoad="init();" style="margin:0px">
    <canvas id="myCanvas" />
  </body>
</html>
```

5. Create the `01.01.canvas.js` file.
6. In the JavaScript file, create the function `init` and call the function `updateCanvas` within it:

```
function init(){
  updateCanvas();
}
```

7. Create the function `updateCanvas`:

```
function  updateCanvas(){
  //rest of the code in the next steps will go in here
}
```

8. In the `updateCanvas` function (for the rest of the steps all the code will be added in this function) create two variables that will store your desired width and height. In our case we will grab the width of our window:

```
function  updateCanvas(){
  var width = window.innerWidth;
  var height = 100;
...
```

9. Access the canvas layer in the HTML document and change its width and height:

```
var myCanvas = document.getElementById("myCanvas");
    myCanvas.width = width;
    myCanvas.height = height;
```

10. Get the 2D context of the canvas:

```
var context = myCanvas.getContext("2d");
```

11. Create a rectangle to fill the full visible area of the canvas:

```
context.fillStyle = "#FCEAB8";
context.fillRect(0,0,width,height);
```

12. Let's create a few helper variables to help us establish the color, size, and count of elements to be drawn:

```
var circleSize=10;
var gaps= circleSize+10;
var widthCount = parseInt(width/gaps);
var heightCount = parseInt(height/gaps);
var aColors=["#43A9D1","#EFA63B","#EF7625","#5E4130"];
var aColorsLength = aColors.length;
```

13. Create a nested loop and create a grid of circles in random colors:

```
for(var x=0; x<widthCount;x++){
  for(var y=0; y<heightCount;y++){
    context.fillStyle = aColors[parseInt
      (Math.random()*aColorsLength)];
    context.beginPath();
    context.arc(circleSize+gaps*x,circleSize+ gaps*y,
      circleSize, 0, Math.PI*2, true);
    context.closePath();
    context.fill();
  }
}
}
```

Woah! That was a lot of steps! If you followed all the steps, you will find a lot of circles in your browser when you run the application.

How it works...

Before we jump right into the JavaScript portion of this application, we need to trigger the `onLoad` event to call our `init` function. We do that by adding the `onLoad` property into our HTML body tag:

```
<body onLoad="init();">
```

Let's break down the JavaScript portion and understand the reason behind doing this. The first step is to create the `init` function:

```
function init(){
  updateCanvas();
}
```

Our `init` function immediately calls the `updateCanvas` function. This is done so that later we can refresh and call `updateCanvas` again.

In the `updateCanvas` function, we start by getting the current width of the browser and set a hardcoded value for the height of our drawing area:

```
var width = window.innerWidth;
var height = 100;
```

Our next step is to get our canvas using its ID, and then set its new width and height based on the previous variables:

```
var myCanvas = document.getElementById("myCanvas");
    myCanvas.width = width;
    myCanvas.height = height;
```

It's time for us to start drawing. To do that, we need to ask our canvas to return its context. There are a few types of contexts such as 2D and 3D. In our case we will focus on the 2D context as follows:

```
var context = myCanvas.getContext("2d");
```

Now that we have the context, we have all that we need to start exploring and manipulating our canvas. In the next few steps, we define the canvas background color by setting the `fillStyle` color using a hex value and by drawing a rectangle that would fit within the entire area of our canvas:

```
var context = myCanvas.getContext("2d");
    context.fillStyle = "#FCEAB8";
    context.fillRect(0,0,width,height);
```

The `fillRect` method takes four parameters. The first two are the (x,y) locations of the rectangle, in our case we wanted to start from (0,0), and the following parameters are the width and height of our new rectangle.

Let's draw our circles. To do so we will need to define the radius of our circle and the space between circles. Let's not space out the circles at all, and create circles with a radius of 10 px.

```
var rad=10;
var gaps= rad*2;
```

The first line assigns the radius for our circles, while the second line captures the gap between the centres of each circle we create, or in our case the diameter of our circle. By setting it up as two times the radius we space out our circles exactly one after the other.

```
var widthCount = parseInt(width/gaps);
var heightCount = parseInt(height/gaps);
var aColors=["#43A9D1","#EFA63B","#EF7625","#5E4130"];
var aColorsLength = aColors.length;
```

Using our new `gaps` variable, we discover how many circles we can create in the width and height of our canvas component. We create an array that stores a few color options for our circles and set a variable `aColorsLength` as the length of `aColors`. We do this to cut down the processing time, as variables are easier to fetch than properties as we are about to call this element many times in our `for` loop:

```
for(var x=0; x<widthCount;x++){
  for(var y=0; y<heightCount;y++){
    context.fillStyle = aColors[parseInt
      (Math.random()*aColorsLength)];
    context.beginPath();
    context.arc(rad+gaps*x,rad+ gaps*y, rad, 0, Math.PI*2, true);
    context.closePath();
    context.fill();
  }
}
```

Our nested `for` loops enable us to create our circles to the width and height of our canvas. The first `for` loop focuses on upgrading the width value while the second `for` loop is in charge of running through every column.

```
context.fillStyle =
aColors[parseInt(Math.random()*aColorsLength)];
```

Using `Math.random`, we randomly select a color from `aColors` to be used as the color of our new circle.

```
context.beginPath();
context.arc(rad+gaps*x,rad+ gaps*y, rad, 0, Math.PI*2, true);
context.closePath();
```

The first and last lines in the previous block of code declare the creation of a new shape. The `beginPath` method defines the start of the shape and the `closePath` method defines the end of it, while `context.arc` creates the actual circle. The `arc` property takes the following format of values:

```
context.arc(x,y,radius,startPoint,endPoint, isCounterClock);
```

The `x` and `y` properties define the center point of the arc (in our case a full circle). In our `for` loops we need to add a buffer of an extra radius to push our content into the screen. We need to do this as only one fourth of our first circle would be visible if we didn't push it to the left and to the bottom by an extra radius.

```
context.fill();
```

Last but not least, we need to call the `fill()` method to fill our newly-created shape with its color.

There's more...

Let's make our element refresh once a second; to do that all we need to do is add two more lines. The first one will trigger a new call to the `updateCanvas` function once every second using `setInterval`.

```
function init(){
  setInterval(updateCanvas,1000);
  updateCanvas();
}
```

If you refresh your browser you will find that our sample is working. If you try really hard to find issues with it you will not, but we have a problem with it. It's not a major problem but a great opportunity for us to learn about another useful functionality of the canvas. At any stage we can clear the canvas or parts of it. Instead of drawing on top of the current canvas, let's clear it before we redraw. In the `updateCanvas` function, we will add the following highlighted code:

```
var context = myCanvas.getContext("2d");
context.clearRect(0,0,width,height);
```

As soon as we get the context we can clear the data that was already present by using the `clearRect` method.

See also

- The *Starting from basic shapes* recipe

Starting from basic shapes

At this stage you know how to create a new canvas area and even create a few basic shapes. Let's expand our skill and start creating flags.

Getting ready

Well, we won't start from the most basic flag as that would just be a green rectangle. If you wanted to learn how to create a green flag you wouldn't need me, so let's move up to a tad more complex flag.

If you followed the *Graphics with 2D canvas* recipe you already know how to do it. This one is dedicated to our Palauan readers and to the perfect arc (also known as circle).

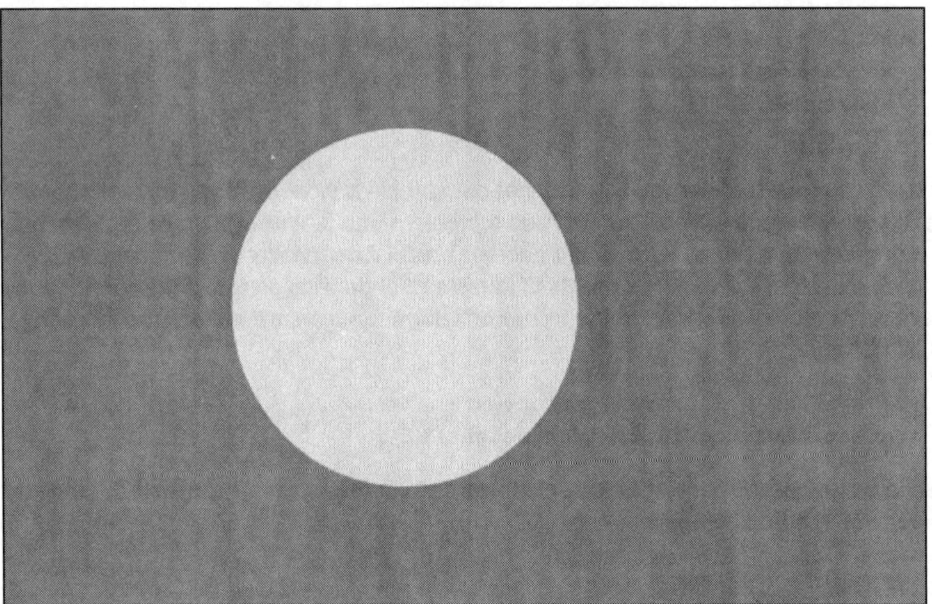

In this recipe we will ignore the HTML part, so if you need a refresher on how to create a canvas with an ID, please go back to the first recipe in this chapter and set up your HTML document. Don't forget to create the canvas with the right ID. You could also download our sample HTML files.

How to do it...

Add the following code block:

```
var cnvPalau = document.getElementById("palau");
  var wid = cnvPalau.width;
  var hei = cnvPalau.height;

  var context = cnvPalau.getContext("2d");
      context.fillStyle = "#4AADD6";
      context.fillRect(0,0,wid,hei);

      context.fillStyle = "#FFDE00";
      context.arc(wid/2.3, hei/2, 40, 0, 2 * Math.PI, false);
      context.fill();
```

That's it, you've just created a perfect arc, and with it your first flag that has a shape within it.

How it works...

A big chunk of this code should look very familiar at this stage. So I'll focus on the new lines compared to the ones used in the first recipe in this chapter.

```
var wid = cnvPalau.width;
var hei = cnvPalau.height;
```

In these lines, we extract the width and height of our canvas. We have two goals here: to shorten our lines of code and to reduce the number of times we make an API call when not needed. As we are using it more than one time, we first fetch the values and store them in `wid` and `hei`.

Now that we know our canvas width and height, it's time for us to draw our circle. Before we start drawing, we will call the `fillStyle` method to define a background color to be used in the canvas, and then we will create the arc followed by triggering the `fill` method when complete.

```
context.fillStyle = "#FFDE00";
context.arc(wid/2.3, hei/2, 40, 0, 2 * Math.PI, false);
context.fill();
```

We then create our first perfect circle using the `arc` method. It's important to note that we can change the colors at any point, such as in this case, where we change our color just before we create a new circle.

Let's take a deeper look at how the `arc` method works. We start by defining the center of our circle with the `x` and `y` positions. The canvas tag follows the standard Cartesian coordinates: (0, 0) is at the top-left (`x` grows to the right and `y` grows towards the bottom).

```
context.arc(x, y, radius, startingAngle, endingAngle, ccw);
```

In our example, we decided to position the circle slightly to the left of the center by dividing the width of the canvas by `2.3`, and we positioned the `y` in the exact center of the canvas. The next parameter is the radius of our circle, It is followed by two parameters that define the starting and ending position of our stroke. As we want to create a full circle we start from `0` and end at two times `Math.PI`, a complete circle (`Math.PI` is equivalent to 180 degrees). The last parameter is the direction of our arc. In our case as we are creating a full circle, it doesn't matter what we set here (ccw = counterclockwise).

```
context.fill();
```

Last but not least, we call the `fill` function to fill and color the shape we created earlier. Contrary to the `fillRect` function that both creates and fills the shape, the `arc` method doesn't. The `arc` method only defines the bounds of a shape to be filled. You can use this method (and others) to create more complex shapes before actually drawing them onto the stage. We will explore this more deeply in the following recipes of this chapter.

Layering rectangles to create the flag of Greece

We learned as we created the flag for Palau that when we create a circle using the `arc` method, we have to trigger a request separately to fill the shape. This is true for all shapes that we create from scratch, and it is true for creating lines as well. Let's move to a slightly more complex flag: the flag of Greece.

Getting ready

As in the previous recipe, we will be skipping the HTML part and will jump right into the JavaScript portion of drawing in the canvas. For a detailed explanation of the steps involved in the creation of the canvas element, please refer to the first recipe of this chapter.

Before you start coding, look at the flag closely and try to come up with an attack plan on the steps you would need to perform to create this flag.

How to do it...

If we look at the flag, it's easy to figure out how to plan this out. There are many ways to do this but the following is our attempt:

1. We will first start our app and create a blank blue canvas:

   ```
   var canvas = document.getElementById("greece");
   var wid = canvas.width;
   var hei = canvas.height;


   var context = canvas.getContext("2d");
       context.fillStyle = "#000080";
       context.fillRect(0,0,wid,hei);
   ```

2. If you take a look at the previous figure, there are four white strips and five blue strips that will be part of the background. Let's divide the total height of our canvas by `9`, so we can find out the right size for our lines:

   ```
   var lineHeight = hei/9;
   ```

3. So far we created shapes using built-in tools, such as `arc` and `fillRect`. Now we are going to draw our lines manually, and to do so we will set the `lineWidth` and `strokeStyle` values, so we can draw lines on the canvas:

   ```
   context.lineWidth = lineHeight;
   context.strokeStyle = "#ffffff";
   ```

4. Now, let's loop through and create four times a line that goes from the right-hand side to the left-hand side, as follows:

   ```
   var offset = lineHeight/2;
   for(var i=1; i<8; i+=2){
     context.moveTo(0,i*lineHeight + offset);
     context.lineTo(wid,i*lineHeight+offset);

   }
   ```

That's it, we got it. Reload your HTML page and you will find the flag of Greece in all its glory. Well not in all its glory yet, but just about enough to guess it's the flag of Greece. Before we move on let's look deeper into how this works.

How it works...

Notice the addition of an offset. This is done because `lineWidth` grows in both directions from the actual point in the center of the line. In other words, a line with the width of 20 pixels that is drawn from (0, 0) to (0, height) would only have 10 pixels visible as the range of the thickness of the line would be between (-10 to 10). As such, we need to take into account that our first line needs to be pushed down by half its width so that it's in the right location.

The `moveTo` function takes in two parameters `moveTo(x,y)`. The `lineTo` function also takes two parameters. I believe you must have guessed the difference between them. One will shift the virtual point without drawing anything while the other will create a line between the points.

There's more...

If you run your HTML file, you will find that our lines were not revealed. Don't worry, you didn't make any mistake (At least, that's what I think ;)). For the lines to become visible, we need to tell the browser that we are ready, just like we called the `fill()` method when we used `arc`. In this case, as we are creating lines we will call the `stroke()` method right after we are done defining our lines, as follows:

```
var offset = lineHeight/2;
  for(var i=1; i<8; i+=2){
    context.moveTo(0,i*lineHeight + offset);
    context.lineTo(wid,i*lineHeight+offset);

  }
  context.stroke();
```

If you refresh the screen now you will see we are getting much closer. It's time for us to add that rectangle on the top-left area of the screen. To do that, we will reuse our `lineHeight` variable. The size of our rectangle is five times the length of `lineHeight`:

```
context.fillRect(0,0,lineHeight*5,lineHeight*5);
```

It is now time to create the cross in the flag:

```
context.moveTo(0, lineHeight*2.5);
context.lineTo(lineHeight*5,lineHeight*2.5);
context.moveTo(lineHeight*2.5,0);
context.lineTo(lineHeight*2.5,lineHeight*5+1);
context.stroke();
```

If you run the application now you will be really disappointed. We did exactly what we learned previously but it's not working as expected.

The lines are all mixed up! OK fear not, it means it's time for us to learn something new.

BeginPath method and closePath method

Our flag didn't pan out that well because it got confused by all the lines we created earlier. To avoid this, we should tell the canvas when we are starting a new drawing and when we are ending it. To do so we can call the `beginPath` and `closePath` methods to let the canvas know that we are done with something or are starting with something new. In our case by adding the method `beginPath` we can fix our flag issue.

```
context.fillRect(0,0,lineHeight*5,lineHeight*5);
context.beginPath();
context.moveTo(0, lineHeight*2.5);
context.lineTo(lineHeight*5,lineHeight*2.5);
context.moveTo(lineHeight*2.5,0);
context.lineTo(lineHeight*2.5,lineHeight*5+1);
context.stroke();
```

Congratulations! You just created your first two flags, and in the process learned a lot about how the canvas API works. This is enough to be able to create 53 country flags out of the 196 flags out there. That's a great start already; 25 percent of the world is in your hands.

The most complex flag you should be able to do right now is the flag of the United Kingdom. If you feel like exploring, give it a go. If you're really proud of it drop me a line at `ben@02geek.com`, I would love to see it.

Creating shapes using paths

We ended the last recipe learning how to create one fourth of the flags of the world, but that can't be the end of it, can it? This recipe will be dedicated to using paths to create more complex shapes. We will start by creating a triangle and progress from there to more complicated shapes.

Getting ready

Let's start from the simplest shape that isn't included in the basic shapes library: a triangle. So if you're ready let's get started...

How to do it...

Let's start with creating our first shape, a triangle:

```
context.fillStyle = color;
context.beginPath();
context.moveTo(x1,y1);
context.lineTo(x2,y2);
context.lineTo(x3,y3);
context.lineTo(x1,y1);
context.closePath();
context.fill();
```

The code here with points `x1,y1` through `x3,y3` is pseudocode. You would need to pick your own points to create a triangle.

How it works...

Most of the elements here aren't new. The most important change here is that we are creating the shape from scratch using the elements we worked with before. When we create a shape we always start by declaring it using the `beginPath()` method. We then create the shape and end the creation with the `closePath()` method. We will still not have anything visible on the screen until we decide what we want to do with the shape we created, such as show its fill or show its strokes. In this case as we are trying to create a triangle we will call the `fill` function.

Let's see this in action in a live flag sample. This time we will visit Mount Roraima in Guyana.

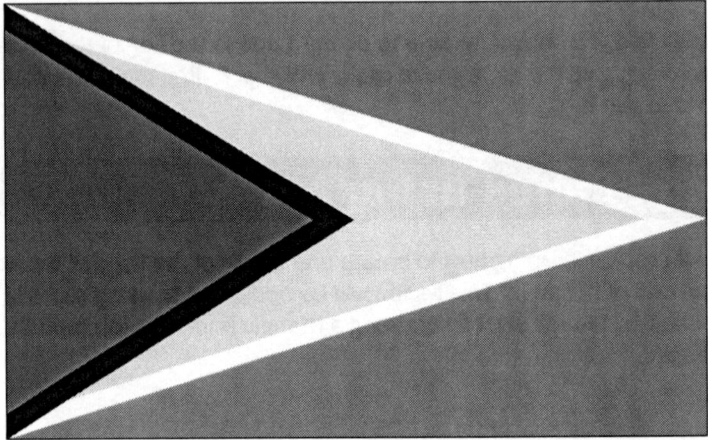

OK, so you get the idea of the triangle. Let's see this in action. I've extracted this code and put it into a function. To create this flag, we will need to create four triangles.

```
var canvas = document.getElementById("guyana");
var wid = canvas.width;
var hei = canvas.height;

var context = canvas.getContext("2d");
    context.fillStyle = "#009E49";
    context.fillRect(0,0,wid,hei);

fillTriangle(context,  0,0,
             wid,hei/2,
             0,hei, "#ffffff");
fillTriangle(context,0,10,
             wid-25,hei/2,
             0,hei-10, "#FCD116");
fillTriangle(context,0,0,
             wid/2,hei/2,
             0,hei, "#000000");
fillTriangle(context,0,10,
             wid/2-16,hei/2,
             0,hei-10, "#CE1126");

function fillTriangle(context,x1,y1,x2,y2,x3,y3,color){
  context.fillStyle = color;
  context.beginPath();
  context.moveTo(x1,y1);
  context.lineTo(x2,y2);
  context.lineTo(x3,y3);
  context.lineTo(x1,y1);
  context.closePath();
  context.fill();
}
```

By creating the `fillTriangle()` function we can now quickly and effectively create triangles just as we created rectangles. This function makes it a breeze to create a flag with such a rich numbers of triangles. Now, with the help of the `fillTriangle` method we can create any flag in the world that has triangles in it.

There's more...

Don't let triangles be your most complex shape, as you can create any number of pointed shapes. Let's create a more complex zigzag pattern. To do so, we will fly over to the Kingdom of Bahrain.

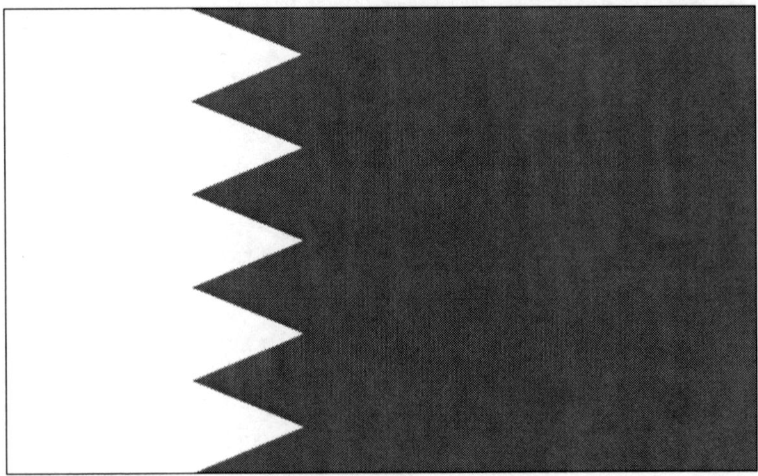

Try to locate the new logic before we break it down and explain it.

```
var canvas = document.getElementById("bahrain");
var wid = canvas.width;
var hei = canvas.height;

var context = canvas.getContext("2d");
    context.fillStyle = "#CE1126";
    context.fillRect(0,0,wid,hei);
var baseX = wid*.25;
    context.fillStyle = "#ffffff";
    context.beginPath();
    context.lineTo(baseX,0);

var zagHeight = hei/5;
for(var i=0; i<5; i++){
  context.lineTo(baseX +25 , (i+.5)*zagHeight);
  context.lineTo(baseX   , (i+1)*zagHeight);

}
context.lineTo(0,hei);
context.lineTo(0,0);
context.closePath();
context.fill();

addBoarder(context,wid,hei);
```

Let's break down this zigzag and understand what's going on here. After starting up with our normal setting up of a canvas element, we jump right into creating our shape. We start by drawing a red background, leaving us to create a shape that will have the white area. It's very much like a rectangle except that it has zigzags in it.

In this code, we start by creating a rectangle but our goal will be to change the highlighted code line with zigzags:

```
var baseX = wid*.25;
context.fillStyle = "#ffffff";
context.beginPath();
context.lineTo(baseX,0);
context.lineTo(wid*.25,hei);
context.lineTo(0,hei);
context.lineTo(0,0);
context.closePath();
context.fill();
```

In this code we set the fill color to white, we set our `beginPath` and then `lineTo` (starting at the point `(0,0)`, the default starting point) and create a rectangle that fills 25 percent of the width of the canvas. I've highlighted the horizontal line as this is the one we want to make zigzags with. By looking at the flag we can see that we are going to create five triangles going across the screen, so let's switch this line with a `for` loop:

```
...
context.lineTo(baseX,0);

var zagHeight = hei/5;
for(var i=0; i<5; i++){
  context.lineTo(baseX +25 , (i+.5)*zagHeight);
  context.lineTo(baseX   , (i+1)*zagHeight);

}

context.lineTo(0,hei);
  ...
```

So our first step before we can run through the loop is to decide how tall each triangle will be:

```
var zagHeight = hei/5;
```

We take the total height of the canvas and divide it by five to give us the height for each triangle.

We draw the zigzags in the `for` loop itself. To do so we need to use the following two lines of code in each round:

```
context.lineTo(baseX +25 , (i+.5)*zagHeight);
context.lineTo(baseX   , (i+1)*zagHeight);
```

In the first line we step away from the current position and expand the line out half way through the height of the triangle, and to the extreme point on the right; and then on the second line we return back to the starting `x` point and update our `y` to the starting point of the next line segment. By the way, the addition of `baseX +25` is totally arbitrary. I just played with it until it looked good, but if you want you could use ratios instead (that way if you expand the canvas it would still look good).

The most amazing part of all of this is just knowing how to create some zigzags, triangles, rectangles, and circles. You can create an even larger number of flags but we are not done yet. Our quest to know how to create all the flags of the world continues.

If you are new to drawing via code or feel you can use some extra practice, just look at the map of the world and challenge yourself to create flags based on the skills we built already.

Creating complex shapes

It's time to take everything we learned and integrate it into the most complex shape we have seen so far, the Star of David. This star is part of the flag of Israel (one of my favorite flags in the world ;)). We need to take a roundabout before we can create it by visiting the magical world of sine and cosine.

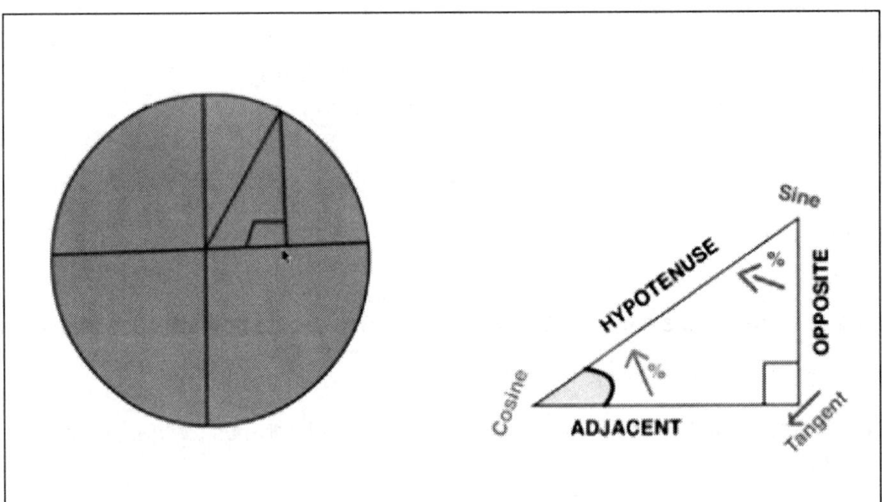

You got to love it, right? I know many people fear cosines and sines but actually they are really easy and fun to work with. Let's break them down here in a more programming-for-drawing type of way. The most basic idea is that you have a triangle that has a 90 degree angle. You have some information about this triangle, and that's all you need to be able to start working with sine and cosine. Once you know that you have a 90 degree angle and know the sine/cosine, you have all the information you need and with it you can discover any missing information. In our case we know all the angles and we know the length of the hypotenuse (it's our radius; take a look at the image with the circle to see it in action). In JavaScript, the methods `Math.cos()` and `Math.sin()` are both representing a circle with a radius of one located on the (0,0) point on the screen. If we input the angle we are looking for into the `sin` function, it would return the `x` value (in this case the length of the adjacent) and the `cos` function would return the length of the opposite, in our case the required value `y`.

I've made a nice video which goes deeper into the logic. You can check it out at `http://02geek.com/courses/video/58/467/Using-Cos-and-Sin-to-animate.html`.

Getting ready

The easiest way to understand how sine/cosine work is by a live example, and in our case we will use it to help us figure out how to create the Star of David in the flag of Israel. We will take a step back and learn how we figured out the points on the screen to create the shapes. Again we will be skipping the creation of the HTML file and will go right into the JavaScript code. For an overview of how to get your HTML set, please review the *Graphics with 2D canvas* recipe.

How to do it...

After creating the JavaScript file add the following code in your `init` function.

1. Create our basic canvas variables:

   ```
   var canvas = document.getElementById("israel");
   var wid = canvas.width;
   var hei = canvas.height;
   var context = canvas.getContext("2d");
   ```

2. Define one degree in radians. We do that since `Math.cos` and `Math.sin` expect a radian value and not a degree value (`radian` is one degree measured in radians):

   ```
   var radian = Math.PI/180;
   ```

3. Create a `tilt` variable. This variable will define the tilt of the triangle that will be created. Imagine the triangle is in a circle and we are rotating the circle with this `tilt` variable:

   ```
   var tilt = radian*180;
   ```

4. Define the center point of the canvas:

   ```
   var baseX = wid / 2;
   var baseY = hei / 2;
   ```

5. Set the radius of the invisible bounding circle of the Star of David:

   ```
   var radius = 24;
   ```

6. Define the height of the strips in the flag:

   ```
   var stripHeight = 14;
   ```

7. Define a line width:

   ```
   context.lineWidth=5;
   ```

8. Create two triangles (one tilted and one not):

   ```
   createTrinagle(context,
     baseX+ Math.sin(0) * radius,
     baseY + Math.cos(0) * radius,
     baseX+ Math.sin(radian*120) * radius,
     baseY + Math.cos(radian*120) * radius,
     baseX+ Math.sin(radian*240) * radius,
     baseY + Math.cos(radian*240) * radius,
     null,"#0040C0");

   createTrinagle(context,
     baseX+ Math.sin(tilt) * radius,
     baseY + Math.cos(tilt) * radius,
     baseX+ Math.sin(radian*120+tilt) * radius,
     baseY + Math.cos(radian*120+tilt) * radius,
   ```

```
    baseX+ Math.sin(radian*240+tilt) * radius,
    baseY + Math.cos(radian*240+tilt) * radius,
    null,"#0040C0");
```

9. Draw flag strips:

```
context.lineWidth=stripHeight;
context.beginPath();
context.moveTo(0,stripHeight);
context.lineTo(wid,stripHeight);
context.moveTo(0,hei- stripHeight);
context.lineTo(wid,hei- stripHeight);
context.closePath();
context.stroke();
```

10. Create the `createTriangle` function:

```
function createTriangle(context,x1,y1,x2,y2,x3,y3,fillColor,stroke
Color){
  context.beginPath();
  context.moveTo(x1,y1);
  context.lineTo(x2,y2);
  context.lineTo(x3,y3);
  context.lineTo(x1,y1);
  context.closePath();
  if(fillColor) {
    context.fillStyle = fillColor;
    context.fill();
  }
  if(strokeColor){
  context.strokeStyle = strokeColor;
  context.stroke();

  }
}
```

You are done. Run your application and you will find the flag of Israel with the Star of David in the center of the flag.

How it works...

Before we dig into the creation of the flag and how it was done, we need to understand how we locate points in a circle. To do so let's look at a simpler example:

```
var rad = Math.PI/180;
context.fillStyle = "#FFDE00";
context.arc(wid / 2, hei / 2, 30, 0, 2 * Math.PI, false);
context.fill();
```

```
context.beginPath();
context.strokeStyle = "#ff0000";
context.lineWidth=6;
context.moveTo(Math.sin(0) * 30 + wid / 2,
  Math.cos(0) * 30 + hei/2);
context.lineTo(Math.sin(rad*120) * 30 + wid / 2,
  Math.cos(rad*120) * 30 + hei/2);
context.stroke();
```

The following is the output the code will generate:

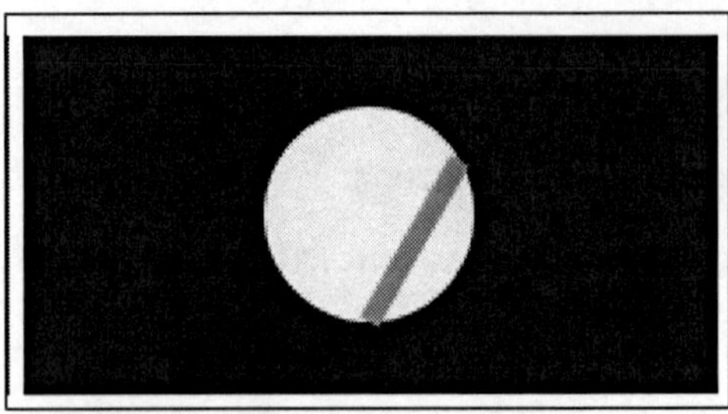

Although a circle, in our human-friendly head, is a shape that has 360 degrees, it's actually best represented in most programming languages in radians.

Radians are just like degrees, only instead of being human-friendly numbers between 0 and 360 these are numbers between 0 and two times Pi. You might be wondering what Pi is, so a bit more on Pi. Pi is in essence the value that is created when you take the circumference of any circle and divide it by the diameter of the same circle. The result that would come back would be Pi or about 3.14159. It is a magical number and the good news is you don't need to know much more about it if you don't want to. All you need to know is that 3.142 is equal to half of a circle. With that fact we can now divide Pi by `180` to get a value in radian that equals one degree:

```
var rad = Math.PI/180;
```

We then create a circle with a radius of `30` in the center of the screen, to help us visualize this, and move on to start creating a line that will start at angle `0` of our circle and end at angle `120` (as we want to create a triangle 360/3).

```
context.strokeStyle = "#ff0000";
context.lineWidth=6;
context.moveTo(Math.sin(0) * 30 + wid / 2,
  Math.cos(0) * 30 + hei/2);
context.lineTo(Math.sin(rad*120) * 30 + wid / 2,
  Math.cos(rad*120) * 30 + hei/2);
context.stroke();
```

Let's break down the most complex line:

```
context.lineTo(Math.sin(rad*120) * 30 + wid / 2,
  Math.cos(rad*120) * 30 + hei/2);
```

As `Math.sin` and `Math.cos` return a value for a radius of `1`, we will multiply any value returned by the radius of our circle (in this case `30`). In the parameters of `Math.sin` and `Math.cos`, we will provide the exact same values; in this example `120` radians. As our circle would be centered at the top left-hand side of the canvas we want to shift the circle to start from the center of the screen by adding to our values `wid/2` and `hei/2`.

At this stage, you should know how to find points on a circle, and with that how to draw lines between two points. Let's go back to our flag of Israel and take a deeper look into the new function `createTriangle`. It was based on the function `fillTriangle` created in the *Creating shapes using paths* recipe.

```
function
createTriangle(context,x1,y1,x2,y2,x3,y3,fillColor,strokeColor){

...

  if(fillColor) {
    context.fillStyle = fillColor;
    context.fill();
  }

if(stokeColor){
    context.strokeStyle = fillColor;
    context.stroke();

  }

}
```

I've highlighted the new components of this function compared to the function `fillTriangle`. The two new parameters `fillColor` and `strokeColor` define if we should fill or stroke the triangle. Notice that we moved the `strokeStyle` and `fillStyle` methods to the bottom of our function to reduce our code footprint. Great! We now have a modern triangle creator that could deal with the Star of David.

There's more...

OK, time to connect the dots (literally speaking) and create the flag of Israel. Looking back at our original code we find ourselves using the `createTriangle` function twice to create the full Star of David shape. Let's take a deeper look at the logic here by looking at the second triangle (the one that is turned upside down):

```
createTriangle(context,
  baseX+ Math.sin(tilt) * radius,
  baseY + Math.cos(tilt) * radius,
  baseX+ Math.sin(radian*120+tilt) * radius,
  baseY + Math.cos(radian*120+tilt) * radius,
baseX+ Math.sin(radian*240+tilt) * radius,
  baseY + Math.cos(radian*240+tilt) * radius,
  null,"#0040C0");
```

We are sending in three points on the virtual circle to create a triangle. We split our virtual circle to three equal parts and find the point values at the `0`, `120`, and `240` degrees. This way if we drew a line between these points we would get a perfect triangle in which all of the sides were equal.

Let's take a deeper look at one of the points sent to the `createTriangle` function:

```
baseX + Math.sin(radian*120+tilt) * radius,
baseY + Math.cos(radian*120+tilt) * radius
```

We start from `baseX` and `baseY` (the center of the screen) as the center point of our circle before we figure out the actual point gap from that base starting point. We then add to it the value that we get from `Math.sin` and `Math.cos` respectively. In this example, we are trying to get `120` degrees plus the tilt value. In other words, `120` degrees plus `180` degrees (or `300` degrees).

To make it easier to comprehend, in pseudocode it would look similar to the following code snippet:

```
startingPositionX + Math.sin(wantedDegree) * Radius
startingPositionY + Math.cin(wantedDegree) * Radius
```

Not much more to say besides congrats. We just finished creating another flag and in the process, learned how to create complex shapes, use math to help us figure out points on the screen, and mix together different shapes to create more advanced shapes.

Adding more vertices

There are many flags that contain stars that just cannot be created by overlapping triangles. In this recipe, we will figure out how to create a star that contains an arbitrary number of points We will use the same key concept we discovered in the previous recipe by taking advantage of a virtual circle to calculate positions, this time with only two virtual circles. In this recipe, we will create the flag of Somalia and in the process figure out how to create a function that will enable us to create stars.

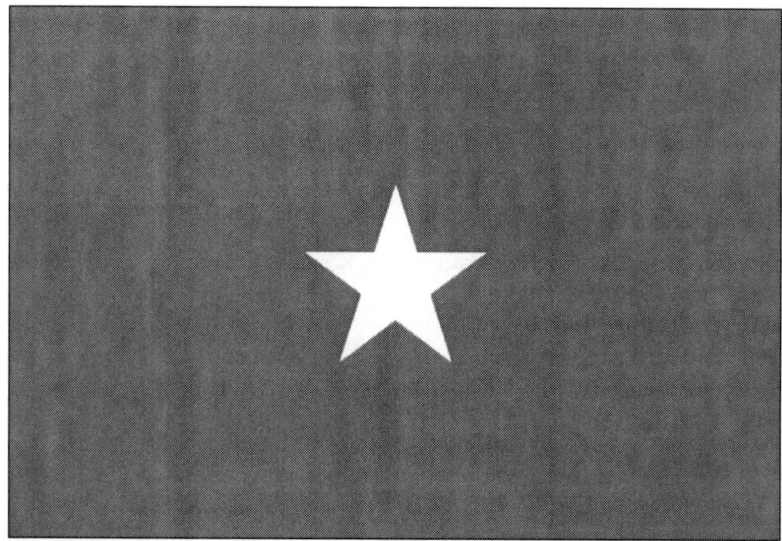

Getting ready

Please continue working on the sample from the previous recipe. If you haven't worked on it yet, I strongly encourage you to do so as this recipe is the next logical step of the previous recipe. As in the previous recipe, we will be skipping the HTML portion of this sample. Please review the first recipe in the book to refresh on the required HTML code.

How to do it...

Let's jump right in and create the flag of Somalia.

1. Create the canvas standard logic:

```
var canvas = document.getElementById("somalia");
var wid = canvas.width;
var hei = canvas.height;

var context = canvas.getContext("2d");
```

2. Fill the background color of canvas:

```
context.fillStyle = "#4189DD";
context.fillRect(0,0,wid,hei);
```

3. Draw the star by calling the `createStar` function:

```
createStar(context,wid/2,hei/2,7,20,5,"#ffffff",null,0);
```

4. Create the `createStart` function:

```
function createStar(context,baseX,baseY,
                    innerRadius,outerRadius,
                    points,fillColor,
                    strokeColor,tilt){
// all the rest of the code in here
}
```

5. From this point on we will be working within the `createStart` function. Add a few helper variables:

```
function createStar(context,baseX,baseY,innerRadius,outerRadius,
  points,fillColor,strokeColor,tilt){
  var radian = Math.PI/180;
  var radianStepper = radian * ( 360/points) /2;
  var currentRadian =0;
  var radianTilt = tilt*radian;
```

6. Call the `beginPath` method before starting to draw any shape:

```
  context.beginPath();
```

7. Move the drawing pointer to the angle `0` in the internal circle:

```
  context.moveTo(baseX+ Math.sin(currentRadian +
    radianTilt) * innerRadius,baseY+
    Math.cos(currentRadian + radianTilt) * innerRadius);
```

8. Loop through the total points of the star and draw a line back and forth between the outer circle and inner circle to create a star:

```
for(var i=0; i<points; i++){
  currentRadian +=  radianStepper;
  context.lineTo(baseX+ Math.sin(currentRadian +
    radianTilt) * outerRadius,baseY+
    Math.cos(currentRadian + radianTilt) * outerRadius);
  currentRadian +=  radianStepper;
  context.lineTo(baseX+ Math.sin(currentRadian +
    radianTilt) * innerRadius,baseY+
    Math.cos(currentRadian + radianTilt) * innerRadius);
}
```

9. Close the path of the drawing and fill or stroke according to the function parameters:

```
context.closePath();

  if(fillColor){
    context.fillStyle = fillColor;
    context.fill();
  }

  if(strokeColor){
    context.strokeStyle = strokeColor;
    context.stroke();

  }

}
```

When you run your HTML wrapper, you will find your first star and with it another flag will be under your belt.

How it works...

Let's start by understanding what the function we are going to create expects. The idea is simple, to create a star we want to have a virtual inner circle and a virtual outer circle. We can then draw lines between the circles back and forth to create the star. To do so, we need some basic parameters.

```
function createStar(context,baseX,baseY,
     innerRadius,outerRaduis,points,fillColor,
                              strokeColor,tilt){
```

Our regular context, `baseX` and `baseY` don't need further introductions. The virtual `innerRadius` and `outerRadius` are there to help define the length of the line segments that create a star and their positions. We want to know how many points our star will have. We do so by adding in the `points` parameters. We want to know the `fillColor` and/or `strokeColor` so we can define the actual colors of the star. We top it with a `tilt` value (it can be useful as we've seen when creating the Star of David for the flag of Israel).

```
var radian = Math.PI/180;
var radianStepper = radian * ( 360/points) / 2;
var currentRadian =0;
var radianTilt = tilt*radian;
```

We then move on to configure our facilitator variables for our star. It's not the first time we see the radian variable, but it is our first `radianStepper`. The goal of the radian stepper is to simplify calculations in our loop. We divided 360 degrees by the number of points our triangle will have. We divided the value by `2`, as we will have two times the number of points as lines. Last but not least, we want to convert this value into radians so we are duplicating the full results by our radian variable. We then create a simple `currentRadian` variable to store the current step we are in and finish off by converting the `tilt` value to be a radian value, so we can add it into all our lines without extra calculations within the loop.

As always, we start and complete our shapes with the `beginPath` and `closePath` methods. Let's take a deeper look at the starting position for our soon-to-be shape:

```
context.moveTo(baseX+ Math.sin(currentRadian + radianTilt) *
  innerRadius,baseY+ Math.cos(currentRadian + radianTilt) *
  innerRadius);
```

Although at first glance this probably looks a bit scary, it's actually very similar to how we created the Star of David. We are starting at `currentRadian` (that is currently `0`) using `innerRadius` as our start point.

In our loop, our goal will be to weave back and forth between the inner and external circles. To do so we will need to progress the `currentRadian` value each time the loop cycles by a `radianStepper`:

```
for(var i=0; i<points; i++){
  currentRadian +=  radianStepper;
  context.lineTo(baseX+ Math.sin(currentRadian + radianTilt) *
    outerRadius,baseY+ Math.cos(currentRadian + radianTilt) *
    outerRadius);
  currentRadian +=  radianStepper;
  context.lineTo(baseX+ Math.sin(currentRadian + radianTilt) *
    innerRadius,baseY+ Math.cos(currentRadian + radianTilt) *
    innerRadius);
}
```

We start a loop based on the number of points in our parameter. In this loop, we go back and forth between the external radius and the internal one each time we draw two lines between the inner circle and the external one. Our step size is defined by the number of points (the value we configured with the `radianStepper` variable).

We covered the rest of the functions when we created the `createTriangle` function in an earlier recipe. There you have it! You can now run the app and find our seventh flag. With this new complex function, we can create all solid stars and all non-solid stars that are hollow within.

OK I hope you are sitting down... with the newly-acquired star powers, you can now create at least 109 flags including the United States of America and all the other countries that have stars in their flag (57 percent of the countries in the world and counting!).

Overlapping shapes to create other shapes

There are many flags and many shapes in general that can be created by combining the shapes we created so far. One of the most popular shapes in 82 flags we don't know how to create is the crescent shape like the one in the flag of Turkey. With it we learn a new skill of using subtraction to create more in-depth shapes.

Getting ready

The previous recipe is our starting point in this recipe. From here, we will continue working to create more advanced shapes that are built out of two shapes when combined. As such, we will be using the code created in the last recipe located in `01.02.flags.js`.

How to do it...

Let's jump right into our code and see it in action.

1. Gain access to the context and save the width and height of the canvas into variables:

```
var canvas = document.getElementById("turkey");
var wid = canvas.width;
var hei = canvas.height;

var context = canvas.getContext("2d");
```

2. Fill the rectangle canvas area:

```
context.fillStyle = "#E30A17";
context.fillRect(0,0,wid,hei);
```

3. Create a full circle:

```
context.fillStyle = "#ffffff";
context.beginPath();
context.arc(wid / 2 - 23, hei / 2, 23, 0, 2 *
  Math.PI, false);
context.closePath();
context.fill();
```

4. Change the color of canvas fill. Fill a circle within its bound with another circle that hides part of the last circle that was created. This effect creates a shape that looks like a crescent moon:

```
context.fillStyle = "#E30A17";
context.beginPath();
context.arc(wid / 2 - 18, hei / 2, 19, 0, 2 *
  Math.PI, false);
context.closePath();
context.fill();
```

5. Reuse `createStart` from the previous recipe to add the Turkish star:

```
createStar(context,wid/2 +
  13,hei/2,5,16,5,"#ffffff",null,15);
```

There you go! You've just created a shape that is not possible without masking one shape with another.

How it works...

The catch here is we are using two circles, one overlaps the other to create a crescent shape. By the way, notice how we are tilting the star as well so that one of its points will point to the middle of the circle.

We've gone through a lot in the last few examples and at this stage you should be very comfortable creating many shapes and elements in the canvas. There is still much to explore before we can say we have mastered canvas, but we can definitely say we have mastered creating most of the flags of the world and that's very cool. I would love to see your flags. Drop me a line when you create one not in the book! :)

2
Advanced Drawing in Canvas

- Drawing arcs
- Drawing curves with a control point
- Creating a Bezier curve
- Integrating images into our art
- Drawing with text
- Understanding pixel manipulation

Introduction

This is the last chapter where we will dig deep into canvas as the remaining chapters will focus on building charts and interactivity.

In this chapter, we will continue to master our skills with canvas by adding curves, images, text, and even pixel manipulation to our tool belt.

Drawing arcs

There are three types of curves we can create in canvas—using the arc, quadratic curves, and Bezier curves. Let's get started.

Getting ready

If you recall in *Chapter 1, Drawing Shapes in Canvas*, in our first recipe we used the arc method to create perfect circles. The arc method is much more than just that. We can actually create any partial curve in a circular shape. If you don't recall drawing circles, I strongly encourage you to scan through *Chapter 1, Drawing Shapes in Canvas* again, and while you are there, you will find the template for creating the HTML documents as well. We are exclusively going to focus on the JavaScript code in this recipe.

How to do it...

Let's jump into it and create our first noncircle that has curves:

1. Access the `pacman` canvas element and fetch its width and height by using the following code snippet:

   ```
   var canvas = document.getElementById("pacman");
   var wid = canvas.width;
   var hei = canvas.height;
   ```

2. Create a `radian` variable (one degree in radians):

   ```
   var radian = Math.PI/180;
   ```

3. Get the canvas context and fill its background in black by using the following code snippet:

   ```
   var context = canvas.getContext("2d");
     context.fillStyle = "#000000";
     context.fillRect(0,0,wid,hei);
   ```

4. Begin a new path before starting to draw:

   ```
     context.beginPath();
   ```

5. Change fill style color:

   ```
     context.fillStyle = "#F3F100";
   ```

6. Move the pointer to the center of the screen:

   ```
     context.moveTo(wid/2,hei/2);
   ```

7. Draw a curve that starts at 40 degrees and ends at 320 degrees (with a radius of 40) in the center of the screen:

   ```
     context.arc(wid / 2, hei / 2, 40, 40*radian, 320*radian,
     false);
   ```

8. Close the shape by drawing a line back to the starting point of our shape:

```
context.lineTo(wid/2,hei/2);
```

9. Close the path and fill the shape:

```
context.closePath();
context.fill();
```

You have just created a PacMan.

How to do it...

For the first time, we take advantage and create a pie-type shape, known as PacMan (you can see how this can be very useful when we get into creating the pie graph). Very simple—again we connect to that idea of radians:

```
context.arc(wid / 2, hei / 2, 40, 40*radian, 320*radian, false);
```

Notice how our 4th and 5th parameters—instead of being a complete circle by starting from 0 and ending at `2*Math.PI`—are setting the angle to start the arc at radian 40 and end at radian 320 (leaving 80 degrees open to create the mouth of a PacMan). All that is left is to start drawing from the center of the circle:

```
context.moveTo(wid/2,hei/2);
context.arc(wid / 2, hei / 2, 40, 40*radian, 320*radian, false);
context.lineTo(wid/2,hei/2);
```

We start by moving our pointer to the center of our circle. We then create the arc. As our arc isn't a complete shape it's continuing where we left off—drawing a line from the center of the arc to the starting point (40 degrees). We complete the action by drawing a line back to the center of the arc to complete the shape. Now we are ready to fill it and complete our work.

Now that we have got arcs out of the way, you can see how useful this will be for creating pie charts.

Drawing curves with a control point

If the world was just two points with a perfect arc this would be the end of the book, but alas or lucky for us, there are still many more complex shapes to learn and explore. There are many curves that are not perfectly aligned curves. Till now all the curves that we created were part of a perfect circle, but not any more. In this recipe, we will explore quadratic curves. The quadratic curves enable us to create curves that are not circular, by adding a third point—a controller to control the curve. You can easily understand this by looking at the following diagram:

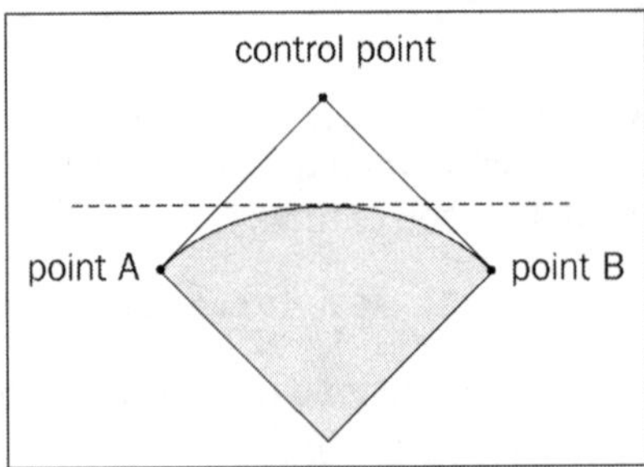

A **quadratic curve** is a curve that has one control point. Consider the case when creating a line, we draw it between two points (A and B in this illustration). When we want to create a quadratic curve, we use an external gravity controller that defines the direction of the curve while the middle line (the dotted line) defines how far will the curve reach.

Getting ready

As done in previous recipes, we are skipping the HTML part here too—not that it's not needed, it just repeats itself in every recipe and if you need to refresh yourself on how to get the HTML setup, please take a look at the *Graphics with 2D Canvas* recipe in *Chapter 1, Drawing Shapes in Canvas*.

How to do it...

In this example, we will create a closed shape that looks like a very basic eye.
Let's get started:

1. We always need to start with extracting our canvas element, setting up our width and height variables, and defining a radian (as we find it useful to have one around):

```
var canvas = document.getElementById("eye");
  var wid = canvas.width;
  var hei = canvas.height;
  var radian = Math.PI/180;
```

2. Next, fill our canvas with a solid color and after that begin a new shape by triggering the `beginPath` method:

```
var context = canvas.getContext("2d");
  context.fillStyle = "#dfdfdf";
  context.fillRect(0,0,wid,hei);
  context.beginPath();
```

3. Define the line width and stroke color for our eye shape:

```
  context.lineWidth = 1;
  context.strokeStyle = "#000000"; // line color
  context.fillStyle = "#ffffff";
```

4. Move our drawing pointer to the left-centered point as we will need to draw a line from left to right in the center of the screen and back (only with a curve):

```
  context.moveTo(0,hei/2);
```

5. Draw two quadratic curves from our initial point to the other side of the canvas and back to the initial point by using an anchor point, which is in the extreme top followed by the extreme bottom of the canvas area:

```
  context.quadraticCurveTo(wid / 2, 0, wid,hei/2);
  context.quadraticCurveTo(wid / 2, hei, 0,hei/2);
```

6. Close the path. Fill the shape and use the `stroke` method on the shape (`fill` for filling the content and `stroke` for outlines):

```
  context.closePath();
  context.stroke();
  context.fill();
```

Great job! You have just created your first shape by using the `quadraticCurveTo` method.

How it works...

Let's look at this method closely:

```
context.quadraticCurveTo(wid / 2, 0, wid,hei/2);
```

As we are already at the origin point (point A), we input two other points—the control point and point B.

```
context.quadraticCurveTo(controlX, controlY, pointB_X, pointB_Y);
```

In our sample, we create a contained shape—the starting point to create an eye. Play with the controller to see how it affects the direction and size of the curve. The thumb rule is that the closer to the vertical line the less steep the curve will be, and the further away it is from the center point the more curved shape would be to the offset.

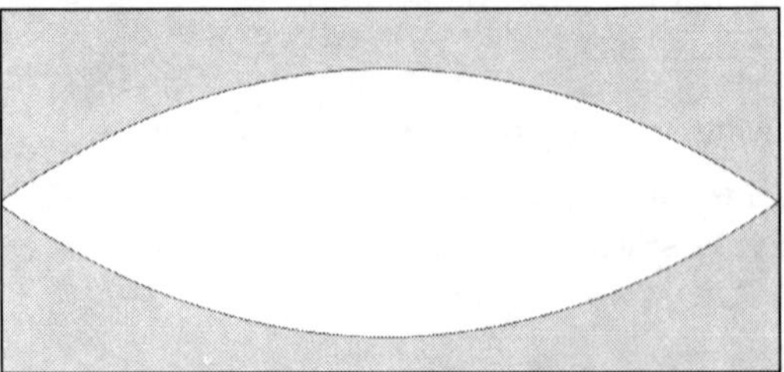

Creating a Bezier curve

We've just learned that with the quadratic curve we have one control point. Although we can do many things with one control point, we don't really have full control over the curve. So let's take it one step further by adding one more control point. Adding a second control point actually adds the relationship between these two points as well making it three control factors. If we include the actual anchor points (we have got two of them), we end up with five points that control the shape of the curve. That does sound complicated; it's because the more control we get the more complicated it is to actually understand how it works. It's really not easy to figure out complicated curves by code alone and as such we actually use other tools to help us figure out the right curves.

To prove the preceding point, we can find a very complex shape and start with that one (don't worry, later on in this recipe, we will practice on a very simple shape to make the concept clear). We will pick to draw the flag of Canada and mainly the maple leaf.

Getting ready

This recipe is difficult to understand, but we will break it down into details in the following *How it works...* section. So if you are new to curves, I strongly encourage you to start learning from this *How it works...* section before implementing it.

How to do it...

Let's create the flag of Canada. Let's jump right into the JavaScript code:

1. Create the canvas and context:

```
var canvas = document.getElementById("canada");
var wid = canvas.width;
var hei = canvas.height;

var context = canvas.getContext("2d");
```

2. Fill the background to match the background of the Canadian flag:

```
context.fillStyle="#FF0000";
context.fillRect(0,0,50,100);
context.fillRect(wid-50,0,50,100);
```

3. Begin a new path and move the pointer to `84,19`:

```
context.beginPath();
context.moveTo(84,19);
```

4. Draw curves and lines to create the maple leaf:

```
context.bezierCurveTo(90,24,92,24,99,8);
context.bezierCurveTo(106,23,107,23,113,19);
context.bezierCurveTo(108,43,110,44,121,31);
context.bezierCurveTo(122,37,124,38,135,35);
context.bezierCurveTo(130,48,131,50,136,51);
context.bezierCurveTo(117,66,116,67,118,73);
context.bezierCurveTo(100,71,99,72,100,93);
context.lineTo(97,93);
context.bezierCurveTo(97,72,97,71,79,74);
context.bezierCurveTo(81,67,80,66,62,51);
context.bezierCurveTo(67,49,67,48,63,35);
context.bezierCurveTo(74,38,75,37,77,31);
context.bezierCurveTo(88,44,89,43,84,19);
```

5. Close the path and fill the shape:

```
context.closePath();
context.fill();
```

Now, you have created the flag of Canada. I don't know if you already know why it works or how we got to the apparently random numbers that we put into our curves to create the flag, but you've created the flag of Canada! Don't worry, we are about to decrypt the magic of curves right away in the next section.

How it works...

Before we can explain the details of how the Canadian flag works, we should take a step back and create a simpler example. In this short example, we will create an oval shape by using the `bezierCurveTo` method.

```
context.moveTo(2,hei/2);
  context.bezierCurveTo(0, 0,wid,0, wid-2,hei/2);
  context.bezierCurveTo(wid, hei,0,hei, 2,hei/2);
  context.closePath();
  context.stroke();
  context.fill();
```

That's it. The following is the outcome you get out of this:

If you get this, you are in great shape. We will now explain how this works and then move into how we figured out all the points for the Canadian flag. We are taking advantage of the full canvas again and we are keeping our controllers under control by setting two of our controllers to be the corners of the canvas:

```
context.bezierCurveTo(controlPointX1, controlPointY1, controlPointX2,
controlPointY2, pointBX, pointBY);
```

Play around with the controllers to see how much more control you get by using two dots—this is very useful when you need more detailed control over a curve.

This is the heart of the full example of our full flag. I strongly encourage you to explore the effects of changing the values of the control points to get a better understanding and sensitivity to it. It's time for us to get back to our flag and see how we structured it.

It's time to take our most complex drawing style—Bezier curves—and put them to action with something a bit more interesting than an oval. I have a confession: when I decided to create the flag of Canada from scratch I got scared. I was thinking "How am I going to get this done? This is going to take me hours," and then it hit me... it was clear that this flag needs to be created with a lot of Bezier points but how would I know where the points should be? So for a shape this advanced, I opened up my graphics editor (in my case, Flash Editor) and added pivot points to the maple shape:

If you closely look at the previous diagram, I basically traced the flag of Canada and placed a black dot on every sharp corner. Then I created a canvas and drew lines to see if the base shape I got was in the right overall position (by the way, I got the dots just by selecting the dots in Flash to see if their (x, y) coordinates as Flash and canvas coordinate systems are the same).

```
var context = canvas.getContext("2d");
context.beginPath();
context.moveTo(84,19);
context.lineTo(99,8);
context.lineTo(113,19);
context.lineTo(121,31);
context.lineTo(135,35);
context.lineTo(136,51);
context.lineTo(118,73);
context.lineTo(100,93);
context.lineTo(97,93);
context.lineTo(79,74);
context.lineTo(62,51);
context.lineTo(63,35);
context.lineTo(77,31);
context.lineTo(84,19);

context.closePath();
context.stroke();
```

I got a shape that was far from what I was looking for. But now I knew that my shape was getting formed in the right direction. What were missing were the curves to connect between the dots. If you look at the preceding diagram again, you will notice that I've placed two blue points between each sharp corner to define where the curves would be and how sharp or soft they would be. I then moved back into canvas and then updated the values to have the two control points. I added all the curves and switched from creating strokes to creating a fill.

```
var context = canvas.getContext("2d");
  context.fillStyle="#FF0000";
  context.fillRect(0,0,50,100);
  context.fillRect(wid-50,0,50,100);

  context.beginPath();
  context.moveTo(84,19);
  context.bezierCurveTo(90,24,92,24,99,8);
  context.bezierCurveTo(106,23,107,23,113,19);
  context.bezierCurveTo(108,43,110,44,121,31);
  context.bezierCurveTo(122,37,124,38,135,35);
  context.bezierCurveTo(130,48,131,50,136,51);
  context.bezierCurveTo(117,66,116,67,118,73);
  context.bezierCurveTo(100,71,99,72,100,93);
  context.lineTo(97,93);
  context.bezierCurveTo(97,72,97,71,79,74);
  context.bezierCurveTo(81,67,80,66,62,51);
  context.bezierCurveTo(67,49,67,48,63,35);
  context.bezierCurveTo(74,38,75,37,77,31);
  context.bezierCurveTo(88,44,89,43,84,19);
  context.closePath();
  context.fill();
```

Bingo! I just got an almost perfect flag and I feel this is enough for this sample.

Don't try to create very complex shapes on your own just yet. Maybe there are a few people out there who can do that, but for the rest of us the best way to do it is to trace the elements by using a visual editor of some sort. We can then grab the graphic information and update the values in canvas as I've done with the Canadian flag example.

At this stage, we have covered the most complex shapes that we can cover in canvas. The rest of the chapter is dedicated to other ways of manipulating content on the screen.

Integrating images into our art

Lucky for us, we don't need to start from scratch always and we can leave the more complex art for external images. Let's figure out how we can integrate images into our canvas.

Getting ready

We've been in a flag theme in this chapter and getting another flag under our belt sounds real good to me right now. So let's turn our heads to Haiti and get their flag up and running. To create this flag, we need to have the image of the symbol that is placed in the center of the flag.

In the source files, you will find an image of the center graphic (at `img/haiti.png`). By the way, when integrating art into canvas it's always best to avoid resizing the image whenever possible via code to preserve the image quality.

How to do it...

We will prepare the background to match the flag and then put the entire image above it in the center of the canvas/flag:

1. Follow the basic steps that we need to access the canvas. Set the width, height, and the actual context:

```
var canvas = document.getElementById("haiti");
  var wid = canvas.width;
  var hei = canvas.height;

  var context = canvas.getContext("2d");
```

2. Draw the background elements:

```
context.fillStyle="#00209F";
context.fillRect(0,0,wid,hei/2);
context.fillStyle="#D21034";
context.fillRect(0,hei/2,wid,hei/2);
```

3. Create a new `Image` object:

```
var oIMG = new Image();
```

4. Create an `onLoad` function (that will be called when the image is loaded):

```
oIMG.onload = function(){
context.drawImage(this, (wid-this.width)/2, (hei-this.height)/2);
};
```

5. Set the source of the image:

```
oIMG.src = "img/haiti.png";
```

Yes, it's that easy to add images into canvas, but let's review more deeply what we have just done.

How it works...

The steps involved in creating an image are downloading its data and then creating a new image container in the same way as it is done in canvas:

```
var oIMG = new Image();
```

The next step is to create a listener that will be triggered when the image is loaded and ready to be used:

```
oIMG.onload = theListenerFunctionHere;
```

The last step in the loading process is to tell canvas what image should be loaded. In our case we are loading `img/haiti.png`:

```
oIMG.src = "img/haiti.png";
```

Loading an image and having it ready to be used is only the first step. If we ran our application without actually telling canvas what to do with it, nothing would happen beyond the loading of the image.

In our case, when our listener is triggered, we add the image as it is to the center of the screen:

```
context.drawImage(this, (wid-this.width)/2, (hei-this.height)/2);
```

That is all it takes to integrate an image into a canvas project.

There's more...

There are more operations that we can do with images in canvas beyond using them as backgrounds. We can define exactly what parts of the image we want (scaling). We can resize and manipulate the full image (scaling). We can even pixel manipulate our images. There are many things that we can do with images, but in the next few topics we will cover some of the more often used ones.

Scaling images

We can scale the image by adding two more parameters to the `drawImage` function, which sets the width and height of our image. Try the following:

```
context.drawImage(this, (wid-this.width)/2, (hei-this.height)/2 , 100,
120);
```

In the previous sample, we are loading the same image but we are forcing a resized image (note that the positions are not going to be in the actual center of the stage).

Adding even more control

You can control many aspects of an image. If you need more control than the preceding sample, you would need to input the full number of possible coordinates:

```
context.drawImage(this, sourceX, sourceY, sourceWidth, sourceHeight,
destX, destY, destWidth, destHeight);
```

In this case, the order has changed (notice that!). Now, the first two parameters after `this` are the local x and y coordinates of the image followed by the width and height (creating the crop that we were talking about) followed by the position on the canvas and its controlling information (x, y, width, and height).

In our case:

```
context.drawImage(this, 25,25,20,20,0,0,50,50);
```

The preceding code line means we want to take the image from its internal position of (25,25) and we want to slice a 20 x 20 rectangle out of there. We then want to position this new cropped image at (0,0) that is, the top corner of the canvas and we want that output to be a 50 x 50 rectangle.

Using images as a fill

We can use our loaded image as a way to fill up objects as well:

```
var oIMG = new Image();
  oIMG.onload = function(){
    var pattern = context.createPattern(this, "repeat");
    createStar(context,wid/2,hei/2,20,50,20,pattern,"#ffffff",20);
  };
  oIMG.src = "img/haiti.png";
```

After the image is loaded (always after the image is loaded, you start manipulating it), we create a pattern that repeats based on our image:

```
var pattern = context.createPattern(this, "repeat");
```

We can then use this pattern as our fill. So in this case, we are calling the `createStar` that we created in an earlier task—drawing a star in the center of the screen—by using the following pattern:

```
createStar(context,wid/2,hei/2,20,50,20,pattern,"#ffffff",20);
```

This ends our flag obsession to move on to shapes that just don't appear in flags. By the way, at this stage you should be able to create all the flags in the world and take advantage of integrating images when it's just not fun to draw it yourself from scratch—such as detailed country logos.

Drawing with text

I agree, we've been working on some complicated things. Now, its time for us to lay back, kick off the shoes, and do something a bit easier.

Getting ready

The good news is, if you are on this page, you should already know the basics of getting a canvas up and running. So there isn't much more that you need to do besides picking the font, size, and position of your text.

Here, we aren't covering how you can embed fonts that aren't created within JavaScript, but instead, via CSS, we will use a basic font and hope for the best in this sample.

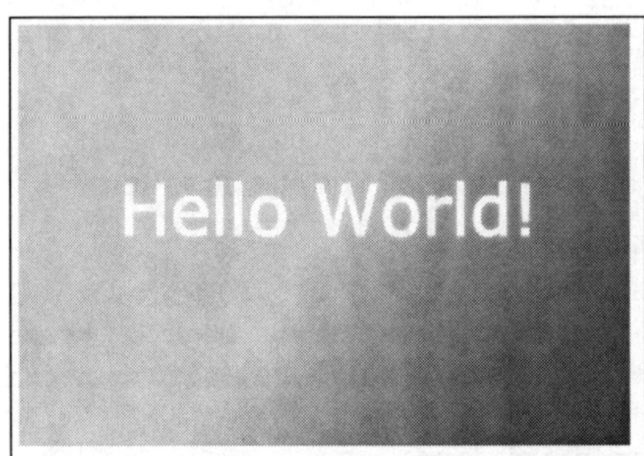

How to do it...

In this example, we are going to create a text field. In this process, we are going to use gradients and shadows for the first time. Perform the following steps:

1. Gain access to the canvas 2D API:

```
var canvas = document.getElementById("textCanvas");
  var wid = canvas.width;
  var hei = canvas.height;

  var context = canvas.getContext("2d");
```

2. Create a gradient style and fill the background with it:

```
var grd = context.createLinearGradient(wid/2, hei/2, wid, hei);
  grd.addColorStop(0, "#8ED6FF");
  grd.addColorStop(1, "#004CB3")
  context.fillStyle= grd;
  context.fillRect(0,0,wid,hei);
```

3. Create a gradient to be used by the text:

```
grd = context.createLinearGradient(100, hei/2, 200,
hei/2+110);
grd.addColorStop(0, "#ffff00");
grd.addColorStop(1, "#aaaa44");
```

4. Define the font to be used and set the style:

```
context.font = "50pt Verdana, sans-serif";
context.fillStyle = grd;
```

5. Add shadow details before drawing the text:

```
context.shadowOffsetX = 0;
context.shadowOffsetY = 0;
context.shadowBlur    = 8;
context.shadowColor   = 'rgba(255, 255, 255, 0.5)';
```

6. Use `fillText` to fill the shape and `strokeText` for outlines of the shape (notice that I call the text a shape; this is because as soon as we draw it, it will just be a part of our canvas and not live text):

```
context.fillText("Hello World!", 100, hei/2);
context.strokeStyle = "#ffffff";
context.strokeText("Hello World!", 100, hei/2);
```

That's it, we just integrated our first drawn text into canvas.

How it works...

Until now, we were stuck with the solid colors. We will now break out of that and move to a new world of gradient colors. Refer to the following code snippet:

```
var grd = context.createLinearGradient(wid/2, hei/2, wid, hei);
  grd.addColorStop(0, "#8ED6FF");
  grd.addColorStop(1, "#004CB3");
```

There are a few steps involved with creating a gradient. The first step is defining its scope:

```
var grd = context.createLinearGradient(x1, y1, x2, y2);
```

Contrary to many other languages, it's really easy to define the rotation and size of a gradient in canvas. If you have worked with Photoshop before, you will find this really easy (even if you haven't, it will be easy).

All you need to do is define where you want the gradient to start and where you want it to end. You can send two dots into the method `createLinearGradient`:

```
grd.addColorStop(0, "#8ED6FF");
grd.addColorStop(1, "#004CB3");
```

In this transition, we are using only two colors. Position them at a value between 0 and 1. These values are ratios, so we are, in other words, requesting to spread the color transition from the start of the gradient area all the way to the end. We could add more colors, but our goal is to bind them all within the ratio 0 to 1. The more colors you add, the more playing around you would need to do with the values sent into the first parameter.

You just completed creating a gradient. Time to use it:

```
context.fillStyle= grd;
context.fillRect(0,0,wid,hei);
```

In this part again, we will use the `fillStyle` method and then create a rectangle.

Please note the importance of the range of values that you may send to the `addColorStop` method. As you add more colors into your gradient, the more noticeable the importance of the values sent here will be. The points are not counters but ratios of colors in our sample. The transition is between the two colors' range from 0 to 1 or in other words they transition all the way through from our first point that we send into the `createLinearGradient` method all the to the last point. As we are working with two colors, this is the perfect ratio for us.

Although we are not getting into radial gradients, they should be really easy for you as we have already learned a lot about radial shapes and gradients. The signature of this method is as follows:

```
context.createRadialGradient(startX,startY,startR, endX,endY,endR);
```

The only difference here is that our shape is a radial shape. We also want to add the starting radius and ending radius into it. You might be wondering why we need two or even more radii. So why can't we figure out the radius based on the distance between the two dots (start point and end point)? I hope you are wondering about that and if you are not, wonder about it for a second before reading the next paragraph.

We have a separate control over the radius, mainly to enable us to separate the radius and to enable us to move the focal point within the drawing without changing the actual art or recalculating the ratios of colors. A really great way to see this in use is when drawing the moon. The moon's gradients over time will change or more accurately the radius of the colors and position of the radius would change over time depending on the moon's position compared to the sun.

We are not done yet. We just mastered everything that we need to know about gradients and it's time for us to integrate some text into it.

```
context.font = "50pt Verdana, sans-serif";
context.fillText("Hello World!", 100, hei/2);
```

We set the global font value and then create a new text element. The `fillText` method gets three parameters; the first is the text to be used while the other two are the x and y positions of the new element.

```
context.strokeStyle = "#ffffff";
context.strokeText("Hello World!", 100, hei/2);
```

In our example, we are giving our text drawing both a fill and an outline. The two functions are called separately. The `fillText` method is used to fill the content of the shape while the `strokeText` method is called to outline the text. We can use any one of them or both of the methods and they can get the exactly same parameters.

There's more...

There are some more options that you can explore.

Using gradients in your text

If you can do anything to any graphical element in canvas, you can do it to text as well—for example, in our sample we are using a gradient for our text.

```
grd = context.createLinearGradient(100, hei/2, 200, hei/2+110);
  grd.addColorStop(0, "#ffff00");
  grd.addColorStop(1, "#aaaa44");

  context.font = "50pt Verdana, sans-serif";
  context.fillStyle = grd;
```

Notice that we are updating our gradient. Our last gradient was too big for such a small text area. As such, we are drawing a line from around the start of our text going horizontally for 110 pixels.

Adding shadows and glows

You can add a shadow/glow to any filled element:

```
context.shadowOffsetX = 0;
  context.shadowOffsetY = 0;
  context.shadowBlur    = 8;
  context.shadowColor   = 'rgba(255, 255, 255, 0.5)';
  context.fillText("Hello World!", 100, hei/2);
```

You can control the position of the offset of the shadow. In our case, we want it to be a glow, so we placed our shadow exactly under our element. When setting the blur values to a shadow, try using values that are powers of 2 for efficiency (its easier to render values that are powers of 2).

Notice that when we defined our shadow color, we opted to use an RGBA as we wanted to set that alpha value to 50 percent.

Understanding pixel manipulation

Now that you have mastered drawing in canvas, it's time for us to turn to a new aspect of working with canvas. In canvas, you can manipulate pixels. It's not only a vector drawing tool, but a very smart pixel editor (raster).

Getting ready

Now that we are about to start reading data that is present on the canvas, we need to understand how security works when it comes to pixels. In an effort to protect content that isn't yours, there are security issues involved in working with data that isn't hosted on the same host as yours. We will not cover these security issues in this section and will be always working with images in the same domain as our code (or all locally).

Your first step is to find an image that you wish to work with (I've added an old image of my own into the source files). In this sample, we will recreate a pixel fade-out animation—really cool and useful for slides.

How to do it...

Let's get our code working and then break it down to see how it works. Perform the following steps:

1. Create a few helper global variables:

```
var context;
var imageData;
var pixelData;
var pixelLen;
var currentLocation=0;
var fadeOutImageInterval;
```

2. Create an `init` function (for the rest of the steps, all code will be in this function):

```
function init(){
  //all the rest of the code will go in here
}
```

3. Create a context variable for the 2D Canvas API:

```
function init(){
  var canvas = document.getElementById("textCanvas");
  var wid = canvas.width;
  var hei = canvas.height;

  context = canvas.getContext("2d");
```

4. Create a new image:

```
var oIMG = new Image();
```

5. Add the `onload` listener logic:

```
oIMG.onload = function(){
  context.drawImage(this,
  0,0,this.width,this.height,0,0,wid,hei);
  imageData = context.getImageData(0, 0, wid, hei);
  pixelData = imageData.data;
  pixelLen = pixelData.length;
  fadeOutImageInterval = setInterval(fadeOutImage, 25);
};
```

6. Define the image source:

```
oIMG.src = "img/slide2.jpg";

} //end of init function
```

7. Create a new function called `fadeOutImage`. This image will transition our image in:

```
function fadeOutImage(){
  var pixelsChanged=0;
  for (var i = 0; i < pixelLen; i +=4) {
    if(pixelData[i]) {
      pixelData[i] =  pixelData[i]-1; // red
      pixelsChanged++;
    }
    if(pixelData[i + 1]){
      pixelData[i + 1] = pixelData[i+1]-1; // green
      pixelsChanged++;
    }
    if(pixelData[i + 2]){
      pixelData[i + 2] = pixelData[i+2]-1; // green
      pixelsChanged++;
    }

  }
  context.putImageData(imageData, 0, 0);

  if(pixelsChanged==0){
    clearInterval(fadeOutImageInterval);
    alert("we are done fading out");
  }
}
```

Your outcome should look something like the following screenshot:

How it works...

We will skip explaining things that we have already covered in earlier samples such as how to load images and how to work with the `drawImage` method (covered in the *Integrating images into our art* recipe discussed earlier in this chapter).

```
var context;
var imageData;
var pixelData;
var pixelLen;
var currentLocation=0;
var fadeOutImageInterval;
```

We will see the usage of these variables in our code, but all these variables have been saved as global variables so there is no need to redefine them in our functions. By defining these variables once, we improve the efficiency of our application.

The real new logic starts within the `onLoad` listener. Right after we draw our image onto the canvas, our new logic is added. It is highlighted in the following code snippet:

```
var oIMG = new Image();
  oIMG.onload = function(){
    context.drawImage(this,
    0,0,this.width,this.height,0,0,wid,hei);
    imageData = context.getImageData(0, 0, wid, hei);
    pixelData = imageData.data;
```

```
        pixelLen = pixelData.length;
        fadeOutImageInterval = setInterval(fadeOutImage, 25);
    };
    oIMG.src = "img/slide2.jpg";
```

We are now taking advantage of storing information in our canvas area and storing it globally. The first variable we are storing is `imageData`. This variable contains all the information of our canvas. We get this variable by calling the `context.getImageData` method.

```
context.getImageData(x, y, width, height);
```

The `getImageData` function returns every single pixel for a rectangular area. We need to set it by defining the area we want. In our case, we want the full canvas area as our image is set in the full canvas area.

The returned object (`imageData`) stores the direct access to the pixel data information in its data property (`imageData.data`) and this is our main focus while working directly with pixels. This object contains all the color information for each pixel in our canvas. The information is stored in four cells (red, green, blue, and alpha). In other words, if there are 100 pixels in total in our application, we would expect our array to contain 400 cells in the `imageData.data` array.

The last thing left to do before finishing the logic in our `onLoad` listener is to trigger our animation that will transition our image; to do that we will add an interval as follows:

```
fadeOutImageInterval = setInterval(fadeOutImage, 25);
```

Our animation is triggered after every 25 milliseconds until it's completed. The logic that fades our view happens within our `fadeOutImage` function.

Now that we have got all the prep work done, it's time to delve into the `fadeoutImage` function. Here, we will be doing the actual pixel manipulation logic. The first step in this function is to create a variable that will count how many changes our `imageData.data` array has made. When we hit the required number of changes, we terminate our interval (or in a real application maybe animate the next image):

```
var pixelsChanged=0;
```

We now start to run through all the pixels by using a `for` loop:

```
for (var i = 0; i < pixelLen; i +=4) {
  //pixel level logic will go in here
}
```

Each pixel stores RGBA values, thus, every pixel gets four positions in our array and as such we are jumping four steps at a time to move between pixels.

```
context.putImageData(imageData, 0, 0);
```

When we are done with manipulating our data, it's time for us to update our canvas. To do that we just need to send our new data back into our context. The second and third parameters are for the x and y starting point.

```
if(pixelsChanged==0){
  clearInterval(fadeOutImageInterval);
  alert("we are done fading out");
}
```

When we have no more changes (you can adjust that to fit your wishes such as when there are less than 100 pixels changed), we terminate the interval and trigger an alert.

In our `for` loop, we will lower the values of red, green, and blue until they get to 0. In our case, as we are counting changes we also add the counter into the loop:

```
for (var i = 0; i < pixelLen; i +=4) {
  if(pixelData[i]) {
    pixelData[i] =  pixelData[i]-1; // red
    pixelsChanged++;
  }
  if(pixelData[i + 1]){
    pixelData[i + 1] = pixelData[i+1]-1; // green
    pixelsChanged++;

  if(pixelData[i + 2]){
    pixelData[i + 2] = pixelData[i+2]-1; // blue
    pixelsChanged++;
  }

}
```

Earlier we mentioned that each pixel gets four cells of information in the array. The first three cells store the RGB values, while the fourth stores the alpha channel. As such I thought it would be important to notice that we are skipping position `i+3` as we don't want the alpha channel to get affected. Every element in the `pixelData` array is a value between `0` and `255`. In other words, if that pixel's value was `#ffffff` (white), all three RGB cells would be equal to `255`. By the way, it would take 255 calls to our function to get the values down to `0` as the value in the cells would start from `255` and go down by 1 each time.

We always skip the position `i+3`, as we don't want to change anything in our array. Our values are between `255` and `0`; in other words, if our image has a value `#ffffff` (totally white pixel), it would go down `255` times for our function to get `0`.

Making an image grayscale

To make an image or our canvas grayscale, we need to take all of our colors (red, green, blue) into account and mix them together. After mixing them together, get to a brightness value, which we can then apply to all the pixels. Let's see it in action:

```
function grayScaleImage(){
  for (var i = 0; i < pixelLen; i += 4) {
    var brightness = 0.33 * pixelData[i] + 0.33 * pixelData[i + 1]
    + 0.34 * pixelData[i + 2];
    pixelData[i] = brightness; // red
    pixelData[i + 1] = brightness; // green
    pixelData[i + 2] = brightness; // blue
  }
  context.putImageData(imageData, 0, 0);
}
```

In this case, we are taking the red (`pixelData[i]`), green (`pixelData[i+1]`), and blue (`pixelData[i+2]`), and using a one third of each to combine together to get one color and then we are assigning them all with this new averaged value.

Try only changing two out of the three values and see what comes out.

Pixel reversing

Color reversing an image is very easy as all we need to do is flip its value pixel by pixel by taking the maximum possible value (`255`) and subtracting the current value from it:

```
function colorReverseImage(){
  for (var i = 0; i < pixelLen; i += 4) {
    pixelData[i] = 255-pixelData[i];
    pixelData[i + 1] = 255-pixelData[i+1];
    pixelData[i + 2] = 255-pixelData[i+2];
  }
  context.putImageData(imageData, 0, 0);
}
```

There you go! We visited a few options of pixel manipulation, but the limit is really just up to your imagination. Experiment, you never know what might come out of it!

3
Creating Cartesian-based Graphs

In this chapter, we will cover the following topics:

- Building a bar chart from scratch
- Spreading data in a scatter chart
- Building line charts
- Creating the flying brick chart (waterfall chart)
- Building a candlestick chart (stock chart)

Introduction

Our first graph/chart under the microscope is the most popular and simplest one to create. We can classify them all roughly under Cartesian-based graphs. Altogether this graph style is relatively simple; it opens the door to creating amazingly creative ways of exploring data. In this chapter we will lay down the foundations to building charts in general and hopefully motivate you to come up with your own ideas on how to create engaging data visualizations.

Building a bar chart from scratch

The simplest chart around is the one that holds only one dimensional data (only one value per type). There are many ways to showcase this type of data but the most popular, logical, and simple way is by creating a simple bar chart. The steps involved in creating this bar chart will be very similar even in very complex charts. The ideal usage of this type of chart is when the main goal is to showcase simple data, as follows:

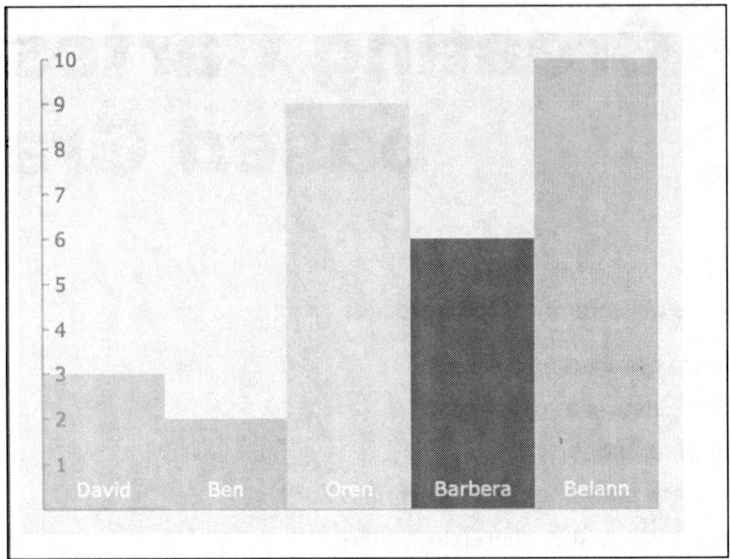

Getting ready

Create a basic HTML file that contains a canvas and an `onLoad` event that will trigger the `init` function. Load the `03.01.bar.js` script. We will create the content of the JavaScript file in our recipe as follows:

```
<!DOCTYPE html>
<html>
  <head>
    <title>Bar Chart</title>
    <meta charset="utf-8" />
  <script src="03.01.bar.js"></script>
  </head>
  <body onLoad="init();" style="background:#fafafa">
    <h1>How many cats do they have?</h1>
    <canvas id="bar" width="550" height="400"> </canvas>
  </body>
</html>
```

Creating a graph in general has three steps: defining the work area, defining the data sources, and then drawing in the data.

How to do it...

In our first case, we will compare a group of friends and how many cats they each own. We will be performing the following steps:

1. Define your data set:

```
var data = [{label:"David",
         value:3,
         style:"rgba(241, 178, 225, 0.5)"},
         {label:"Ben",
         value:2,
         style:"#B1DDF3"},
         {label:"Oren",
         value:9,
         style:"#FFDE89"},
         {label:"Barbera",
         value:6,
         style:"#E3675C"},
         {label:"Belann",
         value:10,
         style:"#C2D985"}];
```

   For this example I've created an array that can contain an unlimited number of elements. Each element contains three values: a label, a value, and a style for its fill color.

2. Define your graph outlines.

   Now that we have a data source, it's time to create our basic canvas information, which we create in each sample:

```
var can = document.getElementById("bar");
  var wid = can.width;
  var hei = can.height;
  var context = can.getContext("2d");
  context.fillStyle = "#eeeeee";
  context.strokeStyle = "#999999";
  context.fillRect(0,0,wid,hei);
```

3. The next step is to define our chart outlines:

```
var CHART_PADDING = 20;

  context.font = "12pt Verdana, sans-serif";
  context.fillStyle = "#999999";

  context.moveTo(CHART_PADDING,CHART_PADDING);
  context.lineTo(CHART_PADDING,hei-CHART_PADDING);
  context.lineTo(wid-CHART_PADDING,hei-CHART_PADDING);

  var stepSize = (hei - CHART_PADDING*2)/10;
  for(var i=0; i<10; i++){
    context.moveTo(CHART_PADDING, CHART_PADDING + i*  stepSize);
    context.lineTo(CHART_PADDING*1.3,CHART_PADDING + i*
stepSize);
    context.fillText(10-i, CHART_PADDING*1.5, CHART_PADDING + i*
stepSize + 6);
  }
  context.stroke();
```

4. Our next and final step is to create the actual data bars:

```
var elementWidth =(wid-CHART_PADDING*2)/ data.length;
  context.textAlign = "center";
  for(i=0; i<data.length; i++){
    context.fillStyle = data[i].style;
    context.fillRect(CHART_PADDING +elementWidth*i ,hei-
CHART_PADDING - data[i].value*stepSize,elementWidth,data[i].
value*stepSize);
    context.fillStyle = "rgba(255, 255, 225, 0.8)";
    context.fillText(data[i].label, CHART_PADDING
+elementWidth*(i+.5), hei-CHART_PADDING*1.5);

  }
```

That's it. Now, if you run the application in your browser, you will find a bar chart rendered.

How it works...

I've created a variable called `CHART_PADDING` that is used throughout the code to help me position elements (the variable is in uppercase because I want it to be a constant; so it's to remind myself that this is not a value that will change in the lifetime of the application).

Let's delve deeper into the sample we created starting from our outline area:

```
context.moveTo(CHART_PADDING,CHART_PADDING);
context.lineTo(CHART_PADDING,hei-CHART_PADDING);
context.lineTo(wid-CHART_PADDING,hei-CHART_PADDING);
```

In these lines we are creating the L-shaped frame for our data; this is just to help and provide a visual aid.

The next step is to define the number of steps that we will use to represent the numeric data visually.

```
var stepSize = (hei - CHART_PADDING*2)/10;
```

In our sample we are hardcoding all of the data. So in the step size we are finding the total height of our chart (the height of our canvas minus our padding at the top and bottom), which we then divide by the number of the steps that will be used in the following `for` loop:

```
  for(var i=0; i<10; i++){
    context.moveTo(CHART_PADDING, CHART_PADDING + i*  stepSize);
context.lineTo(CHART_PADDING*1.3,CHART_PADDING + i*  stepSize);
    context.fillText(10-i, CHART_PADDING*1.5, CHART_PADDING + i*
stepSize + 6);
  }
```

We loop through 10 times going through each step to draw a short line. We then add numeric information using the `fillText` method.

Notice that we are sending in the value `10-i`. This value works well for us as we want the top value to be 10. We are starting at the top value of the chart; we want the displayed value to be 10 and as the value of `i` increases, we want our value to get smaller as we move down the vertical line in each step of the loop.

Next we want to define the width of each bar. In our case, we want the bars to touch each other and to do that we will take the total space available, and divide it by the number of data elements.

```
var elementWidth =(wid-CHART_PADDING*2)/ data.length;
```

At this stage we are ready to draw the bar but before we do that, we should calculate the width of the bars.

We then loop through all the data we have and create the bars:

```
context.fillStyle = data[i].style;
context.fillRect(CHART_PADDING +elementWidth*i ,hei-CHART_PADDING -
data[i].value*stepSize,elementWidth,data[i].value*stepSize);
context.fillStyle = "rgba(255, 255, 225, 0.8)";
context.fillText(data[i].label, CHART_PADDING +elementWidth*(i+.5),
hei-CHART_PADDING*1.5);
```

Notice that we are resetting the style twice each time the loop runs. If we didn't, we wouldn't get the colors we are hoping to get. We then place our text in the middle of the bar that was created.

```
context.textAlign = "center";
```

There's more...

In our example, we created a non-flexible bar chart, and if this is the way we create charts we will need to recreate them from scratch each time. Let's revisit our code and tweak it to make it more reusable.

Revisiting the code

Although everything is working exactly as we want it to work, if we played around with the values, it would stop working. For example, what if I only wanted to have five steps; if we go back to our code, we will locate the following lines:

```
var stepSize = (hei - CHART_PADDING*2)/10;
for(var i=0; i<10; i++){
```

We can tweak it to handle five steps:

```
var stepSize = (hei - CHART_PADDING*2)5;
for(var i=0; i<5; i++){
```

We would very quickly find out that our application is not working as expected.

To solve this problem let's create a new function that will deal with creating the outlines of the chart. Before we do that, let's extract the data object and create a new object that will contain the steps. Let's move the data and format it in an accessible format:

```
var data = [...];
var chartYData = [{label:"10 cats", value:1},
          {label:"5 cats", value:.5},
          {label:"3 cats", value:.3}];
var range = {min:0, max:10};

var CHART_PADDING = 20;
var wid;
var hei;
function init(){
```

Take a deep look into `chartYData` object as it enables us to put in as many steps as we want without a defined spacing rule and the range object that will store the minimum and maximum values of the overall graph. Before creating the new functions, let's add them into our `init` function (changes marked in bold).

```
function init(){
  var can = document.getElementById("bar");
  wid = can.width;
   hei = can.height;
  var context = can.getContext("2d");
  context.fillStyle = "#eeeeee";
  context.strokeStyle = "#999999";
  context.fillRect(0,0,wid,hei);

  context.font = "12pt Verdana, sans-serif";
  context.fillStyle = "#999999";


  context.moveTo(CHART_PADDING,CHART_PADDING);
  context.lineTo(CHART_PADDING,hei-CHART_PADDING);
  context.lineTo(wid-CHART_PADDING,hei-CHART_PADDING);
  fillChart(context,chartYData);
  createBars(context,data);
}
```

All we did in this code is to extract the creation of the chart and its bars into two separate functions. Now that we have an external data source both for the chart data and the content, we can build up their logic.

Using the fillChart function

The `fillChart` function's main goal is to create the foundation of the chart. We are integrating our new `stepData` object information and building up the chart based on its information.

```
function fillChart(context, stepsData){
  var steps = stepsData.length;
  var startY = CHART_PADDING;
  var endY = hei-CHART_PADDING;
  var chartHeight = endY-startY;
  var currentY;
  var rangeLength = range.max-range.min;
  for(var i=0; i<steps; i++){
    currentY = startY + (1-(stepsData[i].value/rangeLength)) *
chartHeight;
    context.moveTo(CHART_PADDING, currentY );
```

```
      context.lineTo(CHART_PADDING*1.3,currentY);
      context.fillText(stepsData[i].label, CHART_PADDING*1.5,
currentY+6);
    }
    context.stroke();

}
```

Our changes were not many, but with them we turned our function to be much more dynamic than it was before. This time around we are basing the positions on the `stepsData` objects and the range length that is based on that.

Using the createBars function

Our next step is to revisit the `createBars` area and update the information so it can be created dynamically using external objects.

```
function createBars(context,data){
  var elementWidth =(wid-CHART_PADDING*2)/ data.length;
  var startY = CHART_PADDING;
  var endY = hei-CHART_PADDING;
  var chartHeight = endY-startY;
  var rangeLength = range.max-range.min;
  var stepSize = chartHeight/rangeLength;
  context.textAlign = "center";
  for(i=0; i<data.length; i++){
    context.fillStyle = data[i].style;
    context.fillRect(CHART_PADDING +elementWidth*i ,hei-CHART_PADDING
- data[i].value*stepSize,elementWidth,data[i].value*stepSize);
    context.fillStyle = "rgba(255, 255, 225, 0.8)";
    context.fillText(data[i].label, CHART_PADDING
+elementWidth*(i+.5), hei-CHART_PADDING*1.5);
  }
}
```

Almost nothing changed here apart from a few changes in the way we positioned the data and extracted hardcoded values. Compare the two samples in our source code and find the differences between them.

Spreading data in a scatter chart

The scatter chart is a very powerful chart and is mainly used to get a bird's-eye view while comparing two data sets. For example, comparing the scores in an English class and the scores in a Math class to find a correlative relationship. This style of visual comparison can help find surprising relationships between unexpected data sets.

This is ideal when the goal is to show a lot of details in a very visual way.

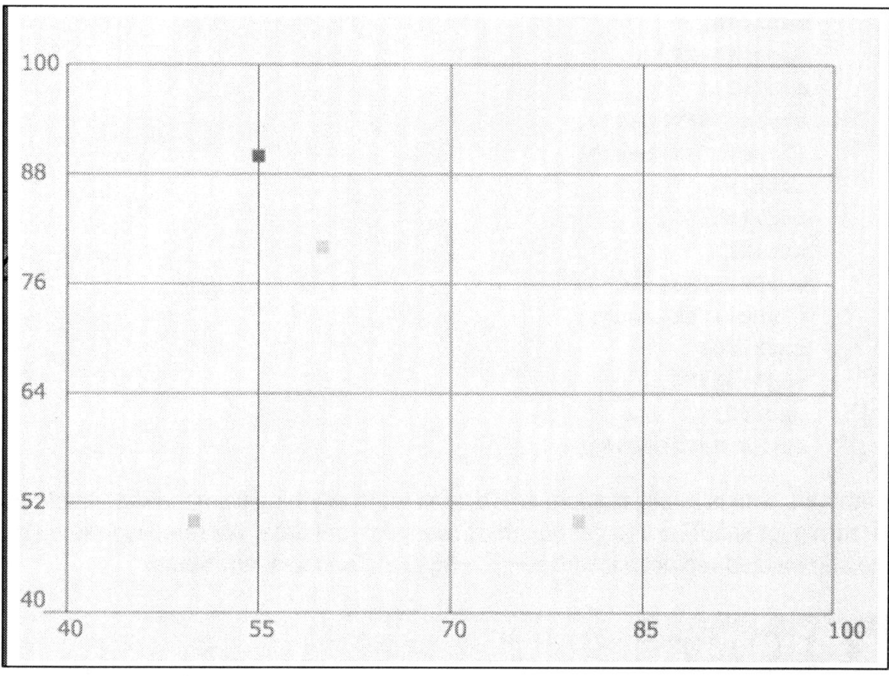

Getting ready

If you haven't had a chance yet to scan through the logic of our first recipe in this chapter, I recommend you take a peek at it as we are going to base a lot of our work on that while expanding and making it a bit more complex to accommodate two data sets.

The regular HTML start-up code can be found in the code bundle or go through *Chapter 1, Drawing Shapes in Canvas*, for more information on creating the HTML document.

I've revisited our data source from the previous recipe and modified it to store three variables of students' exam scores in Math, English, and Art.

```
var data = [{label:"David",
        math:50,
        english:80,
        art:92,
        style:"rgba(241, 178, 225, 0.5)"},
        {label:"Ben",
        math:80,
        english:60,
        art:43,
```

```
style:"#B1DDF3"},
{label:"Oren",
math:70,
english:20,
art:92,
style:"#FFDE89"},
{label:"Barbera",
math:90,
english:55,
art:81,
style:"#E3675C"},
{label:"Belann",
math:50,
english:50,
art:50,
style:"#C2D985"}];
```

Notice that this data is totally random so we can't learn anything from the data itself; but we can learn a lot about how to get our chart ready for real data. We removed the `value` attribute and instead replaced it with `math`, `english`, and `art` attributes.

How to do it...

Let's dive right into the JavaScript file and the changes we want to make:

1. Define the `y` space and `x` space. To do that, we will create a helper object that will store the required information:

   ```
   var chartInfo= { y:{min:40, max:100, steps:5,label:"math"},
           x:{min:40, max:100, steps:4,label:"english"}
         };
   ```

2. It's time for us to set up our other global variables and start up our `init` function:

   ```
   var CHART_PADDING = 30;
   var wid;
   var hei;
   function init(){

     var can = document.getElementById("bar");

     wid = can.width;
     hei = can.height;
     var context = can.getContext("2d");
     context.fillStyle = "#eeeeee";
     context.strokeStyle = "#999999";
   ```

```
    context.fillRect(0,0,wid,hei);

    context.font = "10pt Verdana, sans-serif";
    context.fillStyle = "#999999";

    context.moveTo(CHART_PADDING,CHART_PADDING);
    context.lineTo(CHART_PADDING,hei-CHART_PADDING);
    context.lineTo(wid-CHART_PADDING,hei-CHART_PADDING);

    fillChart(context,chartInfo);
    createDots(context,data);
  }
```

Not much is new here. The major changes are highlighted. Let's get on and start creating our `fillChart` and `createDots` functions.

3. If you worked on our previous recipe, you might notice that there are a lot of similarities between the functions in the previous recipe and this function. I've deliberately changed the way we create things just to make them more interesting. We are now dealing with two data points as well, so many details have changed. Let's review them:

```
function fillChart(context, chartInfo){
  var yData = chartInfo.y;
  var steps = yData.steps;
  var startY = CHART_PADDING;
  var endY = hei-CHART_PADDING;
  var chartHeight = endY-startY;
  var currentY;
  var rangeLength = yData.max-yData.min;
  var stepSize = rangeLength/steps;
  context.textAlign = "left";
  for(var i=0; i<steps; i++){
    currentY = startY + (i/steps) *     chartHeight;
    context.moveTo(wid-CHART_PADDING, currentY );
    context.lineTo(CHART_PADDING,currentY);
    context.fillText(yData.min+stepSize*(steps-i), 0, currentY+4);
  }

  currentY = startY +      chartHeight;
  context.moveTo(CHART_PADDING, currentY );
  context.lineTo(CHART_PADDING/2,currentY);
  context.fillText(yData.min, 0, currentY-3);
```

```
  var xData = chartInfo.x;
  steps = xData.steps;
  var startX = CHART_PADDING;
  var endX = wid-CHART_PADDING;
  var chartWidth = endX-startX;
  var currentX;
  rangeLength = xData.max-xData.min;
  stepSize = rangeLength/steps;
  context.textAlign = "left";
  for(var i=0; i<steps; i++){
    currentX = startX + (i/steps) *      chartWidth;
    context.moveTo(currentX, startY );
    context.lineTo(currentX,endY);
    context.fillText(xData.min+stepSize*(i), currentX-6,
endY+CHART_PADDING/2);
  }

  currentX = startX +       chartWidth;
  context.moveTo(currentX, startY );
  context.lineTo(currentX,endY);
  context.fillText(xData.max, currentX-3, endY+CHART_PADDING/2);


  context.stroke();

}
```

When you review this code you will notice that our logic is almost duplicated twice. While in the first loop and first batch of variables we are figuring out the positions of each element in the `y` space, we move on in the second half of this function to calculate the layout for the `x` area. The y axis in canvas grows from top to bottom (top lower, bottom higher) and as such we need to calculate the height of the full graph and then subtract the value to find positions.

4. Our last function is to render the data points and to do that we create the `createDots` function:

```
function createDots(context,data){
  var yDataLabel = chartInfo.y.label;
  var xDataLabel = chartInfo.x.label;
  var yDataRange = chartInfo.y.max-chartInfo.y.min;
  var xDataRange = chartInfo.x.max-chartInfo.x.min;
  var chartHeight = hei- CHART_PADDING*2;
  var chartWidth = wid- CHART_PADDING*2;

  var yPos;
  var xPos;
```

```
    for(var i=0; i<data.length;i++){
      xPos = CHART_PADDING + (data[i][xDataLabel]-chartInfo.x.min)/
  xDataRange * chartWidth;
      yPos = (hei - CHART_PADDING)  -(data[i][yDataLabel]-
  chartInfo.y.min)/yDataRange * chartHeight;

      context.fillStyle = data[i].style;
      context.fillRect(xPos-4 ,yPos-4,8,8);

    }
  }
```

Here we are figuring out the same details for each point—both the `y` position and the `x` position—and then we draw a rectangle. Let's test our application now!

How it works...

We start by creating a new `chartInfo` object:

```
var chartInfo= { y:{min:40, max:100, steps:5,label:"math"},
      x:{min:40, max:100, steps:4,label:"english"}
    };
```

This very simple object encapsulates the rules that will define what our chart will actually output. Looking closely you will see that we set an object named `chartInfo` that has information on the y and x axes. We have a minimum value (`min` property), maximum value (`max` property), and the number of steps we want to have in our chart (`steps` property), and we define a label.

Let's look deeper into the way the `fillChart` function works. In essence we have two numeric values; one is the actual space on the screen and the other is the value the space represents. To match these values we need to know what our data range is and also what our view range is, so we first start by finding our `startY` point and our `endY` point followed by calculating the number of pixels between these two points:

```
var startY = CHART_PADDING;
var endY = hei-CHART_PADDING;
var chartHeight = endY-startY;
```

These values will be used when we try to figure out where to place the data from the `chartInfo` object. As we are already speaking about that object, let's look at what we do with it:

```
var yData = chartInfo.y;
var steps = yData.steps;
var rangeLength = yData.max-yData.min;
var stepSize = rangeLength/steps;
```

As our focus right now is on the height, we are looking deeper into the `y` property and for the sake of comfort we will call it `yData`. Now that we are focused on this object, it's time to figure out what is the actual data range (`rangeLength`) of this value, which will be our converter number. In other words we want to take a visual space between the points `startY` and `endY` and based on the the range, position it in this space. When we do so we can convert any data into a range between 0-1 and then position them in a dynamic visible area.

Last but not least, as our new data object contains the number of steps we want to add into the chart, we use that data to define the step value. In this example it would be 12. The way we get to this value is by taking our `rangeLength` (100 - 40 = 60) value and then dividing it by the number of `steps` (in our case 5). Now that we have got the critical variables out of the way, it's time to loop through the data and draw our chart:

```
var currentY;
context.textAlign = "left";
  for(var i=0; i<steps; i++){
    currentY = startY + (i/steps) *  chartHeight;
    context.moveTo(wid-CHART_PADDING, currentY );
    context.lineTo(CHART_PADDING,currentY);
    context.fillText(yData.min+stepSize*(steps-i), 0, currentY+4);
  }
```

This is where the magic comes to life. We run through the number of steps and then calculate the new `Y` position again. If we break it down we will see:

```
currentY = startY + (i/steps) *      chartHeight;
```

We start from the start position of our chart (upper area) and then we add to it the steps by taking the current `i` position and dividing it by the total possible steps (0/5, 1/5, 2/5 and so on). In our demo it's 5, but it can be any value and should be inserted into the `chartInfo` steps attribute. We multiply the returned value by the height of our chart calculated earlier.

To compensate for the fact that we started from the top we need to reverse the actual text we put into the text field:

```
yData.min+stepSize*(steps-i)
```

This code takes our earlier variables and puts them to work. We start by taking the minimal value possible and then add into it `stepSize` times the total number of steps subtracted by the number of the current step.

Let's dig into the `createDots` function and see how it works. We start with our setup variables:

```
var yDataLabel = chartInfo.y.label;
var xDataLabel = chartInfo.x.label;
```

This is one of my favorite parts of this recipe. We are grabbing the label from our `chartInfo` object and using that as our ID; this ID will be used to grab information from our data object. If you wish to change the values, all you need to do is switch the labels in the `chartInfo` object.

Again it's time for us to figure out our ranges as we've done earlier in the `fillChart` function. This time around we want to get the actual ranges for both the x and y axes and the actual width and height of the area we have to work with:

```
var yDataRange = chartInfo.y.max-chartInfo.y.min;
var xDataRange = chartInfo.x.max-chartInfo.x.min;
var chartHeight = hei- CHART_PADDING*2;
var chartWidth = wid- CHART_PADDING*2;
```

We also need to get a few variables to help us keep track of our current `x` and `y` positions within loops:

```
var yPos;
var xPos;
```

Let's go deeper into our loop, mainly into the highlighted code snippets:

```
for(var i=0; i<data.length;i++){
    xPos = CHART_PADDING + (data[i][xDataLabel]-chartInfo.x.min)/
    xDataRange * chartWidth;
    yPos = (hei - CHART_PADDING)  -(data[i][yDataLabel]-
    chartInfo.y.min)/yDataRange * chartHeight;

    context.fillStyle = data[i].style;
    context.fillRect(xPos-4 ,yPos-4,8,8);

  }
```

The heart of everything here is discovering where our elements need to be. The logic is almost identical for both the `xPos` and `yPos` variables with a few variations. The first thing we need to do to calculate the `xPos` variable is:

```
(data[i][xDataLabel]-chartInfo.x.min)
```

In this part we are using the label, `xDataLabel`, we created earlier to get the current student score in that subject. We then subtract from it the lowest possible score. As our chart doesn't start from 0, we don't want the values between 0 and our minimum value to affect the position on the screen. For example, let's say we are focused on math and our student has a score of 80; we subtract 40 out of that (80 - 40 = 40) and then apply the following formula:

```
(data[i][xDataLabel] - chartInfo.x.min) / xDataRange
```

We divide that value by our data range; in our case that would be (100 - 40)/60. The returned result will always be between 0 and 1. We can use the returned number and multiply it by the actual space in pixels to know exactly where to position our element on the screen. We do so by multiplying the value we got, that is between 0 and 1, by the total available space (in this case, width). Once we know where it needs to be located we add the starting point on our chart (the padding):

```
xPos = CHART_PADDING + (data[i][xDataLabel]-chartInfo.x.min)/
xDataRange * chartWidth;
```

The `yPos` variable has the same logic as that of the `xPos` variable, but here we focus only on the height.

Building line charts

The line charts are based on scatter charts. Contrary to scatter charts that show isolated correlation between two variables, the line chart tells a story in many ways; we can go back to our previous recipe, *Spreading data in a scatter chart*, and draw a line between the dots to create the connection. This type of chart is usually used in website statistics, tracking things over time, speed, age, and so on. Let's jump right into it and see it in action.

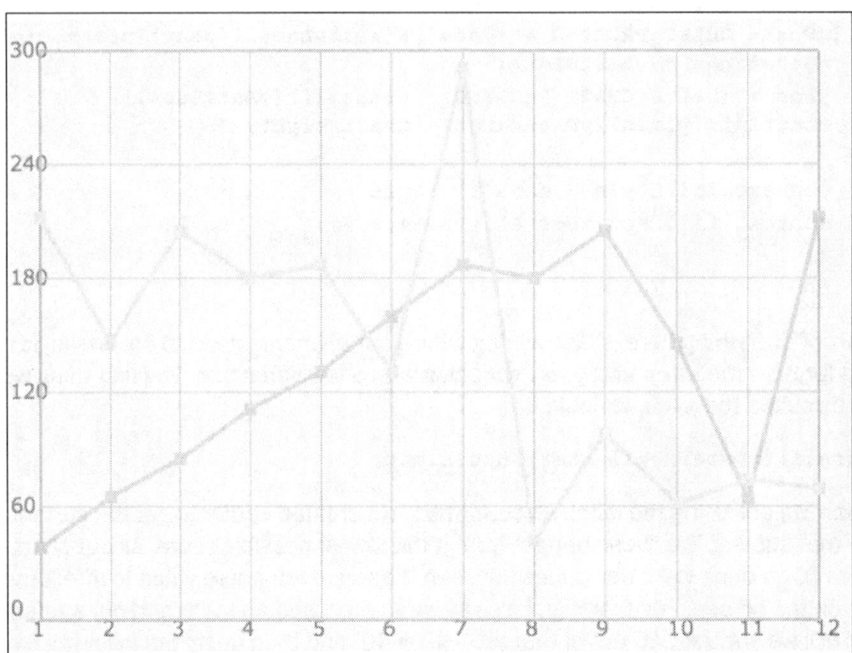

Getting ready

As usual get your HTML wrapper ready. In this recipe we actually are going to base our changes on the previous recipe, *Spreading data in a scatter chart*.

In our case study for this example, we will create a chart that shows how many new members joined my site, `02Geek.com`, in 2011 and 2010. I've gathered the information month by month and gathered it into two arrays:

```
var a2011 = [38,65,85,111,131,160,187,180,205,146,64,212];
var a2010 = [212,146,205,180,187,131,291,42,98,61,74,69];
```

Both arrays have a length of 12 (for 12 months of the year). I've deliberately created a new data source that is totally different than the one we used earlier. I did that to render our old map useless in this example. I've done it to add some extra value into this recipe (a good lesson in manipulating data to fit even when it doesn't, instead of rebuilding things).

```
var chartInfo= { y:{min:0, max:300, steps:5,label:"users"},
        x:{min:1, max:12, steps:11,label:"months"}
      };
```

For our chart information we are using the same object type and for the `y` position we will assume a range from 0 to 300 (as I haven't had the privilege of having more than 300 members in one month, yet I'm hopeful). For our `x` position we are setting it to output values from 1 through 12 (for the 12 months of the year).

OK, it's time to build it!

How to do it...

As always, our `init` function is going to look very similar to the one we used in the previous recipe. Let's take a look at the modifications that have taken place in this recipe:

1. Update/create the global variables:

```
var a2011 = [38,65,85,111,131,160,187,180,205,146,64,212];
var a2010 = [212,146,205,180,187,131,291,42,98,61,74,69];

var chartInfo= { y:{min:0, max:300, steps:5,label:"users"},
        x:{min:1, max:12, steps:11,label:"months"}
      };

var CHART_PADDING = 20;
var wid;
var hei;
```

2. Update the `init` function:

```
function init(){

  var can = document.getElementById("bar");

  wid = can.width;
  hei = can.height;
  var context = can.getContext("2d");
  context.fillStyle = "#eeeeee";
  context.strokeStyle = "#999999";
  context.fillRect(0,0,wid,hei);

  context.font = "10pt Verdana, sans-serif";
  context.fillStyle = "#999999";


  context.moveTo(CHART_PADDING,CHART_PADDING);
  context.rect(CHART_PADDING,CHART_PADDING,wid-CHART_
  PADDING*2,hei-CHART_PADDING*2);
  context.stroke();
  context.strokeStyle = "#cccccc";
  fillChart(context,chartInfo);
  addLine(context,formatData(a2011, "/2011","#B1DDF3"),"#B1DDF3");
  addLine(context,formatData(a2010, "/2010","#FFDE89"),"#FFDE89");
}
```

3. Change the name of the function `createDots` to `addLine` and update the logic:

```
function addLine(context,data,style){
  var yDataLabel = chartInfo.y.label;
  var xDataLabel = chartInfo.x.label;
  var yDataRange = chartInfo.y.max-chartInfo.y.min;
  var xDataRange = chartInfo.x.max-chartInfo.x.min;
  var chartHeight = hei- CHART_PADDING*2;
  var chartWidth = wid- CHART_PADDING*2;

  var yPos;
  var xPos;
  context.strokeStyle = style;
  context.beginPath();
  context.lineWidth = 3;
  for(var i=0; i<data.length;i++){
    xPos = CHART_PADDING + (data[i][xDataLabel]-chartInfo.x.min)/
xDataRange * chartWidth;
    yPos = (hei - CHART_PADDING)  -(data[i][yDataLabel]-
chartInfo.y.min)/yDataRange * chartHeight;

    context.fillStyle = data[i].style;
    context.fillRect(xPos-4 ,yPos-4,8,8);
```

```
        i ? context.lineTo(xPos,yPos):context.moveTo(xPos,yPos);

      }
      context.stroke();
    }
```

4. Create the `formatData` function:

```
    function formatData(data , labelCopy , style){
      newData = [];
      for(var i=0; i<data.length;i++){
        newData.push({  label:(i+1)+labelCopy,
                users:data[i],
                months:i+1,
                style:style
                });
      }

      return newData;
    }
```

That's it! We are done!

How it works...

I've added a new method, `rect`, to our tool set for drawing; until now we worked with the `drawRect` method. I've used the `rect` method as it just adds the outlines without drawing anything, so I can perform the stroke or fill function separately and create an outline instead of a fill.

The `fillChart` function did not change at all, cool right? And I've renamed the function `createDots` to `addLine` as it seemed more appropriate for our sample. A few additions have been made into that function and a new function, `formatData`, is being used to format the data to fit what the `addLine` function is expecting.

As you probably noticed we made a few small changes to our code to accommodate the needs of this chart style. Let's dive in and see them in action:

```
addLine(context,formatData(a2011,"/2011","#B1DDF3"),"#B1DDF3")
```

The biggest change we can visibly see in the way we are calling the `addLine` function is that we are calling the `formatData` function to render a data source for us that will be acceptable by the `addLine` function. You might be thinking right now, why didn't I just create the data the way it needs to work for the `addLine` function. When we move to the real, live data sources many times we will find data sources that just don't match our original work. That doesn't mean we need to change our work, often a better solution is to create a converter method that will modify the data and rebuild it to match our application structure so it is in the format we expect.

A reminder from our previous recipe: this is what our data source looked like:

```
var data = [{label:"David",
        math:50,
        english:80,
        art:92
        style:"rgba(241, 178, 225, 0.5)"},
        ...
        ];
```

While currently our array is flat, we need to change that to work with our current system; it expects two properties that will define the `x` and `y` values:

```
var chartInfo= { y:{min:0, max:300, steps:5,label:"users"},
        x:{min:1, max:12, steps:11,label:"months"}
```

In other words the object we need to create needs to look something like the following:

```
var data = [{label: "01/2011",
        users:200,
       months:1,
       style:"#ff0000"} … ];
```

So let's make the function that will create this data format:

```
function formatData(data , labelCopy , style){
  newData = [];
  for(var i=0; i<data.length;i++){
    newData.push({      label:(i+1)+labelCopy,
              users:data[i],
              months:i+1,
              style:style
              });
  }

  return newData;
}
```

Notice how we loop through our old array and restructure it to fit our expected data format using both the array data and external data that was sent to our `formatData` functions. Even though we aren't using all of the information in this recipe, I wanted to keep it up-to-date with all the basics in case you want to expand this sample. We will do so in the future.

This is one of the most powerful tricks in programing in the tool set. I've met many developers, who change their code instead of changing their data to fit their required application structure. There is always a way to modify data to make it more easily consumed by your application and it's much easier to dynamically modify data than it is to change your architecture.

I didn't change anything in the core logic of this `addLine` function, but instead just added drawing lines from one dot to the next one.

In case you're not familiar with the ternary operation, it is a shorthanded `if` statement:

```
condition ? ifStatement: elseStatement;
```

By the way, if you are worried about efficiency, you might want to change the `for` loop by extracting the first instance out of the loop as that's the only occurrence where our ternary operator would trigger the else value.

There's more...

Let's revisit our code and optimize it to be more adaptable. Our goal is to add more flexibility to our chart to render in various modes.

My goal here is to enable our chart to render in three render modes: dot mode (as in the previous sample), line mode (in this sample), and fill mode (new addition):

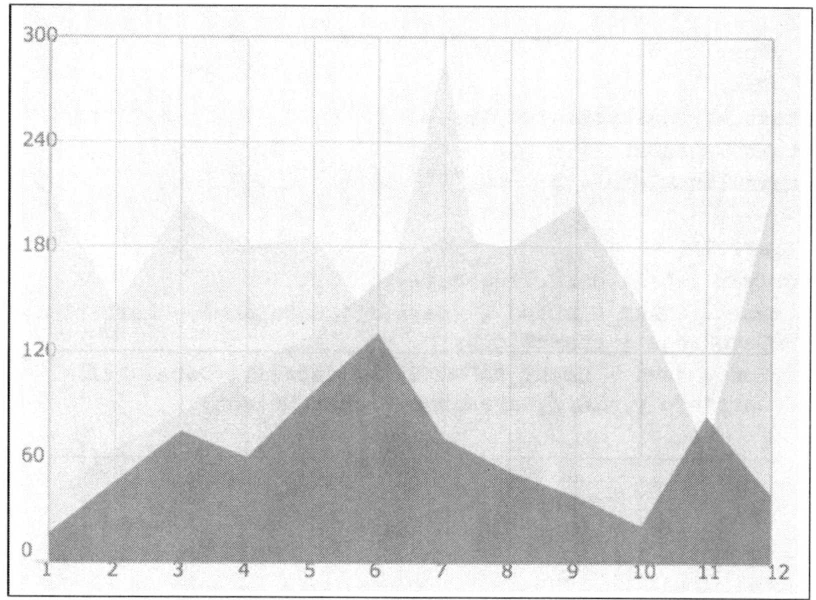

Although, in the preceding screenshot, we have three chart elements and they're all with a fill, with the new code you can pick, per line added, how you wish to treat it. So let's jump right in.

Enabling switching mode between dots and lines

All the work we added into the function doesn't need to go through a big overhaul as nothing is visible until it's actually rendered. That is controlled in one line, where we create the stroke in the `addLine` function. So let's add a new rule that if a style is not sent, it would mean we don't want to create a line:

```
if(style)context.stroke();
```

In other words, only if we have style information will the line we just created be drawn; if not, no line will be drawn.

Creating fill shapes

To create the fill shapes and for the sake of keeping our code simple, we will create an `if...else` statement within our code, and if the user sends a new fourth parameter, we will render it in the fill mode (the changes are highlighted in the following code snippet):

```
function addLine(context,data,style,isFill){
  var yDataLabel = chartInfo.y.label;
  var xDataLabel = chartInfo.x.label;
  var yDataRange = chartInfo.y.max-chartInfo.y.min;
  var xDataRange = chartInfo.x.max-chartInfo.x.min;
  var chartHeight = hei- CHART_PADDING*2;
  var chartWidth = wid- CHART_PADDING*2;

  var yPos;
  var xPos;
  context.strokeStyle = style;
  context.beginPath();
  context.lineWidth = 3;

  if(!isFill){
    for(var i=0; i<data.length;i++){
      xPos = CHART_PADDING + (data[i][xDataLabel]-chartInfo.x.min)/
      xDataRange * chartWidth;
      yPos = (hei - CHART_PADDING)  -(data[i][yDataLabel]-
      chartInfo.y.min)/yDataRange * chartHeight;
```

```
            context.fillStyle = data[i].style;
            context.fillRect(xPos-4 ,yPos-4,8,8);

            i==0? context.moveTo(xPos,yPos):context.lineTo(xPos,yPos);

        }
        if(style)context.stroke();
    }else{
        context.fillStyle = style;
        context.globalAlpha = .6;
        context.moveTo(CHART_PADDING,hei - CHART_PADDING)
        for(var i=0; i<data.length;i++){
            xPos = CHART_PADDING + (data[i][xDataLabel]-chartInfo.x.min)/
            xDataRange * chartWidth;
            yPos = (hei - CHART_PADDING)  -(data[i][yDataLabel]-
            chartInfo.y.min)/yDataRange * chartHeight;

            context.lineTo(xPos,yPos);

        }
        context.lineTo(     CHART_PADDING + chartWidth,
        CHART_PADDING+chartHeight);
        context.closePath();
        context.fill();
        context.globalAlpha = 1;
    }
}
```

The differences are not large in the new code. We just removed some of the code and added a few new lines to create a complete shape. I superimposed the Alpha value as well. A smarter way would be to revisit the values sent and put into them an Alpha value as needed; but that is left for you to improve. Now our `addLine` function can add three types of visualization and we can add multiple types at the same time to our chart (check out the source code to see this in action).

Creating the flying brick chart (waterfall chart)

In each recipe in this chapter we've been advancing the complexity of our code and so we are going to revisit the bar chart and modernize it to fit our evolving charting platform. After we complete this mini task, we will be ready to create our first waterfall chart breaking away from the standard charts into more creative avenues.

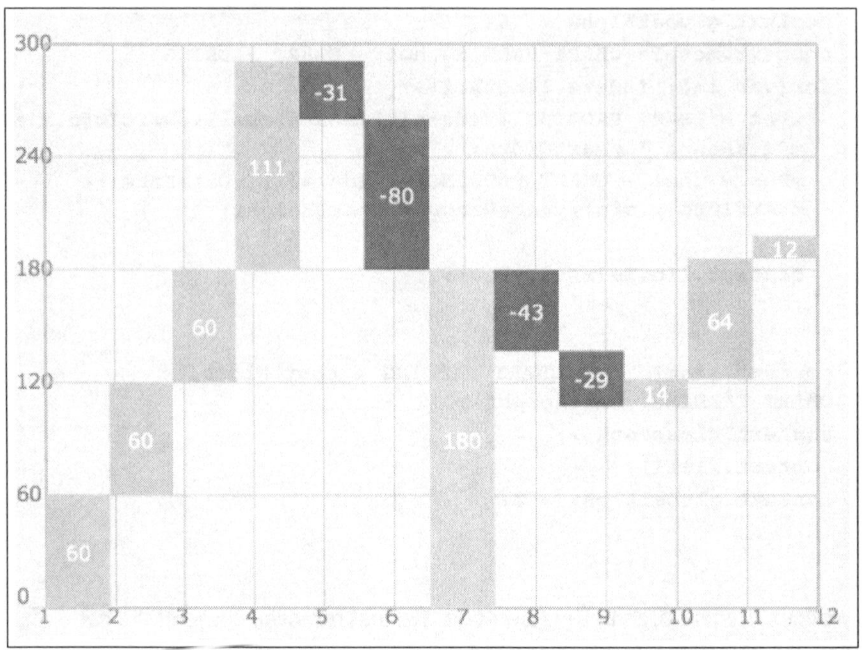

The waterfall chart is a very useful chart to outline trends, such as monthly total changes (positive and negative) while outlining the total value of the big picture. This type of chart helps to outline total assets of a company while showing if they made profits or losses throughout the month. This type of chart is ideal for data that shifts between positive/ negative values.

Getting ready

We will be taking advantage of the interface we created in the earlier recipes and as such we will be integrating the creation of bars into our library of updated functions. To do that, we will need to dig out our old `createBars` function created in `03.02.bar-revamp.js`.

The following is the code before implementing changes:

```
function createBars(context,data){
  var elementWidth =(wid-CHART_PADDING*2)/ data.length;
  var startY = CHART_PADDING;
  var endY = hei-CHART_PADDING;
  var chartHeight = endY-startY;
  var rangeLength = range.max-range.min;
  var stepSize = chartHeight/rangeLength;
  context.textAlign = "center";
  for(i=0; i<data.length; i++){
    context.fillStyle = data[i].style;
    context.fillRect(CHART_PADDING +elementWidth*i ,hei-CHART_PADDING
- data[i].value*stepSize,elementWidth,data[i].value*stepSize);
    context.fillStyle = "rgba(255, 255, 225, 0.8)";
    context.fillText(data[i].label, CHART_PADDING
+elementWidth*(i+.5), hei-CHART_PADDING*1.5);

  }
}
```

And the following is our newly updated function to fit into the new skills we developed in the earlier recipes (changes are highlighted in the following code snippet).

```
function createBars(context,data){

  var range = chartInfo.x;
  var elementWidth =(wid-CHART_PADDING*2)/ data.length;
  var startY = CHART_PADDING;
  var endY = hei-CHART_PADDING;
  var chartHeight = endY-startY;
  var stepSize = chartHeight/(chartInfo.y.max-chartInfo.y.min);
  context.textAlign = "center";
  for(i=0; i<data.length; i++){
    context.fillStyle = data[i].style;
    context.fillRect(CHART_PADDING +elementWidth*i ,endY
    - data[i][chartInfo.y.label]*stepSize,elementWidth,data[i]
    [chartInfo.y.label]*stepSize);
    context.fillStyle = "rgba(255, 255, 225, 0.8)";
    context.fillText(data[i].label, CHART_PADDING
+elementWidth*(i+.5), hei-CHART_PADDING*1.5);

  }

}
```

These changes are more than cosmetic; we are leveraging our external data feeds that have been used throughout a few of our previous samples. Now that our function is up-to-date and working in our latest logic developed in the previous two recipes, it's time to start building our waterfall chart.

How to do it...

The first step to create a waterfall chart is to copy, paste, and rename the function `createBars` and then manipulate it and change the way the data is rendered (mainly where and how we position elements). Notice what we change in this method before I dig deeper into why and how it was done:

1. Let's start with an updated data source:

```
var a2011 = [60,60,60,111,-31,-80,0,-43,-29,14,64,12];
var chartInfo= { y:{min:0, max:300, steps:5,label:"users"},
        x:{min:1, max:12, steps:11,label:"months"}
        };
var CHART_PADDING = 20;
var wid;
var hei;
```

2. In the `init` function we will update the following highlighted code snippets:

```
function init(){

  ...
  context.strokeStyle = "#cccccc";
  fillChart(context,chartInfo);
  createWaterfall(context,formatData(a2011));
}
```

3. Add a few helper variables:

```
function createWaterfall(context,data){

  var range = chartInfo.x;
  var elementWidth =(wid-CHART_PADDING*2)/ data.length;
  var startY = CHART_PADDING;
  var endY = hei-CHART_PADDING;
  var chartHeight = endY-startY;
  var stepSize = chartHeight/(chartInfo.y.max-chartInfo.y.min);
  var currentY= endY;
  var elementValue ;
  var total=0;
  context.textAlign = "center";
```

4. In the `for` loop logic, draw a rectangle if the value is not `0`:

```
for(i=0; i<data.length; i++){
  elementValue = data[i][chartInfo.y.label];
  total +=elementValue;
  if(elementValue!=0){
    context.fillStyle = elementValue>0? "#C2D985" :"#E3675C" ;
    currentY -=(elementValue*stepSize);
    context.fillRect(CHART_PADDING +elementWidth*i ,currentY,ele
    mentWidth,elementValue*stepSize);
  }
```

5. If the current data value is `0` then make it a total column:

```
else{
    context.fillStyle = "#B1DDF3" ;

    context.fillRect(CHART_PADDING +elementWidth*i
    ,currentY,elementWidth,endY-currentY);
    elementValue = total; //hack so we see the right value
  }
  context.fillStyle = "rgba(255, 255, 255, .8)"
;
```

6. Add the changed value inside the element:

```
  context.fillText(elementValue, CHART_PADDING
  +elementWidth*(i+.5), endY - (stepSize*total) +
  (stepSize*elementValue/2) + 6);

 }

}
```

There are a lot of changes here, but in essence these two functions do almost the same thing; only our waterfall chart is smarter and more detailed.

How it works...

The first step and the first problem when we start to think about how to create a waterfall chart is that there is a relationship between each element. To simplify the logic we would want to create a counter that would store the changes (the current summary value).

```
var elementValue ;
var total=0;
```

The first variable is just a helper variable to try to make our code more readable while the total is all about keeping up with what is the current total.

It's time to jump into the `for` loop and see the big changes. Let's focus first on the types of tasks we might need to do within a waterfall chart. There are three types (value goes up, value goes down, and value remains unchanged). Before we start figuring out how to deal with these cases, let's update our variables:

```
for(i=0; i<data.length; i++){
    elementValue = data[i][chartInfo.y.label];
    total +=elementValue;
```

The element value will give us the current numeric value (don't forget this does not correspond to the size on screen; we would still need to duplicate this by the `stepSize` number when we want to draw the element as this is the raw real number). Same is true for our `total` variable; we are just keeping track of the current summary.

So as we stated earlier, we have three possible tasks and there is nothing wrong with creating an `if...else` case as follows:

```
if(elementValue>0){
  //do the positive values
}else if(elementValue<0){
  //do the negative values
}else{
  //do 0
}
```

This would capture all three options but would add some extra code that wouldn't be needed. So, we will use the same `if` statement for both negative and positive values as their logic is very close to each other. That way we can reuse our code and type less.

```
if(elementValue!=0){
  //do positive/negative values
}else{
  // do 0
}
```

Perfecto! Now let's dig into the positive/negative task:

```
context.fillStyle = elementValue>0? "#C2D985" :"#E3675C" ;
currentY -=(elementValue*stepSize);
context.fillRect(CHART_PADDING +elementWidth*i ,currentY,elementWidth,
elementValue*stepSize);
```

Notice that our first line of code in this block is the only difference between positive/negative values. We are literally just changing a color based on whether we are in the positive or negative range using a ternary operation. After figuring out our `currentY` position we create a rectangle in the current position (this current position is after the value was added, so this is our end point). The most important element to notice is the fourth parameter, `elementValue*stepSize`. The fourth parameter captures the size of the rectangle. With it, it captures if it's a negative or positive value. The `elementValue` variable can be positive or negative. This is the trick we are using here as we would draw the bar upwards (if the value is negative) or draw the bar downwards (if the value is positive). If we first created the drawing before updating our `currentY` position, it would be much harder and probably require us to create the three separate `if` cases. Cases like these are really what makes programming so much fun to me; finding these hidden ways to take advantage of the same code to do opposite things.

It's time for us to visit the `else` case:

```
}else{
    context.fillStyle = "#B1DDF3" ;

    context.fillRect(CHART_PADDING +elementWidth*i
    ,currentY,elementWidth,endY-currentY);
    elementValue = total; //hack so we see the right value
    }
```

In the `else` case we want to draw the full length of the bar followed by a small hack. We are assigning the value of our current total into the `elementValue` variable (this will not change our original data as we are doing this as the last thing after we have no more use for the `elementValue` variable). We are doing this to avoid another `if...else` statement when adding the text into the bars. Only if the value is `0`, we want the total to be displayed instead of the current change and that's what this hack captures.

Leaving us the last part of creating a bar for our waterfall chart, which is to get the value of the bar in the center of the element we just created:

```
context.fillStyle = "rgba(255, 255, 255, .8)";
context.fillText(elementValue, CHART_PADDING +elementWidth*(i+.5),
endY - (stepSize*total) + (stepSize*elementValue/2) + 6);
```

Take a deep look at the positioning of the text element; it took a bit of tinkering until I figured it out. What I'm doing here mainly in the last parameter (the `y` position of our new text) is taking the bottom area of our chart, subtracting the current total that would give us exactly the tip of the bar. But that wouldn't work well as for positive values as it would be above the bar while for negative elements it would place it within the bottom area of the bar. Here comes the creative thinking; instead of creating a few cases, how about we position our text exactly in the middle of our element. To do that, we can take advantage of our `elementValue` variable again (as it's positive or negative) and if we take half its size and add it to our total, we will be in the center of the bar leaving only one last tweak adding 6 to our value (as our text is 12 pixels in height).

There you go! You have just created your first waterfall chart. Let's test it; remove any data visualization function calls from our `init` function (such as `createBars` or `addLine`) and instead replace them with our new function:

```
createWaterfall(context,formatData(a2011));
```

Note that I am using the `formatData` object as I'm just reusing our array from an earlier sample. I just updated the values so they don't step out of a total of 300:

```
var a2011 = [60,60,60,111,-31,-80,0,-43,-
29,14,64,12];
```

There's more...

Where we ended, leads us to the issue that we can't control the data and the more we ask of the end user/developer to adjust, the longer the learning curve is. It's great that we have our `chartInfo` object that stores most of our helper information, but what if someone doesn't fill out the attributes? Should our application fail or should we do our best to figure out new default values for the user? So let's say in this example the user does not fill out the `max` and `min` attributes of the `y` object:

```
var chartInfo= { y:{steps:5,label:"users"},
        x:{min:1, max:12, steps:11,label:"months"}
        };
```

The user indicates how many steps they want, but they do not provide any information on the smallest and largest values the chart should output. To solve this issue we need to revisit the way we are creating our charts. So far we created the chart in two totally separate steps (the last two lines in our `init` function):

```
fillChart(context,chartInfo);
createWaterfall(context,formatData(a2011));
```

First we usually create the background and then draw the items, but in this case we have a much clearer relationship between the `fillchart` function and the `createWaterfall` function. As we are trying to reduce the user's code footprint we wouldn't want to add a bunch of logic for each sample that would be unique for each bar type. So instead we will revisit all the graphic functions we created (`addLine`, `createBars`, and `createWaterfall`) and move the `fillChart` function call to be the first thing in the functions. This will enable us to create custom tweaks before calling the `fillChart` function that would be invisible to the end user of our functions (such as you in a few months, so you don't need to remember how everything works). Everything should work the same for now but only our `createWaterfall` function will know how to deal with missing information (I'll leave it up to you to update the other functions).

```
function createWaterfall(context,data){
  fillChart(context,chartInfo);
```

```
//all the rest the same
//do to all 3 functions
```

Now that we have our `fillChart` function and everything is working, let's add some extra logic just before we call the `fillChart` function to help add the `min/max` values dynamically:

```
function createWaterfall(context,data){
  if(!chartInfo.y.min || !chartInfo.y.max)
    updateCumulativeChartInfo(chartInfo,data);
  fillChart(context,chartInfo);
```

Notice that we are checking to see if the `min` or `max` values are missing and if so, we are calling the `updateCumulativeChartInfo` function to update or add the values.

Let's create the `updateCumulativeChartInfo` function:

```
function updateCumulativeChartInfo(chartInfo,data){
  var aTotal=[];
  var total = 0;
  aTotal.push(total);
  for(i=0; i<data.length; i++){
    total +=data[i][chartInfo.y.label]
    aTotal.push(total);

  }
  chartInfo.y.min = Math.min.apply(this,aTotal);
  chartInfo.y.max = Math.max.apply(this,aTotal);
}
```

We are using two variables: `aTotal` and `total`. The `aTotal` variable stores the total in each loop. After we have the value of our `total` variable throughout all phases of our chart within the `aTotal` array, it's time to figure out what the minimum and maximum value will be. We have a problem here. The `Math.min` method can take in an unlimited number of parameters but we have an array that isn't compatible with the requirements of the `Math.min` method. To determine the values we can use a fun hack by using the `apply` method. Every function has an `apply` method. What the `apply` method does is enable you to change the scope of a function and send the parameters as an array.

For more info on the `apply` method check the video at the following website:

`http://02geek.com/catagory/favorites/apply.html`

Now that our data has been dynamically created everything should work. When we run the application we will see we are getting some numbers that are too detailed (such as 3.33333). The next step is to do some format tweaking.

Cleaning the format of numbers

To solve the problem of our numeric values being very ugly, we can create a formatting function and just call it each time we output dynamically created values. So let's first create the function:

```
function formatNumber(num,lead){
  for(var i=0;i<lead;i++) num*=10;
  num = parseInt(num);
  for(var i=0;i<lead;i++) num/=10;
  return num;
}
```

The function parameters are the values to be formatted (`num`) and the number of places we want after the decimal point. In the function, we are multiplying the value by ten; the number of times is based on the value of the `lead` variable. We then convert the number into an integer and divide the number again.

Last but not least, let's track down where we are adding the text; we will find it in the `fillChart` function. All that is left for us is to find the right text that is affected and update it to use our new formatting function:

```
context.fillText(formatNumber(yData.min+stepSize*(steps-i),2), 0,
currentY+4);
```

Our format will look much better. And yes, you probably should leave these details to be configurable in the external `chartInfo` object, but we will leave that to you to make our library even smarter.

Other tasks I've left open

Our new waterfall has one assumption that we always start from zero. In our sample we won't change that, but we will revisit this idea in the next recipe when working with the candlestick chart. If you're bold, try to figure out a solution.

Building a candlestick chart (stock chart)

We are just about to make a super leap. Until now we worked with charts that had one data point, two data points, and a few variations on them, and now we are moving into a new world of four data points in every bar. The stock chart is a way to showcase changes in the market in a given time frame (in our example this is one day). Each day stock prices change many times, but the most important factors are the low and high values of the day and the opening and closing prices. A stock analyst needs to be able to see the information quickly and understand overall trends. We are skipping three data points elements, but we will be back to them in the recipe *Building a bubble chart* in *Chapter 4, Let's Curve Things Up*.

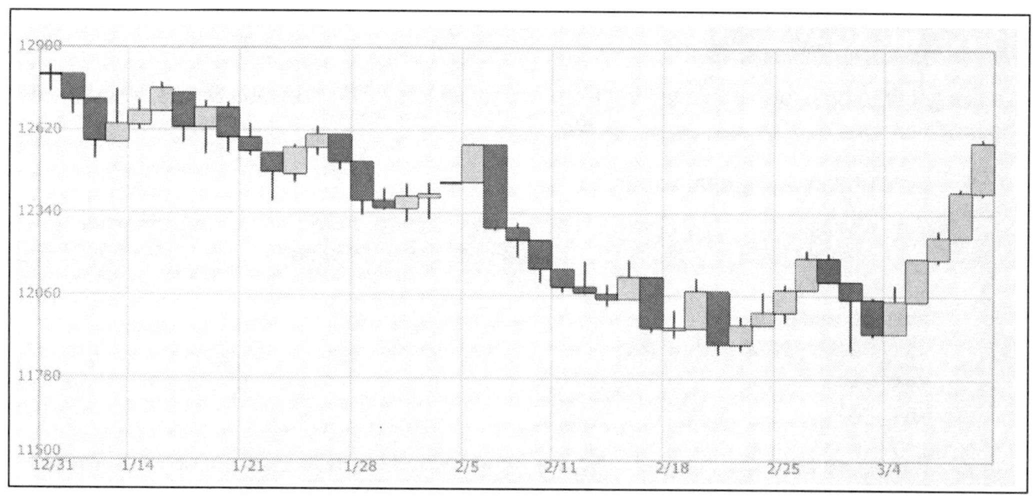

The worst thing you can do is to assume that the only usage of four dimensions of data is in the stock market. This is where you can come up with the next big thing. Visualizing data in a clean and quick way and converting data into logic is one of the most fun things about charts. With that said let's start creating our stock chart.

Getting ready

Our first step is going to be a bit different in this recipe. I've created a sample CSV file called `DJI.txt`; you can find it in our source files. The format is the standard CSV format and the first line names all the data columns:

```
DATE,CLOSE,HIGH,LOW,OPEN,VOLUME
```

And all future lines contain the data (daily data in our case):

```
1309752000000,12479.88,12506.22,12446.05,12505.99,128662688
```

So the steps we will need to go through are loading the file, converting the data to fit our standard data set, and then build the new chart type (and then fixing things as we discover issues; agile development).

How to do it...

We are going to base our work starting from where we left in the previous recipe. We will start the modifications right in the JavaScript file:

1. Let's update our global variables:

```
var chartInfo= { y:{min:11500, max:12900,steps:5,label:"close"},
        x:{min:1, max:12, steps:11,label:"date"}
        };
var stockData;
var CHART_PADDING = 20;
var wid;
var hei
```

2. Before we start our internal logic, we need to load our new external CSV file. We will rename the `init` function and call it `startUp` and then create a new `init` function:

```
function init(){

  var client = new XMLHttpRequest();
  client.open('GET', 'data/DJI.txt');

  client.onreadystatechange = function(e) {
   if(e.target.readyState==4){

     var aStockInfo = e.target.responseText.split("\n");
     stockData = translateCSV(aStockInfo,7);

      startUp()

   }
  }

  client.send();
}

function startUp(){
  //old init function
}
```

3. The data we get back from the CSV file needs to be formatted to a structure we can work with. For that we create the `translateCSV` function that takes in the raw CSV data and converts it into an object that matches our architecture needs:

```
function translateCSV(data,startIndex){
  startIndex|=1; //if nothing set set to 1
  var newData = [];
  var aCurrent;
```

```
    var dataDate;
    for(var i=startIndex; i<data.length;i++){
      aCurrent = data[i].split(",");
      dataDate = aCurrent[0].charAt(0)=="a"?parseInt(aCurrent[0].sli
  ce(1)):parseInt(aCurrent[0]);
      newData.push({  date:dataDate,
              close:parseFloat(aCurrent[1]),
              high:parseFloat(aCurrent[2]),
              low:parseFloat(aCurrent[3]),
              open:parseFloat(aCurrent[4]),
              volume:parseFloat(aCurrent[5])
              });
    }

    return newData;
  }
```

4. Our `startUp` function, formally known as `init`, will remain the same besides changing the `createWaterfall` method to call `addStock`:

```
function startUp(){
  ...
addStock(context,stockData);
}
```

5. It is time to create the `addStock` function:

```
function addStock(context,data){
  fillChart(context,chartInfo);
  var elementWidth =(wid-CHART_PADDING*2)/ data.length;
  var startY = CHART_PADDING;
  var endY = hei-CHART_PADDING;
  var chartHeight = endY-startY;
  var stepSize = chartHeight/(chartInfo.y.max-chartInfo.y.min);
  var openY;
  var closeYOffset;
  var highY;
  var lowY;
  var currentX;
  context.strokeStyle = "#000000";
  for(i=0; i<data.length; i++){
    openY = (data[i].open-chartInfo.y.min)*stepSize;
    closeYOffset = (data[i].open-data[i].close)*stepSize;
    highY = (data[i].high-chartInfo.y.min)*stepSize;
    lowY =(data[i].low-chartInfo.y.min)*stepSize;
    context.beginPath();
    currentX = CHART_PADDING +elementWidth*(i+.5);
    context.moveTo(currentX,endY-highY);
```

```
        context.lineTo(currentX,endY-lowY);
        context.rect(CHART_PADDING +elementWidth*i ,endY-openY,element
Width,closeYOffset);
        context.stroke();
        context.fillStyle = closeYOffset<0? "#C2D985" :"#E3675C" ;
        context.fillRect(CHART_PADDING +elementWidth*i ,endY-openY,ele
mentWidth,closeYOffset);
      }

}
```

All these steps are required to create a new candlestick chart.

How it works...

Let's review the steps to load our external file. If you are working with open source tools such as jQuery you will be better off using them to load external files but, to avoid using other libraries, we will work with the `XMLHttpRequest` object as it's supported in all modern browsers that support HTML5.

We start with creating a new `XMLHttpRequest` object:

```
var client = new XMLHttpRequest();
client.open('GET', 'data/DJI.txt');
```

The next step is to set what we want to do (`GET/POST`) and the name of the file, followed by creating a handler function for the `onreadystatechange` callback and sending our request.

```
client.onreadystatechange = function(e) {
   if(e.target.readyState==4){
     var aStockInfo = e.target.responseText.split("\n");
     stockData = translateCSV(aStockInfo,1);
      startUp()

   }
  }
  client.send();
```

The event handler `onreadystatechange` gets called a few times throughout the loading process of a file. We only want to listen in and act once the file is loaded and ready to be played with; to do that we will check whether the `readyState` variable is equal to four (ready and loaded). When the file is loaded, we want to split our file into an array based on line breaks.

Note that the file was created on a Mac. The \n does the trick, but when you create your own files or download files, you might need to use \r or a combination \n\r or \n\r. Always confirm that you made the right selection by outputting the length of your array and validating its right size (then test to see if its content is what you expect it to be).

After our array is ready we want to format it to the user-friendly format followed by starting up the old `init` function that is now known as `startUp`.

Let's quickly review the `translateCSV` formatting function. We are literally looping through our data array that was created earlier and replacing each line with a formatted object that will work for our needs. Notice that we have an optional parameter `startIndex`. If nothing or zero is set then on the first line we are assigning it the value of `1`:

```
startIndex||=1; //if nothing set set to 1
```

The former is a shorthand way of writing:

```
startIndex = startIndex || 1;
```

If the `startIndex` parameter has a value that is equivalent to true then it would remain as it was; if not, it would be converted to `1`.

By the way, if you don't know how to work with these shortcuts, I really recommend getting familiar with them; they are really fun and save time and typing. If you want to learn more on this check the following links:

- `http://www.jquery4u.com/javascript/shorthand-javascript-techniques/`
- `http://02geek.com/javascript/objects-and-arrays.html`

Great! Now we have a data source that is formatted in the style we've been using so far.

We will hardcode our `chartInfo` object. It will work out well for our `y` values but not that well for our date requirements (in the `x` values). We will revisit that issue later after we get our chart running. We created a dynamic range generator in an earlier exercise, so if you want to keep up with that then review it and add that type of logic into this chart as well, but for our needs we will keep it hardcoded for now.

Ok, so let's dig deeper into the `addStock` function. By the way, notice that as we are working with the same format and overall tools, we can mix charts together with ease. But before we do that, let's understand what the `addStock` function actually does. Let's start with our base variables:

```
fillChart(context,chartInfo);
var elementWidth =(wid-CHART_PADDING*2)/ data.length;
```

```
var startY = CHART_PADDING;
var endY = hei-CHART_PADDING;
var chartHeight = endY-startY;
var stepSize = chartHeight/(chartInfo.y.max-chartInfo.y.min);
```

We are gathering information that will make it easier to work in our loop when creating the bars from the width of elements (`elementWidth` to the ratio between our values and the height of our chart). All these variables have been covered in earlier recipes in this chapter.

```
var openY;
var closeYOffset;
var highY;
var lowY;
var currentX;
context.strokeStyle = "#000000";
```

These variables are going to be our helper variables (updated after every round of our loop) to establish the position of the high, low, open, and close offsets (as we are drawing a rectangle, it expects the height and not a second `y` value).

The first thing we do in each round of our loop is to find out the values for these variables:

```
for(i=0; i<data.length; i++){
    openY = (data[i].open-chartInfo.y.min)*stepSize;
    closeYOffset = (data[i].open-data[i].close)*stepSize;
    highY = (data[i].high-chartInfo.y.min)*stepSize;
    lowY =(data[i].low-chartInfo.y.min)*stepSize;
```

You will notice that the logic is almost the same in all of the variables. We are just subtracting the minimum from the value (as our chart doesn't cover values under our minimum value), and then multiplying it by our `stepSize` ratio to have the value fit within our chart dimensions (this way even if we change our chart size everything should continue working). Note that only the `closeYOffset` variable doesn't subtract the `min` property but instead it subtracts the `close` property.

The next step is to draw our candlestick chart starting with a line from the low to the high of the day:

```
    context.beginPath();
    currentX = CHART_PADDING +elementWidth*(i+.5);
    context.moveTo(currentX,endY-highY);
    context.lineTo(currentX,endY-lowY);
```

This will be followed by the rectangle that represents the full open and close values:

```
    context.rect(CHART_PADDING +elementWidth*i ,endY-openY,elementWidt
h,closeYOffset);
    context.stroke();
```

```
    context.fillStyle = closeYOffset<0? "#C2D985" :"#E3675C" ;
    context.fillRect(CHART_PADDING +elementWidth*i ,endY-openY,element
Width,closeYOffset);
}
```

After this, we will create a fill to this rectangle and set the style color based on the value of the `closeYOffset` variable. At this stage we have a running application, although it can use a few more tweaks to make it work better.

There's more...

It's time to fix our `x` coordinate values:

```
var chartInfo= { y:{min:11500, max:12900,steps:5,label:"close"},
        x:{min:1, max:12, steps:11,label:"date"}
        };
```

We didn't change this variable before as until now there was a clear separation between the outline and our content (the chart itself); but at this stage as our `x` outline content isn't a linear number anymore but a date; we need to somehow introduce into the `fillChart` method external data that is related to the content of the chart. The biggest challenge here is that we don't want to introduce into this method something that is only relevant to our chart as this is a globally used function. Instead we want to put our unique data in an external function and send that function in as a formatter. So let's get started:

```
var chartInfo= { y:{min:11500, max:12900,steps:5,label:"close"},
        x:{label:"date",formatter:weeklyCapture}
        };
```

Our `x` space in a stock chart represents time and as such our previous usage based on linear data does not apply (the properties such as `min`, `max`, and `steps` have no meaning in this case). We will remove them in favor of a new property `formatter` that will take a function as its value. We will use this `formatter` function instead of the default function. If this function is set we will let an external function define the rules. We will see more on this when we describe the `weeklyCapture` function. This method of coding is called **plugin coding**. Its name is derived out of the idea of enabling us to create replaceable functions without reworking our core logic in the future. Before we create the `weeklyCapture` function, let's tweak the `chartInfo` object so we have the right range and number of steps:

```
function addStock(context,data){
  if(!chartInfo.x.max){
    chartInfo.x.min = 0;
    chartInfo.x.max = data.length;
    chartInfo.x.steps = data.length;
  }

  fillChart(context,chartInfo);

...
```

What we are doing here is, before we call the `fillChart` function in our `addStock` function, we are checking to see if the `max` value is set; if it isn't set, we are going to reset all the values, setting the `min` to `0` and the `max` and `steps` to the length of our data array. We are doing this as we want to travel through all of our data elements to test and see if there is a new weekday.

Now we integrate our `weeklyCapture` function into the `fillChart` function.

```
function fillChart(context, chartInfo){
  // ....
  var output;
  for(var i=0; i<steps; i++){
    output = chartInfo.x.formatter && chartInfo.x.formatter(i);
    if(output || !chartInfo.x.formatter){
      currentX = startX + (i/steps) *      chartWidth;
      context.moveTo(currentX, startY );
      context.lineTo(currentX,endY);
      context.fillText(output?output:xData.min+stepSize*(i),
      currentX-6, endY+CHART_PADDING/2);
    }
  }

  if(!chartInfo.x.formatter){
    currentX = startX +chartWidth;
    context.moveTo(currentX, startY );
    context.lineTo(currentX,endY);
    context.fillText(xData.max, currentX-3, endY+CHART_PADDING/2);
  }

  context.stroke();

}
```

In our first step, we are going to fetch the value that comes back from our `formatter` function.

```
output = chartInfo.x.formatter && chartInfo.x.formatter(i);
```

The logic is simple, we are checking to see if the `formatter` function exists and if it does we are calling it and sending the current value of `i` (as we are in the loop).

The next step is if our output isn't empty (negative or has a value equivalent to false) or if our output is empty but our formatter isn't active then render the data:

```
if(output || !chartInfo.x.formatter){
  currentX = startX + (i/steps) *    chartWidth;
  context.moveTo(currentX, startY );
  context.lineTo(currentX,endY);
  context.fillText(output?output:xData.min+stepSize*(i), currentX-6,
endY+CHART_PADDING/2);
}
```

Only if we have an output from the `formatter` function and/or if the `formatter` function does not exist we don't need to do anything. As such we need the `if` statement to capture both the scenarios, if we do not have the `if` statement, then our output will not conform to our earlier recipes. The only content we are changing within this block of code is the `fillText` method. If we are working with our output, we want to use that for the text. If not, we want to keep the logic that was there before the same:

```
if(output || !chartInfo.x.formatter){
  currentX = startX + (i/steps) *    chartWidth;
  context.moveTo(currentX, startY );
  context.lineTo(currentX,endY);
  context.fillText(output?output:xData.min+stepSize*(i), currentX-6,
endY+CHART_PADDING/2);
}
```

We have one last thing we need to cover before we can run our application and see it in action and that is to create our `weeklyCapture` function. So let's create it now:

```
var DAY = 1000*60*60*24;
function weeklyCapture(i){
  var d;
  if(i==0){
    d =  new Date(stockData[i].date);
  }else if ( i>1 && stockData[i].date != stockData[i-1].date+1 ){
    d = new Date(stockData[i].date + DAY*stockData[i].date );
  }

  return d? d.getMonth()+1+"/"+d.getDate():false;

}
```

We start by creating a helper variable called `DAY` that will store how many milliseconds there are in a day:

```
var DAY = 1000*60*60*24;
```

If you take a peek at our external data, you will see that only on day `0` we have an actual date (formatted in milliseconds since 1970). All we need to do is send that to the `date` object to create a date:

```
var d;
  if(i==0){
    d =  new Date(stockData[i].date);
  }
```

While all other data lines contain only a number that represents how many days passed since that original date, we want to test and see if the current date is only one day after the last day. Only if the date change is greater than one day, we will create a new date format for it:

```
}else if ( i>1 && stockData[i].date != stockData[i-1].date+1 ){
    d = new Date(stockData[0].date + DAY*stockData[i].date );
  }
```

Note that to create the date object we need to take our current original date from row `0` and then add to it the total days in milliseconds (multiplying our `DAY` variable with the current day value).

With this method all that is left to check is if we have a valid date. Let's format it and send it back, and if not, we will send back `false`:

```
return d? d.getMonth()+1+"/"+d.getDate():false;
```

Congratulations! Now our sample is a fully fledged integrated candlestick chart with live dynamic dates.

Adding other render options to our stock chart

Although the candlestick chart is a very popular option, there is another popular technical chart view. One that is used when there are no colors to use. Instead of the usage of colors, on the left-hand side we draw a line to define the opening price, and on the right-hand side we capture the closing price. Let's integrate that logic into our chart as an optional render mode. We will add a new parameter to the `addStock` function:

```
function addStock(context,data,isCandle){
```

We are now going to adjust our internal `for` loop to change the render depending on the value of this variable:

```
for(i=0; i<data.length; i++){
    openY = (data[i].open-chartInfo.y.min)*stepSize;
    closeYOffset = (data[i].open-data[i].close)*stepSize;
    highY = (data[i].high-chartInfo.y.min)*stepSize;
    lowY =(data[i].low-chartInfo.y.min)*stepSize;
    context.beginPath();
    currentX = CHART_PADDING +elementWidth*(i+.5);
    context.moveTo(currentX,endY-highY);
    context.lineTo(currentX,endY-lowY);
    if(!isCandle){
      context.moveTo(currentX,endY-openY);
      context.lineTo(CHART_PADDING +elementWidth*(i+.25),endY-openY);
      context.moveTo(currentX,endY-openY+closeYOffset);
      context.lineTo(CHART_PADDING +elementWidth*(i+.75),endY-
openY+closeYOffset);
```

```
            context.stroke();
        }else{
            context.rect(CHART_PADDING +elementWidth*i ,endY-openY,elementWi
dth,closeYOffset);
            context.stroke();
            context.fillStyle = closeYOffset<0? "#C2D985" :"#E3675C" ;
            context.fillRect(CHART_PADDING +elementWidth*i ,endY-openY,eleme
ntWidth,closeYOffset);

        }

    }
```

There we go. We set the default to be `false` for our `isCandle` Boolean variable. If we run our application again, we will find it rendering in the new format. To change that, all we need to do is provide that third parameter as `true` when calling the `addStock` function:

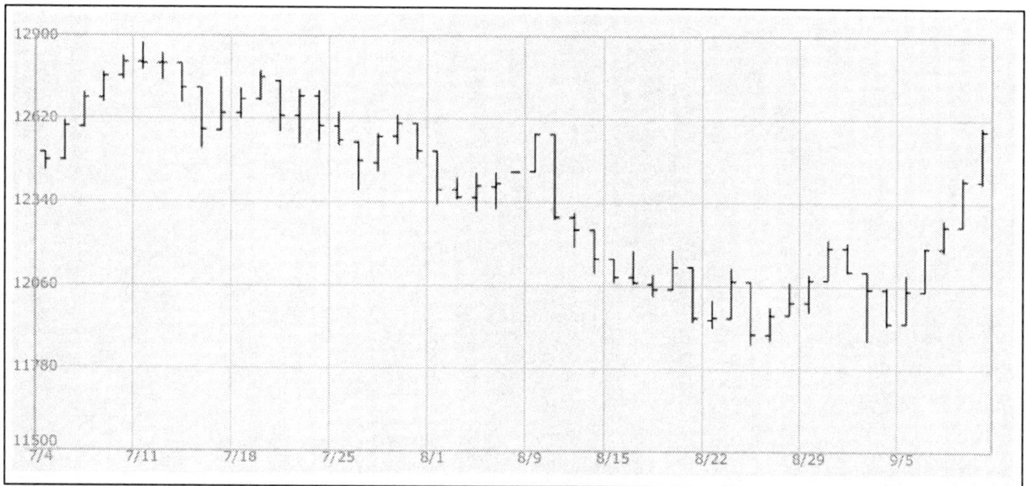

This chapter has been self-contained and really the hub of all the charts if you need to strengthen your chart building skills. I recommend you to revisit some of the earlier recipes in this chapter.

4
Let's Curve Things Up

In this chapter we will cover:

- Building a bubble chart
- Creating a pie chart
- Using a doughnut chart to show relationships
- Leveraging a radar
- Structuring a tree chart

Introduction

In the last chapter, we built a component for linear graphs ranging through dots, lines, and bars. Most of the data we worked with was two-dimensional, while we ended our lesson with a four-dimensional chart. It was still represented using linear art. In this chapter, we will leverage the capability of creating non-linear data to represent data.

Building a bubble chart

Although many items in our chart will have correlations with earlier charts that we created in *Chapter 3, Creating Cartesian-based Graphs*, we will start from scratch. Our goal is to create a chart that has bubbles in it—the bubbles enable us to showcase data with three data points (x, y, and the size of the bubble). This type of chart is really ideal when animated as it can showcase changes over time (it could showcase many years in a few seconds).

A great demo of the powers of bubble charts can be seen in a TED presentation by Hans Rosling (`http://blog.everythingfla.com/2012/05/hans-rosling-data-vis.html`).

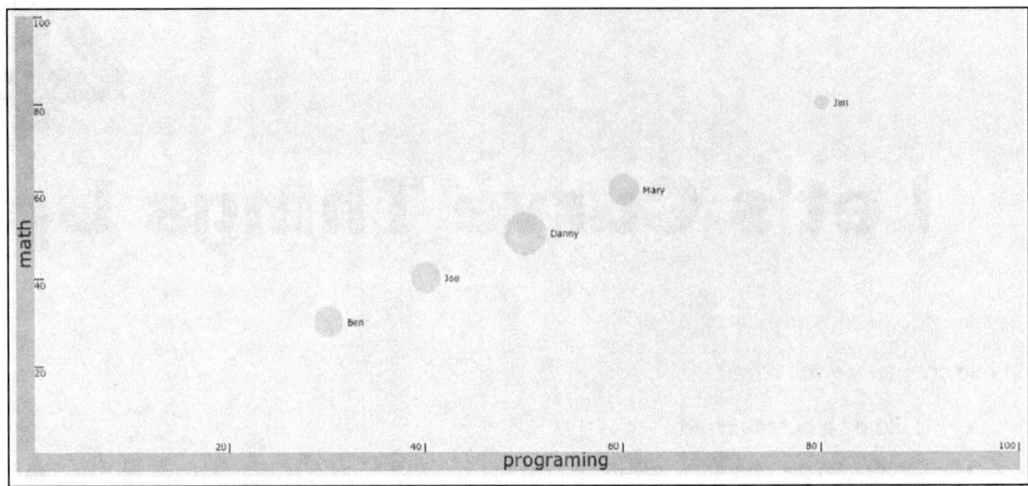

Getting ready

We will start up our project with a canvas setup and skip the HTML end. If you have forgotten how to create it please refer to the *Graphics with 2D Canvas* recipe in *Chapter 1, Drawing Shapes in Canvas*.

There are three major steps:

- Creating the data source
- Creating the background
- Adding the chart data info into the chart

How to do it...

Let's list the steps required to create a bubble chart:

1. The next data object should look familiar in an array that has objects within it with student scores in English, Math, and programming. Build the data object:

```
var students2001 = [{name:"Ben",
  math:30,
  english:60,
  programing:30},
  {name:"Joe",
  math:40,
```

```
    english:60,
    programing:40},
    {name:"Danny",
    math:50,
    english:90,
    programing:50},
    {name:"Mary",
    math:60,
    english:60,
    programing:60},
    {name:"Jim",
    math:80,
    english:20,
    programing:80}];
```

2. Create our chart information; contrary to previous charts, this chart has a third parameter for our bubble information. Define our chart rules:

```
var chartInfo= { y:{min:0, max:100,steps:5,label:"math"},
  x:{min:0, max:100,steps:5,label:"programing"},
  bubble:{min:0, max:100, minRaduis:3,
  maxRaduis:20,label:"english"}
};
```

3. The last data object will contain all the styling information that we might want to change in the future. Add a styling object:

```
var styling = { outlinePadding:4,
  barSize:16,
  font:"12pt Verdana, sans-serif",
  background:"eeeeee",
  bar:"cccccc",
  text:"605050"
};
```

4. We create an event callback when the document is ready to trigger `init`, so let's create the `init` function:

```
var wid;
var hei;
function init(){
  var can = document.getElementById("bar");

  wid = can.width;
  hei = can.height;
  var context = can.getContext("2d");

  createOutline(context,chartInfo);
```

```
  addDots(context,chartInfo,students2001,
  ["math","programing","english"],"name");
}
```

5. We start creating our outline when we create our style object. Now it's time to draw everything into our canvas. So we start by setting up our base canvas style:

```
function createOutline(context,chartInfo){
  var s = styling;
  var pad = s.outlinePadding;
  var barSize = s.barSize;
  context.fillStyle = s.background;
  context.fillRect(0,0,wid,hei);
  context.fillStyle = s.bar;
  context.fillRect(pad,pad,barSize,hei-pad*2);
  context.font = s.font;
  context.fillStyle = s.text;
```

6. We need to save our current, canvas-based graphic layout information, change it to make it easier to position elements and then return it back to its original state:

```
context.save();
context.translate(17, hei/2 );
context.rotate(-Math.PI/2);
context.textAlign = "center";
context.fillText(chartInfo.y.label, 0, 0);
context.restore();

context.fillStyle = s.bar;
context.fillRect(pad+barSize,hei-pad-barSize,wid-pad*2-
barSize,barSize);
context.font = s.font;
context.fillStyle = s.text;
context.fillText(chartInfo.x.label,( wid-pad*2-barSize)/2, hei-
pad*2);

context.translate(pad+barSize,hei-pad-barSize);
context.scale(1, -1);
//SET UP CONSTANTS - NEVER CHANGE AFTER CREATED
styling.CHART_HEIGHT = hei-pad*2-barSize;
styling.CHART_WIDTH = wid-pad*2-barSize;
```

7. Now it is time to draw the outlines with the help of our `chartInfo` object:

```
var steps = chartInfo.y.steps;
var ratio;
chartInfo.y.range = chartInfo.y.max-chartInfo.y.min;
var scope = chartInfo.y.range;
```

```
context.strokeStyle = s.text;
var fontStyle = s.font.split("pt");
var pointSize = fontStyle[0]/2;
fontStyle[0]=pointSize;
fontStyle = fontStyle.join("pt");
context.font = fontStyle; // making 1/2 original size of bars
  for(var i=1; i<=steps; i++){
    ratio = i/steps;
    context.moveTo(0,ratio*styling.CHART_HEIGHT-1);
    context.lineTo(pad*2,ratio*styling.CHART_HEIGHT-1);
    context.scale(1,-1);

    context.fillText(chartInfo.y.min +
    (scope/steps)*i,0,(ratio*styling.CHART_HEIGHT-3 -
    pointSize)*-1);
    context.scale(1,-1);

  }

  steps = chartInfo.x.steps;
  chartInfo.x.range = chartInfo.x.max-chartInfo.x.min;
  scope = chartInfo.x.max-chartInfo.x.min;
  context.textAlign = "right";
  for(var i=1; i<=steps; i++){
    ratio = i/steps;
    context.moveTo(ratio*styling.CHART_WIDTH-1,0);
    context.lineTo(ratio*styling.CHART_WIDTH-1,pad*2);
    context.scale(1,-1);
    context.fillText(chartInfo.x.min +
    (scope/steps)*i,ratio*styling.CHART_WIDTH-pad,-
    pad/2);
    context.scale(1,-1);

  }

context.stroke();
}
```

8. Now it is time to add the data into our chart by creating the `addDots` method. The function `addDots` will take in the data with the definition of rules (keys) to be used, contrary to what we did in the earlier recipes.

```
function addDots(context,chartInfo,data,keys,label){
  var rangeX = chartInfo.y.range;
  var _y;
```

```
var _x;

var _xoffset=0;
var _yoffset=0;

if(chartInfo.bubble){
  var range = chartInfo.bubble.max-
  chartInfo.bubble.min;
  var radRange = chartInfo.bubble.maxRadius-
  chartInfo.bubble.minRadius;
  context.textAlign = "left";
}


for(var i=0; i<data.length; i++){
  _x = ((data[i][keys[0]] - chartInfo.x.min )/
  chartInfo.x.range) * styling.CHART_WIDTH;
  _y = ((data[i][keys[1]] - chartInfo.y.min )/
  chartInfo.y.range) * styling.CHART_HEIGHT;
  context.fillStyle = "#44ff44";


  if(data[i][keys[2]]){
    _xoffset = chartInfo.bubble.minRadius +
    (data[i][keys[2]]-chartInfo.bubble.min)/range
    *radRange;
    _yoffset = -3;
    context.beginPath();
    context.arc(_x,_y, _xoffset , 0, Math.PI*2, true);
    context.closePath();
    context.fill();

    _xoffset+=styling.outlinePadding;
  }else{
    context.fillRect(_x,_y,10,10);
  }

  if(label){
    _x+=_xoffset;
    _y+=_yoffset;
    context.fillStyle = styling.text;
    context.save();
    context.translate(_x,_y );
    context.scale(1,-1);
    context.fillText("Bluping",0,0);
```

```
            context.restore();

          }
        }
      }
```

This block of code, although redone from scratch, bears a lot of resemblance to the *Spreading data in a scatter chart* recipe in *Chapter 3, Creating Cartesian-based Graphs*, with modifications to enable the third level of data and the new charting format.

That's it. You should have a running bubble chart. Now when you run the application, you will see that the `x` parameter is showcasing the math score, the `y` parameter is showcasing the programming score, while the size of our bubble showcases the student's score in English.

How it works...

Let's start with the `createOutline` function. In this method, apart from the regular canvas drawing methods that we grow to love, we introduce a new style of coding where we manipulate the actual canvas to help us define our code in an easier way. The two important key methods here are as follows:

```
context.save();
context.restore();
```

We will be leveraging both the methods a few times. The `save` method saves the current view of the canvas while the `restore` method returns users to the last saved canvas:

```
context.save();
context.translate(17, hei/2 );
context.rotate(-Math.PI/2);
context.textAlign = "center";
context.fillText(chartInfo.y.label, 0, 0);
context.restore();
```

In the first use of this style, we are using it to draw our text by rotating it to the right. The `translate` method moves the `0, 0` coordinates of the canvas while the `rotate` method rotates the text using radians.

After drawing the external bars, it's time for us to use this new capability to our advantage. Most charts rely on a y coordinate that grows upwards, but this canvas has the y values growing from the top to the bottom of the canvas area. We can flip this relationship by adding some code before we loop through to add the range values.

```
context.translate(pad+barSize,hei-pad-barSize);
context.scale(1, -1);
```

In the preceding lines, we are first moving the `0,0` coordinates of our canvas to be exactly at the bottom-right range of our chart, and then we are flipping our canvas by switching the scale value. Note that from now on if we try to add text to the canvas, it will be upside down. Keep that in mind as we are now drawing in a canvas that is flipped upside down.

One thing to note in our first loop when we try to type in new text is that when we want to add text, we first undo our scale and then return back our canvas for it to be flipped:

```
context.scale(1,-1);
context.fillText(chartInfo.y.min + (scope/steps)*i,0,(ratio*styling.
CHART_HEIGHT-3 -pointSize)*-1);
context.scale(1,-1);
```

Note that we are multiplying our y coordinate by `*-1`. We are doing this because we actually want the value of our y coordinate to be negative as we have just flipped the screen.

The work around the x bar text is very similar; notice the main differences related to finding the x and y value calculations.

It's time to dig into the `addDots` function. The function will again look familiar if you've been following *Chapter 3, Creating Cartesian-based Graphs*, but this time we are working with a modified canvas.

We start with a few helper variables:

```
var rangeX = chartInfo.y.range;
var _y;
var _x;
var _xoffset=0;
var _yoffset=0;
```

We are adding the bubble effect dynamically, which means that this method can work even if there are only two points of information and not three. We continue by testing to see if our data object contains the bubble information:

```
if(chartInfo.bubble){
  var range = chartInfo.bubble.max-chartInfo.bubble.min;
  var radRange = chartInfo.bubble.maxRaduis-
  chartInfo.bubble.minRaduis;
  context.textAlign = "left";
}
```

If so, we add a few more variables and align our text to the left as we are going to use it in this example.

It's time for us to look through our data object and propagate the data on the chart.

```
for(var i=0; i<data.length; i++){
  _x = ((data[i][keys[0]] - chartInfo.x.min )/ chartInfo.x.range)
  * styling.CHART_WIDTH;
  _y = ((data[i][keys[1]] - chartInfo.y.min )/ chartInfo.y.range)
  * styling.CHART_HEIGHT;
  context.fillStyle = "#44ff44";
```

For each loop, we recalculate the `_x` and `_y` coordinates based on the current values.

If we have a third element, we are ready to develop a bubble. If we do not have it, we need to create a simple dot.

```
if(data[i][keys[2]]){
  _xoffset = chartInfo.bubble.minRaduis + (data[i][keys[2]]-
  chartInfo.bubble.min)/range *radRange;
  _yoffset = -3;
  context.beginPath();
  context.arc(_x,_y, _xoffset , 0, Math.PI*2, true);
  context.closePath();
  context.fill();
  _xoffset+=styling.outlinePadding;
}else{
   context.fillRect(_x,_y,10,10);
}
```

At this stage, we should have an active bubble/dot method. All that is left is for us to integrate our overlay copy.

Before we add a label, let's take a peek at the function signature:

```
function addDots(context,chartInfo,data,keys,label){}
```

The `context` and `chartInfo` parameters are already a standard in our samples. The idea of keys was to enable us to switch what data will be tested dynamically. The keys' values are the array positions `0` and `1` that are correlated to the x and y coordinates, and position `2` is used for bubbles, as we've seen earlier. The `label` parameter enables us to send in a key value for the label. In this way, if the label is there we will add a label and if it is not there we will not.

```
if(label){
  _x+=_xoffset;
  _y+=_yoffset;
  context.fillStyle = styling.text;
  context.save();
  context.translate(_x,_y );
  context.scale(1,-1);
  context.fillText(data[i][label],0,0);
  context.restore();
 }
```

Then we add the preceding `if` statement. If our label is set, we position the style and create the text of the label.

Creating a pie chart

The steps to create a pie chart are relatively easy and short. Pie charts are ideal for showcasing a closed amount of data that we want to easily compare between data fields such as, in our example, dividing the number of people in the world into groups based on their region:

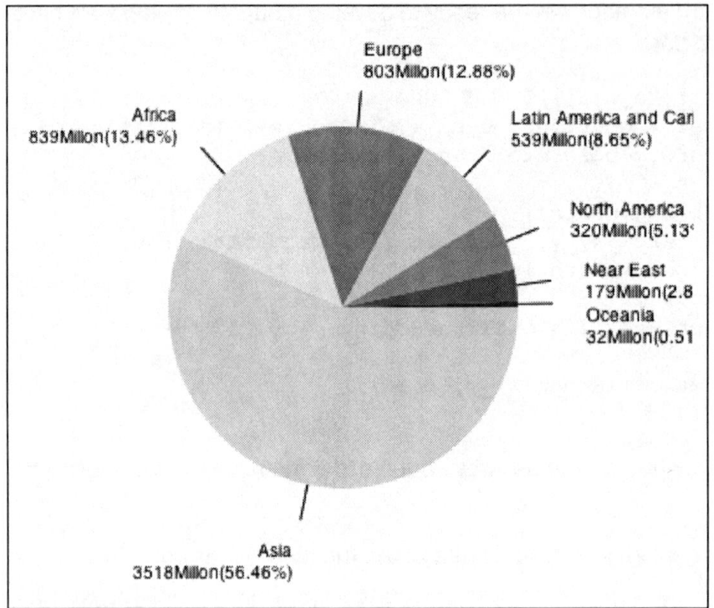

Getting ready

The first step will be to update our canvas size in the HTML area to be a rectangular area. In our sample, we will update the values to 400 x 400. That's about it; let's start building it.

How to do it...

In the following steps we will create our first pie chart. Let's get started:

1. Set up our data source and our global variables:

```
var data= [  {label:"Asia", value:3518000000,style:"#B1DDF3"},
  {label:"Africa", value:839000000,style:"#FFDE89"},
  {label:"Europe", value:803000000,style:"#E3675C"},
  {label:"Latin America and Caribbean", value:
```

```
    539000000,style:"#C2D985"},
    {label:"North America",
    value:320000000,style:"#eeeeee"},
    {label:"Near East", value:179000000,style:"#aaaaaa"},
    {label:"Oceania", value:32000000,style:"#444444"}
    ];
  var wid;
  var hei;
  var radius = 100;
```

2. Prepare our canvas (from here on we are delving into the `init` function):

   ```
   function init(){
     var can = document.getElementById("bar");

     wid = can.width;
     hei = can.height;
     var context = can.getContext("2d");
   ...
   ```

3. Count the total data (world population):

   ```
   var total=0;
   for(var i=0; i<data.length; i++) total+=data[i].value;
   ```

4. Set up 360 degrees in radians and move our pivot point to `0,0`:

   ```
   var rad360 = Math.PI*2;
   context.translate(wid/2,hei/2);
   ```

5. Draw the pie chart by using the following code snippet:

   ```
   var currentTotal=0;
     for(i=0; i<data.length; i++){
     context.beginPath();
     context.moveTo(0,0);
     context.fillStyle = data[i].style;
     context.arc( 0,0,radius,currentTotal/total*rad360,
     (currentTotal+data[i].value)/total*rad360,false);
     context.lineTo(0,0);
     context.closePath();
     context.fill();

     currentTotal+=data[i].value;
     }
   }
   ```

That's it; we have just created a basic pie chart—I told you it would be easy!

How it works...

Our pie chart, as its name indicates, uses pies and always showcases 100 percent of data. As our arc method works based on radians, we need to convert these data points from percentile to radians.

After figuring out what the total of all the values is and the total radians in a circle (`2*PI`), we are ready to loop through and draw the slices.

```
var currentTotal=0;
  for(i=0; i<data.length; i++){
    context.beginPath();
    context.moveTo(0,0);
    context.fillStyle = data[i].style;
```

The logic is relatively simple; we loop through all the data elements, change the fill style based on the data object, and move our pointer to `0,0` (to the center of our screen as we have changed the pivot point of our canvas).

```
context.arc( 0,0,radius,currentTotal/total*rad360,(currentTotal+data
[i].value)/total*rad360,false);
context.lineTo(0,0);
context.closePath();
context.fill();

currentTotal+=data[i].value;
```

Now we draw the arc. Pay attention to the highlighted text; we start with where we left off our current total and through that we calculate the angle in radians:

```
currentTotal/total*rad360
```

We can turn this value into a percentage value that we can duplicate against the total radian of our circle. Our second parameter is very close, so we just add into it the current value of the current region we are in:

```
(currentTotal+data[i].value)/total*rad360
```

And the last point to note here is that we are setting the arc's last parameter to `false` (counter clockwise) as that works best for our calculations.

Last but not least, we update our `currentTotal` value to encompass the newly added region as that will be our starting point in the next round of our `for` loop.

There's more...

A pie chart without any information on its content is probably not going to work as well as a chart with information, but we can figure out the locations... well worry not; we are going to revisit our old friends `cos` and `sin` to help us locate the dots on our circle, to enable us to add textual information on our newly created pie.

Revisiting Math.cos() and Math.sin()

We will start with adding a new global variable to store the color of our lines and then we will call it `copyStyle`:

```
var copyStyle = "#0000000000";
```

Now that we are right back into our `init` function, let's add it into our `for` loop just before the last line:

```
currentTotal+=data[i].value;
```

As expected, we will first set our new `copyStyle` variable as our fill and stroke value:

```
context.strokeStype = context.fillStyle =  copyStyle;
```

Our next step is to locate where in our pie we would like to draw a line out so that we can add the text:

```
midRadian = (currentTotal+data[i].value/2)/total*rad360;
```

To accomplish this, we will use a new variable that will store the mid-value between the last total and the new value (the center of the new slice). So far so good. Now we need to figure out how to get the x and y positions of that point. Lucky for us, there is a very easy way of doing it in a circle by using the `Math.cos` (for the x) and `Math.sin` (for our y) functions:

```
context.beginPath();
context.moveTo(Math.cos(midRadian)*radius,Math.sin(midRadian)*radius);
context.lineTo(Math.cos(midRadian)*(radius+20),Math.
sin(midRadian)*(radius+20));
context.stroke();
```

Armed with our `midRadian` variable, we will get the value for a circle with a radius of `1`, so all that is left for us to do is duplicate that value by our real radius to find our starting point. As we want to draw a line in the same direction to the arc externally, we will find the points of an imaginary circle that is larger; so for that we are going to use the same formula, but instead upgrade our radius values by 20, creating a diagonal line that is correlative to the arc.

All that is left for us to do is figure out what text we would want to have within our chart, using the same arc point with a larger circle size:

```
context.fillText(data[i].label,Math.cos(midRadian)*(radius+40),Math.
sin(midRadian)*(radius+40));
```

Looks good... The only problem is that we don't have our values; let's add them and figure out the challenges involved with them.

Improving our bubbles' text format

In a real-world example, we would probably want to use a rollover if this was a live application (we will visit that idea in a later chapter), but let's try to figure out a way to create the chart capable of containing all the information. We stopped in our preceding line of code with a really large exterior circle (`radius+40`). Well that's because we wanted to slip in a new line of text right under, so let's do it:

```
context.fillText(formatToMillions(data[i].value) +
"(" +formatToPercent(data[i].value/total) + ")" ,Math.
cos(midRadian)*(radius+40),Math.sin(midRadian)*(radius+40) + 12);
```

It's a bit of a mouthful, but it's basically the same as the preceding line with a new line of text and an extra change, as we are shifting the y value by 12 pixels to account for the first line of text on the same area. To get this working, we are using two helper functions that format our text:

```
function formatToPercent(val){
  val*=10000;
  val = parseInt(val);
  val/=100;
  return val + "%"
}

function formatToMillions(val){
  val/=1000000;
  return val + "Million";
}
```

If you run the application in its current format, you will find that the text just doesn't look good on the page, and that is where the artist within you needs to sort things out. I've continued the sample in our source files until it felt right, so check it out or create your own variations from here on.

Using a doughnut chart to show relationships

The doughnut chart is a fancy pie chart. So if you haven't created a pie chart yet, I strongly encourage you to revisit the previous recipe, *Creating a pie chart*. A doughnut chart is a layered pie chart. This chart is ideal for condensing the comparable data between data types that would fit into a pie chart:

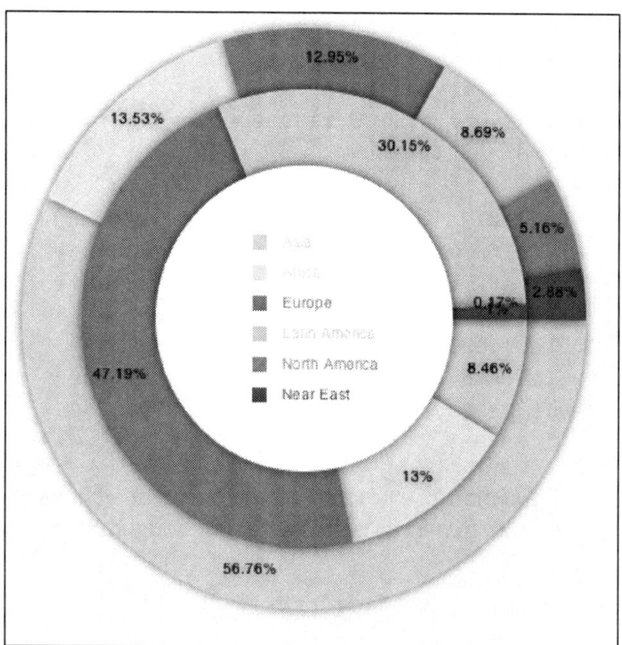

Getting ready

We are going to grab our code from the last example and adjust it to fit our needs. So we will start with the same HTML file and the same code from the last example.

How to do it...

Perform the following steps:

1. Let's update our data with some dummy data (we will create two data objects):

```
var data1= [ {label:"Asia", value:3518000000,style:"#B1DDF3"},
  {label:"Africa", value:839000000,style:"#FFDE89"},
  {label:"Europe", value:803000000,style:"#E3675C"},
  {label:"Latin America and Caribbean", value:
  539000000,style:"#C2D985"},
  {label:"North America",
  value:320000000,style:"#999999"},
  {label:"Near East", value:179000000,style:"#666666"}
];

var data2= [ {label:"Asia", value:151000,style:"#B1DDF3"},
  {label:"Africa", value:232000,style:"#FFDE89"},
  {label:"Europe", value:842000,style:"#E3675C"},
  {label:"Latin America and Caribbean", value:
  538100,style:"#C2D985"},
  {label:"North America", value:3200,style:"#999999"},
  {label:"Near East", value:17900,style:"#666666"}
];
```

2. Modify the `init` function by extracting all the pie-creating lines to a separate function and adding a new function `createHole` (for our doughnut):

```
function init(){
  var can = document.getElementById("bar");

  wid = can.width;
  hei = can.height;
  var context = can.getContext("2d");
  context.translate(wid/2,hei/2);


  createPie(context,data1,190);
  createPie(context,data2,150);
  createHole(context,100);
}
```

3. Modify the pie creation to change the text layout to fit into a pie chart:

```
function createPie(context,data,radius){
  var total=0;
  for(var i=0; i<data.length;i++) total+=data[i].value;
```

```
    var rad360 = Math.PI*2;

    var currentTotal=0;
    var midRadian;
    var offset=0;
    for(i=0; i<data.length; i++){
      context.beginPath();
      context.moveTo(0,0);
      context.fillStyle = data[i].style;
      context.arc( 0,0,radius,currentTotal/total*rad360,
      (currentTotal+data[i].value)/total*rad360,false);
      context.lineTo(0,0);
      context.closePath();
      context.fill();

      context.strokeStype = context.fillStyle =  copyStyle;
      midRadian =
      (currentTotal+data[i].value/2)/total*rad360;
      context.textAlign = "center";
      context.fillText(formatToPercent(data[i].value/total)
      ,Math.cos(midRadian)*(radius-
      20),Math.sin(midRadian)*(radius-20) );

      currentTotal+=data[i].value;

    }

  }
```

4. We need to create the method `createHole` (actually a simple circle):

```
  function createHole(context,radius){
    context.beginPath();
    context.moveTo(0,0);
    context.fillStyle = "#ffffff";
    context.arc( 0,0,radius,0,Math.PI*2,false);
    context.closePath();
    context.fill();

  }
```

That's it! We can now create an endless doughnut with as many layers as we would like by changing the radius, making it smaller each time we add a new layer.

How it works...

The core logic of the doughnut chart is the same as that of the pie chart. Our main focus is really about reformatting and rewiring the content to be outlined at the visual level. As such, part of our work is to delete the things that are not relevant and to make the needed updates:

```
context.fillText(formatToPercent(data[i].value/total),Math.
cos(midRadian)*(radius-20),Math.sin(midRadian)*(radius-20) );
```

The main thing to note is that we are hardcoding a value that is 20 less than the current radius. If we wanted our sample to work for every possible option, we would need to figure out a smarter way of generating this data as ideally we would want the text to be in between the doughnut area and rotated, but we have done things of that nature before so I'll leave that for you to explore.

There's more...

Although our doughnut is created and ready, it would help if we add some more information to it, such as outlines and a legend, as we extracted the majority of the text from the last example.

Adding an outline

We will use shadows to create a glow around our shapes. The easiest and quickest way to do it is to revisit the `init` function and add into it the shadow information to create this effect:

```
function init(){
  var can = document.getElementById("bar");

  wid = can.width;
  hei = can.height;
  var context = can.getContext("2d");
  context.translate(wid/2,hei/2);

  context.shadowOffsetX = 0;
  context.shadowOffsetY = 0;
  context.shadowBlur    = 8;
  context.shadowColor   = 'rgba(0, 0, 0, 0.5)';

  createPie(context,data1,190);
  createPie(context,data2,150);
  createHole(context,100);

}
```

The key here is that we are setting our offset on both the x and y values to be `0`, and as such our shadow is being used as a glow. Every element that will be drawn from here on will have a shadow, and that works perfectly for us.

Creating a legend

Hey, since we have a huge hole in our doughnut, how about we put our legend right in the middle of everything? As sometimes the middle isn't exactly the best-looking thing, it will probably be best to manually figure out what is the perfect position after we create the legend.

```
context.shadowColor   = 'rgba(0, 0, 0, 0)';
context.translate(-35,-55);
createLegend(context,data1);
```

We start by removing our shadow, by setting its alpha to `0` and moving our pivot point. (I tweaked these numbers after the legend was created until I was happy.)

OK, we are ready to create our legend with the `createLegend` function:

```
function createLegend(context,data){
  context.textAlign="left";
  for(var i=0;i<data.length;i++){
    context.fillStyle=data[i].style;
    context.fillRect(0,i*20,10,10);
    context.fillText(data[i].label,20,i*20+8);
  }
}
```

We have completed a fully fledged doughnut chart with a legend.

See also

- The *Creating a pie chart* recipe

Leveraging a radar

Radars are very misunderstood charts but are really amazing. A radar enables us to showcase a really large amount of comparable data in a very condensed way. The radar chart is known as a spider chart as well.

Warning

You really need to be friendly with the `Math.cos` and `Math.sin` functions, as we are going to use them plenty of times in this chart type. With that said, if you don't feel comfortable with them yet, it would be a good idea to start from the start of the chapter to refresh your memory on this.

Getting ready

As always, we are going to start with our base HTML page with an `init` callback.

Note

A radar chart is really a line chart wrapped up into a circular shape with a lot of different math involved; but it's the same idea—instead of spreading our data horizontally, we are spreading our data around a center point.

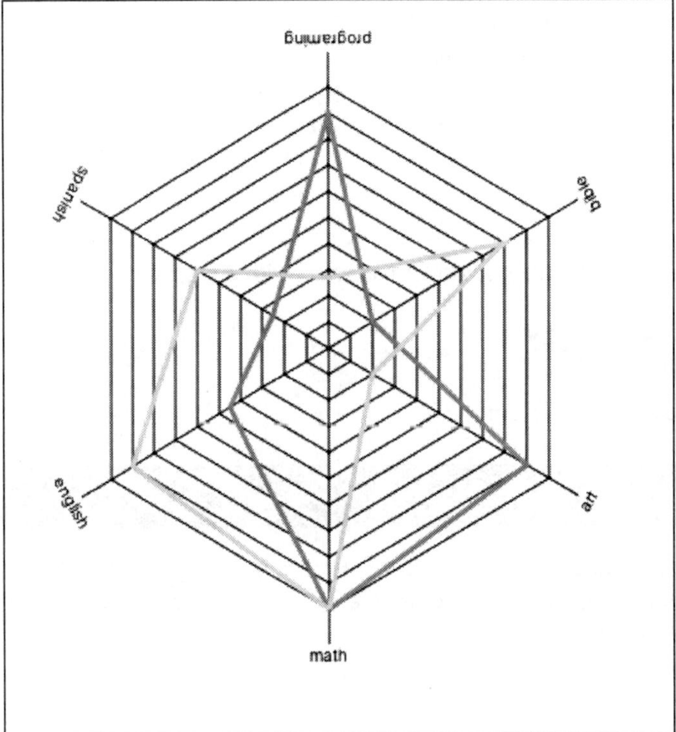

How to do it...

Let's see what are the steps involved in creating a radar chart:

1. Create/Organize the chart data and the actual data:

```
var data=[{label:"Ben", style:"#E3675C", math:90,english:45,spanis
h:25,programing:90,bible:20,art:90},
  {label:"Sharon", style:"#C2D985", math:100,english:90,spanish:60
,programing:27,bible:80,art:20}];

var chartInfo= {steps:10, max:100, types:["math","english","spanis
h","programing","bible","art"]};
```

2. Add a few helper variables and an `init` function:

```
var wid;
var hei;
var copyStyle = "#0000000000";
var radius = 180;
var radianOffset = Math.PI/2

function init(){
  var can = document.getElementById("bar");

  wid = can.width;
  hei = can.height;
  var context = can.getContext("2d");

  createSpider(context,chartInfo,data);
}
```

3. Now it is time to create the `createSpider` function:

```
function createSpider(context,chartInfo,data){
  drawWeb(context,chartInfo,radius);
  drawDataWeb(context,chartInfo,data,radius);

}
```

4. We split the creation of the radar web into two stages. The first is the lines coming out of the center of the web and the other is the actual webs that loop around this center point. Let's start with the first step and continue to the next part in the second loop:

```
function drawWeb(context,chartInfo,radius){
  chartInfo.stepSize = chartInfo.max/chartInfo.steps;
  var hSteps = chartInfo.types.length;
  var hStepSize = (Math.PI*2)/hSteps;
  context.translate(wid/2,hei/2);
```

```
        context.strokeStyle = "#000000";
          for(var i=0; i<hSteps; i++){
            context.moveTo(0,0);
            context.lineTo(Math.cos(hStepSize*i +
            radianOffset)*(radius+20),Math.sin(hStepSize*i +
            radianOffset)*(radius+20));
          }

          var stepSize = radius/chartInfo.steps;
          var cRad;

          for(var i=1; i<=chartInfo.steps; i++){
            cRad = i*stepSize;
            context.moveTo(Math.cos(radianOffset)*cRad,
            Math.sin(radianOffset)*cRad);

          for(var j=0;j<hSteps; j++){
            context.lineTo(Math.cos(hStepSize*j +
            radianOffset)*cRad,Math.sin(hStepSize*j +
            radianOffset)*cRad);
          }
          context.lineTo(Math.cos(radianOffset)*cRad,
          Math.sin(radianOffset)*cRad);

        }

        context.stroke();
      }
```

5. Now it's time to integrate our data:

```
function drawDataWeb(context,chartInfo,data,radius){
  var hSteps = chartInfo.types.length;
  var hStepSize = (Math.PI*2)/hSteps;
  for(i=0; i<data.length; i++){
    context.beginPath();
    context.strokeStyle = data[i].style;
    context.lineWidth=3;
    cRad =
    radius*(data[i][chartInfo.types[0]]/chartInfo.max);
    context.moveTo(Math.cos(radianOffset)*
    cRad,Math.sin(radianOffset)*cRad);

    for(var j=1;j<hSteps; j++){
      cRad =
      radius*(data[i][chartInfo.types[j]]/chartInfo.max);
```

```
            context.lineTo(Math.cos(hStepSize*j +
            radianOffset)*cRad,Math.sin(hStepSize*j +
            radianOffset)*cRad);
          }
          cRad =
          radius*(data[i][chartInfo.types[0]]/chartInfo.max);
          context.lineTo(Math.cos(radianOffset)*
          cRad,Math.sin(radianOffset)*cRad);
          context.stroke();
        }

      }
```

Congratulations, you have just created a radar/spider chart.

How it works...

The radar chart is one of our more complicated chart types. So far it uses a lot of cos/sin functions, but the logic is very consistent and as such relatively simple.

Let's take a deeper look into the `drawWeb` method:

```
chartInfo.stepSize = chartInfo.max/chartInfo.steps;
var hSteps = chartInfo.types.length;
var hStepSize = (Math.PI*2)/hSteps;
context.translate(wid/2,hei/2);
context.strokeStyle = "#000000";
```

We start by creating a few helper variables and repositioning our pivot point to the center of the screen to help us with our calculations.

```
for(var i=0; i<hSteps; i++){
  context.moveTo(0,0);
  context.lineTo(Math.cos(hStepSize*i +
  radianOffset)*(radius+20),Math.sin(hStepSize*i +
  radianOffset)*(radius+20));
}
```

We then create our spikes based on the number of courses, as each course will be represented with a spike.

It's time to create the interwebs of our spider web now that we have our core building blocks (the spikes):

```
var stepSize = radius/chartInfo.steps;
  var cRad;
```

```
    for(var i=1; i<=chartInfo.steps; i++){
      cRad = i*stepSize;
      context.moveTo(Math.cos(radianOffset)*cRad,
      Math.sin(radianOffset)*cRad);

      for(var j=0;j<hSteps; j++){
        context.lineTo(Math.cos(hStepSize*j +
        radianOffset)*cRad,Math.sin(hStepSize*j +
        radianOffset)*cRad);
      }
      context.lineTo(Math.cos(radianOffset)*cRad,
      Math.sin(radianOffset)*cRad);

    }

  context.stroke();
```

In this multidimensional loop, we are running through step by step to draw lines from one dot on a circle to the next (from one spike point to the next), growing our radius each time we are done with creating a complete shape. Each shape we create here represents a growth by 10 in the students' score, as our students can only have scores between 0 and 100. We can ignore extreme cases in this sample. (You might need to adjust this code if your data range doesn't start at 0.)

While our `drawDataWeb` method changes, the radius based on the score assumes a range of 0 to 100. (If your ranges are not the same, you will need to modify this code, or modify your data sets to be between 0 and 100 when sent to the method.)

There's more...

Our radar isn't perfect as it could use a legend and some textual information around our radar so that we know what each bar represents. We will let you sort out a legend as we've done in the previous recipe *Using a doughnut chart to show relationships*.

Adding a rotated legend

To fix this issue and add our text, we will revisit our function `drawWeb` with our first loop in that function, and instead of updating the cos/sin values to find the rotation, we will just rotate our canvas and integrate our text at the edge each time:

```
function drawWeb(context,chartInfo,radius){
  chartInfo.stepSize = chartInfo.max/chartInfo.steps;
  var hSteps = chartInfo.types.length;
  var hStepSize = (Math.PI*2)/hSteps;
  context.translate(wid/2,hei/2);
  context.strokeStyle = "#000000";
```

```
    context.textAlign="center";
    for(var i=0; i<hSteps; i++){
    context.moveTo(0,0); context.lineTo(Math.cos(
    radianOffset)*(radius+20),Math.sin( radianOffset)*(radius+20));
    context.fillText(chartInfo.types[i],Math.cos(
    radianOffset)*(radius+30),Math.sin( radianOffset)*(radius+30));
    context.rotate(hStepSize);
  }
```

The logic here is a bit simpler as we are just rotating our canvas each time and using the exact same code over and over until the rotation comes to a full circle.

Structuring a tree chart

There are many types of trees in the virtual world, although the most intuitive one is a family tree. A family tree is a bit more complex than a basic data tree such as a class inheritance tree, as for the most part classes have only one parent while family trees usually have two.

We will build an inheritance tree for the display objects of ActionScript 3.0.

Getting ready

Please note that this sample is cutting edge in HTML5. One of the new features that no one really knows whether will get adopted or not is E4X. It's been embraced by Firefox, but not all browsers have implemented it (it is fully supported in Flash as well).

ECMAScript for XML (**E4X**) is a programming language extension that adds native XML support to ECMAScript. It has replaced the DOM interface and is implemented as a primitive (such as numbers and Booleans), making it faster and more optimized.

As we are mainly working locally, we are going to save our XML document directly in our JavaScript to avoid sandbox security issues.

To help us space out our elements, we will make our canvas area much larger in this sample (800 x 400). Alright, let's start implementing our tree sample created with E4X.

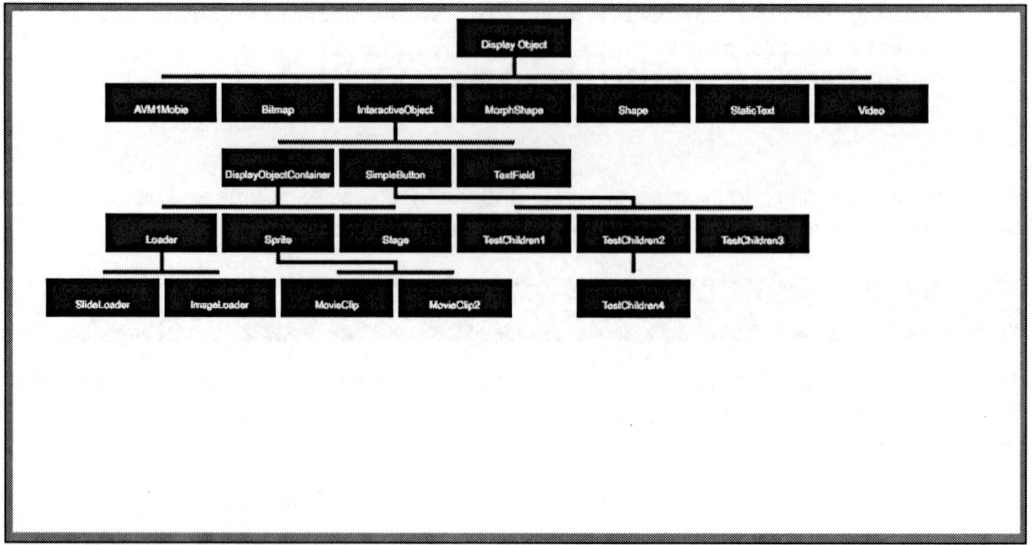

How to do it...

Perform the following steps:

1. We will start by creating our XML object that contains our class tree (please note that this will only work on an up-to-date version of Firefox as at the time of this book being written):

```
var xml = <node name ="Display Object">
<node name="AVM1Mobie" />
  <node name="Bitmap" />
  <node name="InteractiveObject" >
  <node name="DisplayObjectContainer">
  <node name="Loader" />
  <node name="Sprite" >
  <node name="MovieClip"/>
</node>
<node name="Stage" />
</node>
<node name="SimpleButton" />
  <node name="TextField" />
</node>
  <node name="MorphShape" />
  <node name="Shape" />
```

```
    <node name="StaticText" />
    <node name="Video" />
  </node>;
```

2. Then create our standard helper and styling objects:

```
var wid;
var hei;
var style = {boxWidth:90,boxHeight:30, boxColor:"black",boxCopy:"w
hite", boxSpace:4, lines:"black",lineSpace:30 };
```

3. We will implement our `init` function and then call the `drawTree` function:

```
function init(){
  var can = document.getElementById("bar");
  wid = can.width;
  hei = can.height;
  var context = can.getContext("2d");
  context.textAlign = "center";
  context.font = "6pt Arial";
  drawTree(context,wid/2,20, xml );
}
```

4. Time to implement the `drawTree` function (our recursive function):

```
function drawTree(context,_x,_y,node){
  context.fillStyle=style.boxColor;
  context.fillRect(_x-style.boxWidth/2,_y-
  style.boxHeight/2,style.boxWidth,style.boxHeight);
  context.fillStyle=style.boxCopy;
  context.fillText(node.@name,_x,_y+8);

  if(node.hasComplexContent()){
    var nodes = node.node;
    var totalWidthOfNewLayer = nodes.length()*
    style.boxWidth;
    if(nodes.length()>1)totalWidthOfNewLayer += (
    nodes.length()-1)* style.boxSpace;
    var startXPoint = _x-totalWidthOfNewLayer/2 +
    style.boxWidth/2;
    var currentY = _y+style.boxHeight/2;

    context.beginPath();
    context.strokeStyle ="#000000";
    context.lineWidth=3;
    context.moveTo(_x,currentY);
    currentY+=style.lineSpace/2;
    context.lineTo(_x,currentY);
```

```
        context.moveTo(startXPoint,currentY);
        context.lineTo(startXPoint+totalWidthOfNewLayer-
        style.boxWidth,currentY);
        context.stroke();

        for(var i=0; i<nodes.length();i++){
          drawTree(context,startXPoint + i*(style.boxWidth +
          style.boxSpace) ,_y+50,nodes[i]);
        }
      }
    }
```

Tah Dah! We just created our first tree.

How it works...

For more information on how E4X works, I recommend checking out some online resources such as `http://goo.gl/jLWYd` and `http://goo.gl/dsHD4`.

Let's take a deeper look at how our recursive `drawTree` works. The basic idea of `createTree` is to create the current node in focus and to check if the node has children; if it does, to send them to the `drawTree` and have them recursively continue until all the children are created and done. One of the most critical things you need to worry about when creating a recursive function (a function that calls itself) is to make sure that it doesn't end up being endless, and as our scenario has a very defined end that is based on the XML structure, we are safe.

We start by creating the current node in focus, based on the point values that were sent over in our function's parameters:

```
context.fillStyle=style.boxColor;
context.fillRect(_x-style.boxWidth/2,_y-style.boxHeight/2,style.
boxWidth,style.boxHeight);
context.fillStyle=stylc.boxCopy;
context.fillText(node.@name,_x,_y+8);
```

Right after these lines is where it starts getting really interesting. If our node is complex, we are going to assume that it has children, as that's our base rule in creating our XML object; and if so, it's time for us to draw the children:

```
if(node.hasComplexContent()){
```

We start by drawing a visualizer bar to help us see what the children of the current element are, and create a few helper variables in the process:

```
var nodes = node.node;
var totalWidthOfNewLayer = nodes.length()* style.boxWidth;
if(nodes.length()>1)
```

```
    totalWidthOfNewLayer += ( nodes.length()-1)* style.boxSpace;

    var startXPoint = _x-totalWidthOfNewLayer/2 +
    style.boxWidth/2;
    var currentY = _y+style.boxHeight/2;

    context.beginPath();
    context.strokeStyle ="#000000";
    context.lineWidth=3;
    context.moveTo(_x,currentY);
    currentY+=style.lineSpace/2;
    context.lineTo(_x,currentY);
    context.moveTo(startXPoint,currentY);
    context.lineTo(startXPoint+totalWidthOfNewLayer-
    style.boxWidth,currentY);
  context.stroke();
```

After creating our outline helper lines, it's time for us to loop through the children and send them to `drawTree` with their new positions:

```
  for(var i=0; i<nodes.length();i++){
    drawTree(context,startXPoint + i*(style.boxWidth +
    style.boxSpace) ,_y+50,nodes[i]);
    }
  }
```

That covers all the logic. At this stage, the logic will start all over again for each element, one at a time.

There's more...

In a perfect world our work with our tree would be done by now, but many a time in real-world scenarios we would encounter issues. If we play with our current tree enough, we will discover visual issues, such as if a child node has more than one child, its children will overlap the other tree branches. For example, if we update our `Loader` class to have two new children (two dummy classes just for the sake of our example):

```
var xml = <node name ="Display Object">
  <node name="AVM1Mobie" />
  <node name="Bitmap" />
  <node name="InteractiveObject" >
  <node name="DisplayObjectContainer">
  <node name="Loader">
  <node name="SlideLoader"/>
  <node name="ImageLoader"/>
  </node>
```

```
    <node name="Sprite" >
    <node name="MovieClip"/>
    <node name="MovieClip2"/>
    </node>
    <node name="Stage" />
    </node>
    <node name="SimpleButton" />
    <node name="TextField" />
    </node>
    <node name="MorphShape" />
    <node name="Shape" />
    <node name="StaticText" />
    <node name="Video" />
  </node>;
```

If you refresh your browser (currently only Firefox), you will see that our elements are overlapping as we didn't take into account the option of children that have children. If we review our code more deeply, we will see that in the current logic format there is no way to solve the problem as the creation of the children is happening separately. We will need to figure out a way to manage lines so that our elements will have a way to know that they are about to overlap.

To solve this problem, we will need to make our recursive function more complex, as it will need to keep track of its children's x position so that it can offset whenever there is an overlap. Please review the modified code (changes marked in bold):

```
function drawTree(context,_x,_y,node,nextChildX){
  context.fillStyle=style.boxColor;
  context.fillRect(_x-style.boxWidth/2,_y-
  style.boxHeight/2,style.boxWidth,style.boxHeight);
  context.fillStyle=style.boxCopy;
  context.fillText(node.@name,_x,_y+8);

  if(node.hasComplexContent()){
    var nodes = node.node;
    var totalWidthOfNewLayer = nodes.length()* style.boxWidth;
    if(nodes.length()>1)totalWidthOfNewLayer += ( nodes.length()-
    1)* style.boxSpace;
    var startXPoint = _x-totalWidthOfNewLayer/2 +
    style.boxWidth/2;
    var currentY = _y+style.boxHeight/2;

    context.beginPath();
    context.strokeStyle ="#000000";
    context.lineWidth=3;
    context.moveTo(_x,currentY);
```

```
        if(nextChildX>startXPoint){
          currentY+=style.lineSpace/4;
          context.lineTo(_x,currentY);
          context.lineTo(_x + (nextChildX-startXPoint),currentY);

          currentY+=style.lineSpace/4;
          context.lineTo(_x + (nextChildX-startXPoint),currentY);
          startXPoint = nextChildX; // offset correction value
        }else{
          currentY+=style.lineSpace/2;
          context.lineTo(_x,currentY);
        }
        context.moveTo(startXPoint,currentY);
        context.lineTo(startXPoint+totalWidthOfNewLayer-
        style.boxWidth,currentY);
        context.stroke();
        var returnedNextChildX=0;
        for(var i=0; i<nodes.length();i++){
          returnedNextChildX = drawTree(context,startXPoint +
          i*(style.boxWidth + style.boxSpace)
          ,_y+50,nodes[i],returnedNextChildX);
        }
        return startXPoint + i*(style.boxWidth + style.boxSpace);
      }

    return 0;
  }
```

Wow that looks complicated—it's because it is! So let's break the logic down.

The idea is simple, but as for every simple idea, sometimes it's harder to visualize after it's implemented. The idea is that every time we create a new tree element, we will return `0` if it has no children, and if it has children, we will send back the next free position for future children. We added a fourth parameter to the function as well, and we sent that information each time we looped through children. That way each child is aware of where the last child left off. If an element's real position can't be worked out, we draw a redirect line as per the amount of the offset and update `startXPoint`. Take a deeper look at this (so far my favorite code in the cookbook), which was fun to figure out!

5

Getting Out of the Box

In this chapter we will cover:

- Going though a funnel (a pyramid chart)
- Revisiting lines: making the line chart interactive
- Tree mapping and recursiveness
- Adding user interaction into tree mapping
- Making an interactive click meter

Introduction

We have covered our bases with the majority of the standard charts. At this stage, it's time for us to become more creative with our charts. From this chapter onwards, we will progress into more out-of-the-box, less commonly used charts and revisit some of our old charts to incorporate dynamic data into them or to change their layout.

Going through a funnel (a pyramid chart)

It's rare that you see a pyramid chart that is actually created dynamically. For the most part, they're designed and fleshed out creatively and turn into a `.jpg` file when they reach the web, and that's exactly why I wanted to start this chapter with this chart—it's not as complex as it might sound.

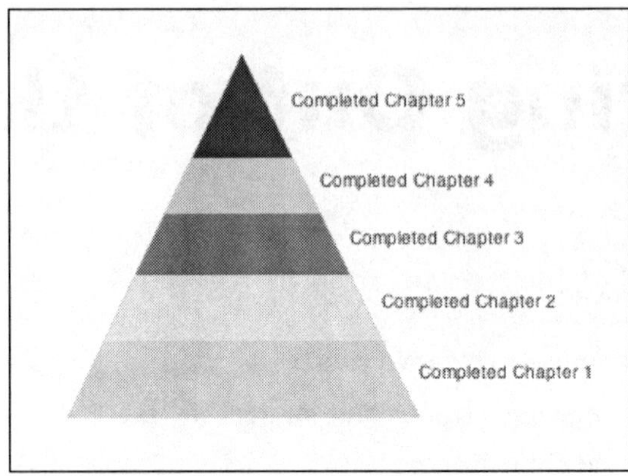

A pyramid chart is in essence a way for us to visualize changes in data that are quantitative by nature. They have a clear relationship between the lower layers and the higher layers. That sounded very vague, so let's explain it through an example.

Imagine that X amount of people complete their eighth year of school in a given year, if we follow the same group of people, how many of them would have completed their twelfth year of education four years later? Fair enough! We can't know the answer to that, but one thing we do know is that it can't be more than the initial X amount of people. The idea of a pyramid chart is exactly that of a body of data, of which less and less goes through the funnel as time or something else changes It's a really great chart to compare between levels of education, finance, involvement in politics, and so on.

Getting ready

Just as always, set up our HTML file logic. For a refresher on how to start up the HTML file, please go back to the *Graphics with 2D canvas* recipe in *Chapter 1, Drawing Shapes in Canvas*.

How to do it...

Beyond our standard HTML preparation, we need to come up with the data sources that we wish to showcase. Let's start building our pyramid. Go right into the JS file and let's start.

1. For our example, we will create a pyramid to find out how many people that read this book from chapter one through chapter five actually reach chapter five (this data is fake; I hope everyone that starts reading will get there!).

```
var layers = [{label:"Completed Chapter 1", amount:23},
  {label:"Completed Chapter 2", amount:15},
  {label:"Completed Chapter 3", amount:11},
  {label:"Completed Chapter 4", amount:7},
  {label:"Completed Chapter 5", amount:3} ];
```

2. Then, provide some charting and styling information.

```
var chartInfo= {height:200, width:200};

var s = { outlinePadding:4,
  barSize:16,
  font:"12pt Verdana, sans-serif",
  background:"eeeeee",
  stroke:"cccccc",
  text:"605050"
};
```

Note that, for the first time, we are differentiating between what we want the size of our canvas to be and the actual size of our chart (funnel/triangle). Another important thing to note is that, for our sample to work in its current format, our triangle height and width (base) must be the same.

3. Define a few global helper variables.

```
var wid;
var hei;
var totalPixels;
var totalData=0;
var pixelsPerData;
var currentTriangleHeight = chartInfo.height;
```

4. It's time for us to create our `init` function. This function will be doing most of the heavy lifting with the help of another function.

```
function init(){
  var can = document.getElementById("bar");

  wid = can.width;
  hei = can.height;
  totalPixels = (chartInfo.height * chartInfo.width) / 2;
  for(var i in layers) totalData +=layers[i].amount;

  pixelsPerData = totalPixels/totalData;


  var context = can.getContext("2d");
  context.fillStyle = s.background;
  context.strokeStyle = s.stroke;

  context.translate(wid/2,hei/2 - chartInfo.height/2);

  context.moveTo(-chartInfo.width/2 , chartInfo.height);
  context.lineTo(chartInfo.width/2,chartInfo.height);
  context.lineTo(0,0);
  context.lineTo(-chartInfo.width/2 , chartInfo.height);

  for(i=0; i+1<layers.length; i++) findLine(context,
  layers[i].amount);

  context.stroke();
}
```

5. Our function performs the normal setup and executes the styling logic and then it creates a triangle, after which it finds the right points (by using the `findLine` function) at which we should cut the triangle:

```
function findLine(context,val){
  var newHeight = currentTriangleHeight;
  var pixels = pixelsPerData * val;
  var lines = parseInt(pixels/newHeight); //rounded

  pixels = lines*lines/2; //missing pixels

  newHeight-=lines;

  lines += parseInt(pixels/newHeight);
  currentTriangleHeight-=lines;

  context.moveTo(-currentTriangleHeight/2 ,
  currentTriangleHeight);
  context.lineTo(currentTriangleHeight/2,
  currentTriangleHeight);
}
```

This function finds the dots on our triangle based on the data of the current line. That's it; now its time to understand what we just did.

How it works...

After setting the code for lines in the `init` function, we are ready to start thinking about our triangle. First, we need to find out the total pixels that are within our triangle.

```
totalPixels = (chartInfo.height * chartInfo.width) / 2;
```

That is easy as we know our height and our width, so the formula is really simple. The next data point that is critical is the total amount of data. We can create a relationship between the pixels and the data.

```
for(var i in layers) totalData +=layers[i].amount;
```

As such, we loop through all the data layers and calculate the summary of all data points. At this stage, we are ready to find out the actual number of pixels. Each data element is equivalent to:

```
pixelsPerData = totalPixels/totalData;
```

After setting up the styles for our stroke and fill, we stop to think about the best translation that would help us build our triangle. For our triangle, I've picked the top edge to be the `0,0` point, after creating the triangle:

```
context.translate(wid/2,hei/2 - chartInfo.height/2);

context.moveTo(-chartInfo.width/2 , chartInfo.height);
context.lineTo(chartInfo.width/2,chartInfo.height);
context.lineTo(0,0);
context.lineTo(-chartInfo.width/2 , chartInfo.height);
```

The last two lines of our `init` function call the `findLine` method for each element in our `layers` array:

```
for(i=0; i+1<layers.length; i++) findLine(context, layers[i].amount);
context.stroke();
```

Time to dig into how the `findLine` function actually finds the points to create the lines. The idea is very simple. The basic idea is to try to find out how many lines it would take to complete the number of pixels in a triangle. As we are not building a math formula, we don't care if it's 100 percent accurate, but it should be accurate enough to work visually.

There's more...

Let's start with introducing color into our pallet.

```
var layers = [{label:"Completed Chapter 1", amount:23,
style:"#B1DDF3"},  {label:"Completed Chapter 2", amount:15,
style:"#FFDE89"},
  {label:"Completed Chapter 3", amount:11, style:"#E3675C"},
  {label:"Completed Chapter 4", amount:7, style:"#C2D985"},
  {label:"Completed Chapter 5", amount:3, style:"#999999"}];
```

OK, we are done with the easy part. Now, it's time to rework our logic.

Making findLine smarter

For us to be able to create a closed shape, we need to have a way to change the direction of the line drawn from right to left or from left to right and not have it go in one direction always. Beyond that, we are using `moveTo` right now and as such can never create a closed shape. What we actually want is to move our point and draw a line:

```
function findLine(context,val,isMove){
  var newHeight = currentTriangleHeight;
  var pixels = pixelsPerData * val;
  var lines = parseInt(pixels/newHeight); //rounded

  pixels = lines*lines/2; //missing pixels

  newHeight-=lines;

  lines += parseInt(pixels/newHeight);

  currentTriangleHeight-=lines;

  if(isMove){
    context.moveTo(currentTriangleHeight/2,
    currentTriangleHeight);
    context.lineTo(-currentTriangleHeight/2 ,
    currentTriangleHeight);
  }else{
    context.lineTo(-currentTriangleHeight/2 ,
    currentTriangleHeight);
    context.lineTo(currentTriangleHeight/2,
    currentTriangleHeight);
  }
}
```

Our next problem is that we don't want to change the actual triangle height as we will be calling this function more times than we did in the past. To come up with a plan for this problem, we need to extract some of the logic. We will return the new number of lines that were created, so that we can remove them externally from the triangle. This action enables us to have more finite control over visuals (a thing that will be important when we incorporate text).

```
function findLine(context,val,isMove){
  var newHeight = currentTriangleHeight;
  var pixels = pixelsPerData * val;
  var lines = parseInt(pixels/newHeight); //rounded

  pixels = lines*lines/2; //missing pixels

  newHeight-=lines;

  lines += parseInt(pixels/newHeight);

  newHeight = currentTriangleHeight-lines;

  if(isMove){
    context.moveTo(newHeight/2,newHeight);
    context.lineTo(-newHeight/2 , newHeight);
  }else{
    context.lineTo(-newHeight/2 , newHeight);
    context.lineTo(newHeight/2,newHeight);
  }


return lines;
}
```

At this stage, our `findLine` function is really smart and is capable of helping us to create closed shapes without controlling more than it needs to control (as it isn't changing any of our global data).

Changing the logic in init to create shapes

Now that we have a smart `findLine` function, it's time for us to rewrite our logic related to drawing lines in the `init` function.

```
var secHeight = 0;
  for(i=0;i<layers.length-1; i++){
    context.beginPath();
    findLine(context, 0,true);
    secHeight = findLine(context, layers[i].amount);
```

```
    currentTriangleHeight -= secHeight;
    context.fillStyle = layers[i].style;
    context.fill();
  }

  context.beginPath();
  findLine(context, 0,true);
  context.lineTo(0,0);
  context.fillStyle = layers[i].style;
  context.fill();
```

First, we draw all elements in our loop, minus the last one (as our last element is actually a triangle and not a line). Then, to help us hide our mathematical inaccuracy, we create a new path each time our loop starts and call our `findLine` function first with no new data (drawing a line in the last place where it drew a line as there is no data) and then drawing a second line, this time with the real new data.

Our exception to the rule is created out of the loop, and there, we just manually draw our shape, starting with the last line, and add the `0,0` point into it, over our triangle.

Adding text into our graph

This one will be simple, as we are already getting back the line count before we resize our triangle. We can use this data to calculate where we want to position our textfield variable, so let's do it:

```
var secHeight = 0;
  for(i=0;i<layers.length-1; i++){
    context.beginPath();
    findLine(context, 0,true);
    secHeight = findLine(context, layers[i].amount);
    currentTriangleHeight -= secHeight;
    context.fillStyle = layers[i].style;
    context.fill();
    context.fillStyle = s.text;
    context.fillText(layers[i].label, currentTriangleHeight/2
    +secHeight/2, currentTriangleHeight+secHeight/2);
  }

  context.beginPath();
  findLine(context, 0,true);
  context.lineTo(0,0);
  context.fillStyle = layers[i].style;
  context.fill();
  context.fillStyle = s.text;
  context.fillText(layers[i].label, currentTriangleHeight/2 ,
  currentTriangleHeight/2);
```

Just see the difference between drawing our text in the loop and out of it. As we don't get new line data out of the loop, we need to change the point logic by using the total size of our leftover triangle.

Revisiting lines: making the line chart interactive

In this recipe, we will travel back in time to one of our earlier recipes, *Building line charts in Chapter 3, Creating Cartesian-based Graphs* and add some user control to it. This control enables the user to turn on and off the streams of data.

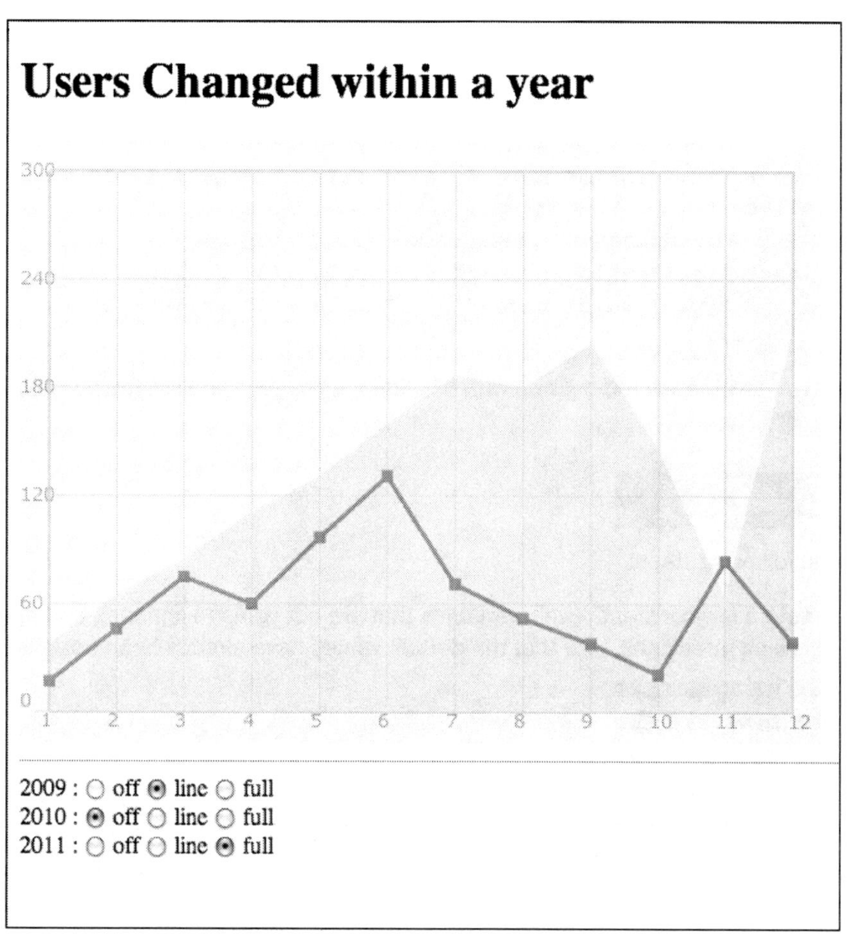

Getting ready

The first step that you will need to take is to grab the source code from *Chapter 3, Creating Cartesian-based Graphs*. We will rename `03.05.line-revamp.html` and `03.05.line-revamp.js` to `05.02.line-revisit`.

Now that we have our files up to date, add our HTML file—three radio groups to represent the three data sources (years 2009, 2010, and 2011).

```
<hr/>

  2009 : <input type="radio" name="i2009" value="-1" /> off
    <input type="radio" name="i2009" value="0" /> line
    <input type="radio" name="i2009" value="1" select="1" />
    full<br/>
  2010 : <input type="radio" name="i2010" value="-1" /> off
    <input type="radio" name="i2010" value="0" /> line
    <input type="radio" name="i2010" value="1" select="1" />
    full<br/>
   2011 : <input type="radio" name="i2011" value="-1" /> off
    <input type="radio" name="i2011" value="0" /> line
    <input type="radio" name="i2011" value="1" select="1" />
    full<br/>
```

Note that I've named each radio group with "i" added to the year and set the possible values to be `-1`, `0`, or `1`.

How to do it...

Perform the following steps:

1. Create a few constants (well, variables that are not going to change), and set the following three lines, now that the default values have already been assigned:

   ```
   var HIDE_ELEMENT = -1;
   var LINE_ELEMENT = 0;
   var FILL_ELEMENT = 1;

   var elementStatus={ i2009:FILL_ELEMENT,
     i2010:FILL_ELEMENT,
     i2011:FILL_ELEMENT};
   ```

2. Time to move the logic of creating the chart into a separate function. Everything after the initalization of our canvas is going to be moved out.

```
var context;

function init(){
  var can = document.getElementById("bar");

  wid = can.width;
  hei = can.height;
  context = can.getContext("2d");

  drawChart();
}
```

3. Update the radio boxes to highlight whatever is currently selected and to add the `onchange` events to all radio buttons.

```
function init(){
  var can = document.getElementById("bar");

  wid = can.width;
  hei = can.height;
  context = can.getContext("2d");

  drawChart();

  var radios ;
    for(var id in elementStatus){
      radios = document.getElementsByName(id);
      for (var rid in radios){
      radios[rid].onchange = onChangedRadio;
      if(radios[rid].value == elementStatus[id] )
      radios[rid].checked = true;
    }
  }

}
```

4. Make some updates in our `drawChart` function. Our goal is to incorporate the new controller `elementStatus` into the drawing of lines.

```
function drawChart(){
  context.lineWidth = 1;
  context.fillStyle = "#eeeeee";
  context.strokeStyle = "#999999";
  context.fillRect(0,0,wid,hei);
```

```
    context.font = "10pt Verdana, sans-serif";
    context.fillStyle = "#999999";

    context.moveTo(CHART_PADDING,CHART_PADDING);
    context.rect(CHART_PADDING,CHART_PADDING,wid-
    CHART_PADDING*2,hei-CHART_PADDING*2);
    context.stroke();
    context.strokeStyle = "#cccccc";
    fillChart(context,chartInfo);


    if(elementStatus.i2011>-1)
    addLine(context,formatData(a2011,    "/2011","#B1DDF3"),"#B1DDF3"
  ,elementStatus.i2011==1);
    if(elementStatus.i2010>-1)
    addLine(context,formatData(a2010,
    "/2010","#FFDE89"),"#FFDE89",elementStatus.i2010==1);
    if(elementStatus.i2009>-1)
    addLine(context,formatData(a2009,
    "/2009","#E3675C"),"#E3675C",elementStatus.i2009==1);

  }
```

5. Last but not least, let's add the logic into our `onChangedRadio` function.

```
  function onChangedRadio(e){
    elementStatus[e.target.name] = e.target.value;
    context.clearRect(0,0,wid,hei);
    context.beginPath();
    drawChart();
  }
```

That's it! We just added user interaction into our chart.

How it works...

We haven't planned for user interaction on this chart in advance. As such, we need to revisit it to change some of the logic. When Canvas draws something, that's it, it's there forever! We can't just delete an object, as there are no objects in Canvas, and as such, we need a way to redraw on demand. To accomplish that, we need to extract all the drawing logic from the `init` function and create the `drawChart` function. Besides adding our logic to the end of the function, we also need to add the start of the function:

```
context.lineWidth = 1;
```

Although we originally worked out the default to use as the width for our background, in a second redraw, our canvas would still have stored its last size (in our case it could be `3`), and as such, we reset it to the original value.

We are using an object called `elementStatus` to store the current status of each line on our chart. The values it can store are as follows:

- `-1`: Do not draw
- `0`: Draw a line with no fill
- `1`: Draw a fill

As such, we are adding the following logic into the end of our function:

```
if(elementStatus.i2011>-1) addLine(context,formatData(a2011, "/2011","
#B1DDF3"),"#B1DDF3",elementStatus.i2011==1);
```

As the logic repeats three times, let's just focus on one of them. If we want, we can use our constant variables to make the logic easier to view.

```
if(elementStatus.i2011!=HIDE_ELEMENT)
  addLine(context,formatData(a2011,
  "/2011","#B1DDF3"),"#B1DDF3",elementStatus.i2011==FILL_ELEMENT);
```

The logic breaks down into a first `if` statement, testing to see if our content should be hidden. If we establish that this line should be added, we draw it by sending into the fill/line parameter the outcome of comparing our current value to `FILL_ELEMENT`, resulting in two variations based on the outcome of this operation.

There's more...

Unfortunately, because we are not using any open source library, the built-in HTML capabilities don't allow us to set events to groups of radios, and as such, we need to find them all and add the `onchange` event to them using the IDs we are storing in our `elementStatus` controller.

```
var radios ;
  for(var id in elementStatus){
    radios = document.getElementsByName(id);
    for (var rid in radios){
      radios[rid].onchange = onChangedRadio;
      if(radios[rid].value == elementStatus[id] )
      radios[rid].checked = true;
    }

  }
```

Pay attention to the highlighted code. Here, we are checking to see whether our current radio button's value matches our element value in `elementStatus`. If it does, it means that the radio button will be selected.

Breaking down the logic of onChangedRadio

Let's take another peek at the logic in this function:

```
elementStatus[e.target.name] = e.target.value;
```

The first thing we do is save the newly selected value into our `elementStatus` controller.

```
context.clearRect(0,0,wid,hei);
```

We follow that by deleting everything from our canvas.

```
context.beginPath();
```

Next, wipe the slate clean and start with a new path.

```
drawChart();
```

And... you guessed it... Then start drawing everything all over, and our new parameter in `elementStatus` will validate that the right things will be drawn.

See also

- The *Building line charts* recipe in *Chapter 3, Creating Cartesian-based Graphs*

Tree mapping and recursiveness

Tree mapping enables us to see in-depth data from a bird's-eye view. Contrary to comparative charts—such as most of the charts that we have created until now—tree mapping displays tree structured data as a set of nested rectangles, enabling us to visualize their quantitative nature and relationship.

Let's start with a tree mapping that showcases only one level of information.

Getting ready

We will start our application with the number of people in the world, in millions, divided by continent (based on public data from 2011).

```
var chartData = [
  {name: "Asia", value:4216},
  {name: "Africa",value:1051},
  {name: "The Americas and the Caribbean", value:942},
  {name: "Europe", value:740},
  {name: "Oceania", value:37}
];
```

We will update this data source later in our example, so keep in mind that this dataset is temporary.

How to do it...

We will start by creating a simple, working, flat tree chart. Let's jump right into it and figure out the steps involved in creating the tree map:

1. Let's add a few helper variables on top of our dataset.

```
var wid;
var hei;
var context;
var total=0;
```

2. Create the `init` function.

```
function init(){
  var can = document.getElementById("bar");

  wid = can.width;
  hei = can.height;
  context = can.getContext("2d");

  for(var item in chartData) total +=
  chartData[item].value;

  context.fillRect(0,0,wid,hei);
  context.fillStyle = "RGB(255,255,255)";
  context.fillRect(5,5,wid-10,hei-10);
  context.translate(5,5);
  wid-=10;
  hei-=10;

  drawTreeMap(chartData);

}
```

3. Create the function `drawTreeMap`.

```
function drawTreeMap(infoArray){
  var percent=0;
  var cx=0;
  var rollingPercent = 0;
  for(var i=0; i<infoArray.length; i++){
    percent = infoArray[i].value/total;
    rollingPercent +=percent
    context.fillStyle =
    formatColorObject(getRandomColor(255));
    context.fillRect(cx,0 ,wid*percent,hei);
    cx+=wid*percent;
    if(rollingPercent > 0.7) break;

  }

  var leftOverPercent = 1-rollingPercent;
  var leftOverWidth = wid*leftOverPercent;
  var cy=0;
  for(i=i+1; i<infoArray.length; i++){
    percent = (infoArray[i].value/total)/leftOverPercent;
    context.fillStyle =
    formatColorObject(getRandomColor(255));
    context.fillRect(cx,cy ,leftOverWidth,hei*percent);
    cy+=hei*percent;
  }

}
```

4. Create a few formatting functions to help us create a random color for our tree map block.

```
function formatColorObject(o){
  return "rgb("+o.r+","+o.g+","+o.b+")";
}

function getRandomColor(val){
  return
  {r:getRandomInt(255),g:getRandomInt(255),
  b:getRandomInt(255)};
}

function getRandomInt(val){
  return parseInt(Math.random()*val)+1
}
```

There is a bit of overkill in the creation of so many formatting functions; their main goal is to help us when we are ready for the next step—to create more depth in our data (refer to the *There's more...* section in this recipe for more details).

How it works...

Let's start with the initial idea. Our goal is to create a map that will showcase the bigger volume areas inside our rectangular area and leave a strip on the side for the smaller areas. So, let's start with our `init` function. Our first task beyond our basic getting started work is to calculate the actual total. We do that by looping through our data source, thus:

```
for(var item in chartData) total += chartData[item].value;
```

We continued with some playing around with the design and making our work area 10 pixels smaller than our total canvas size.

```
CONTEXT.FILLRECT(0,0,WID,HEI);
CONTEXT.FILLSTYLE = "RGB(255,255,255)";
CONTEXT.FILLRECT(5,5,WID-10,HEI-10);
CONTEXT.TRANSLATE(5,5);
WID-=10;
HEI-=10;

drawTreeMap(chartData);
```

It's time to take a look into how our `drawTreeMap` function works. The first thing to notice is that we send in an array instead of working directly with our data source. We do that because we want to be open to the idea that this function will be re-used when we start building the inner depths of this visualization type.

```
function drawTreeMap(infoArray){...}
```

We start our function with a few helper variables (the `percent` variable will store the current `percent` value in a loop). The `cx` (the current x) position of our rectangle and `rollingPercent` will keep track of how much of our total chart has been completed.

```
var percent=0;
var cx=0;
var rollingPercent = 0;
```

Time to start looping through our data and drawing out the rectangles.

```
for(var i=0; i<infoArray.length; i++){
  percent = infoArray[i].value/total;
  rollingPercent +=percent
  context.fillStyle =
  formatColorObject(getRandomColor(255));
  context.fillRect(cx,0 ,wid*percent,hei);
  cx+=wid*percent;
```

Before we complete our first loop, we will test it to see when we cross our threshold (you are welcome to play with that value). When we reach it, we need to stop the loop, so that we can start drawing our rectangles by height instead of by width.

```
if(rollingPercent > 0.7) break;
}
```

Before we start working on our boxes, which take the full leftover width and expand to the height, we need a few helper variables.

```
var leftOverPercent = 1-rollingPercent;
var leftOverWidth = wid*leftOverPercent;
var cy=0;
```

As we need to calculate each element from now on based on the amount of space left, we will figure out the value (`leftOverPercent`), and then we will extract the remaining width of our shape and start up a new `cy` variable to store the current y position.

```
for(i=i+1; i<infoArray.length; i++){
  percent = (infoArray[i].value/total)/leftOverPercent;
  context.fillStyle = formatColorObject(getRandomColor(255));
  context.fillRect(cx,cy ,leftOverWidth,hei*percent);
  cy+=hei*percent;
}
```

We start our loop with one value higher than what we left off (as we broke out of our earlier loop before we had a chance to update its value and draw to the height of our remaining area.

Note that in both loops we are using `formatColorObject` and `getRandomColor`. The breakdown of these functions was created so that we can have an easier way to manipulate the colors returned in our next part.

There's more...

For our chart to really have that extra kick, we need to have a way to make it capable of showing data in at least a second lower-level details of data. To do that, we will revisit our data source and re-edit it:

```
var chartData = [
  {name: "Asia", data:[
    {name: "South Central",total:1800},
    {name: "East",total:1588},
    {name: "South East",total:602},
    {name: "Western",total:238},
    {name: "Northern",total:143}
  ]},
  {name: "Africa",total:1051},
```

```
    {name: "The Americas and the Caribbean", data:[
      {name: "South America",total:396},
      {name: "North America",total:346},
      {name: "Central America",total:158},
      {name: "Caribbean",total:42}
    ]},
    {name: "Europe", total:740},
    {name: "Oceania", total:37}
  ];
```

Now we have two regions of the world with a more in-depth view of their subregions. It's time for us to start modifying our code, so that it will work again with this new data.

Updating the init function – recalculating the total

The first step we need to carry out in the `init` function is to replace the current total loop with a new one that can dig deeper into elements to count the real total.

```
var val;
var i;
for(var item in chartData) {
  val = chartData[item];
  if(!val.total && val.data){
    val.total = 0;
    for( i=0; i<val.data.length; i++)
    val.total+=val.data[i].total;
  }

  total += val.total;
}
```

In essence, we are checking to see whether there is no total and whether there is a data source. If that is the case, we start a new loop to calculate the actual total for our elements—a good exercise for you now would be to try to make this logic into a recursive function (so that you can have more layers of data).

Next, we will change `drawTreeMap` and get it ready to become a recursive function. To make that happen, we need to extract the global variables from it and send them in as parameters of the function.

```
drawTreeMap(chartData,wid,hei,0,0,total);
```

Turning drawTreeMap into a recursive function

Let's update our function to enable recursive operations. We start by adding an extra new parameter to capture the latest color.

```
function drawTreeMap(infoArray,wid,hei,x,y,total,clr){
  var percent=0;
  var cx=x ;
  var cy=y;

  var pad = 0;
  var pad2 = 0;

  var rollingPercent = 0;
  var keepColor = false;
  if(clr){ //keep color and make darker
    keepColor = true;
    clr.r = parseInt(clr.r *.9);
    clr.g = parseInt(clr.g *.9);
    clr.b = parseInt(clr.b *.9);
    pad = PAD*2;
    pad2 = PAD2*2;
  }
```

If we pass a `clr` parameter, we need to keep that color throughout all the new rectangles that will be created, and we need to add a padding around the shapes so that it becomes easier to see them. We make the color a bit darker as well by subtracting 10 percent of its color on all its RGA properties.

The next stage is to add the padding and recursive logic.

```
for(var i=0; i<infoArray.length; i++){
  percent = infoArray[i].total/total;
  rollingPercent +=percent
  if(!keepColor){
    clr = getRandomColor(255);
  }

  context.fillStyle = formatColorObject(clr);
  context.fillRect(cx+pad ,cy+pad ,wid*percent - pad2,hei-pad2);
  context.strokeRect(cx+pad ,cy+pad ,wid*percent - pad2,hei-
  pad2);
  if(infoArray[i].data){
    drawTreeMap(infoArray[i].data,parseInt(wid*percent -
    PAD2),hei - PAD2,cx+ PAD,cy + PAD,infoArray[i].total,clr);
  }
```

```
    cx+=wid*percent;
    if(rollingPercent > 0.7) break;

  }
```

The same logic is then implemented on the second loop as well (to see it check the source files).

Turning the data and total to recursive data

Let's start by updating our tree data to be really recursive (for the full dataset please refer to the source code).

```
...
{name: "Asia", data:[
  {name: "South Central",total:1800},
  {name: "East",total:1588},
  {name: "South East",total:602},
  {name: "Western",total:238},
  {name: "Northern",data:[{name: "1",data:[
    {name: "2",total:30},
    {name: "2",total:30}
  ]},
  {name: "2",total:53},
  {name: "2",total:30}
]}  ...
```

Now, with a tree map that has over four levels of information, we can revisit our code and finalize our last outstanding issue validating that our total is always up-to-date at all levels. To fix that, we will extract the logic of calculating the total into a new function and update the `total` line in the `init` function.

```
function init(){
  var can = document.getElementById("bar");

  wid = can.width;
  hei = can.height;
  context = can.getContext("2d");

  total = calculateTotal(chartData); //recursive function
...
```

Time to create this magical (recursive) function.

```
function calculateTotal(chartData){
  var total =0;
  var val;
  var i;
  for(var item in chartData) {
```

```
      val = chartData[item];
      if(!val.total && val.data)
        val.total = calculateTotal(val.data);

      total += val.total;
    }

  return total;

  }
```

The logic is really similar to what it was, with the exception that all the data entries are internal to the function, and each time there is a need to deal with another level of data, it's re-sent to the same function (in a recursive way) until all data is resolved—until it returns the total.

See also

- The *Adding user interaction into tree mapping* recipe

Adding user interaction into tree mapping

Until now, we have limited our user interaction with our samples. In one of our last samples, we added a controlled way to add and remove chart elements; in this one, we will enable the user to dig deeper into the chart and see more details by creating a truly endless experience (if we only had an endless amount of data to dig into).

In the following image, on the left-hand side, you can see the initial state and what happens after one click of the user (the chart redraws itself to showcase the area that was clicked on).

Consider the case when the user clicks on the chart (for example, the next picture is generated by clicking on the left-hand side rectangle–the tree map will update and zoom into that area).

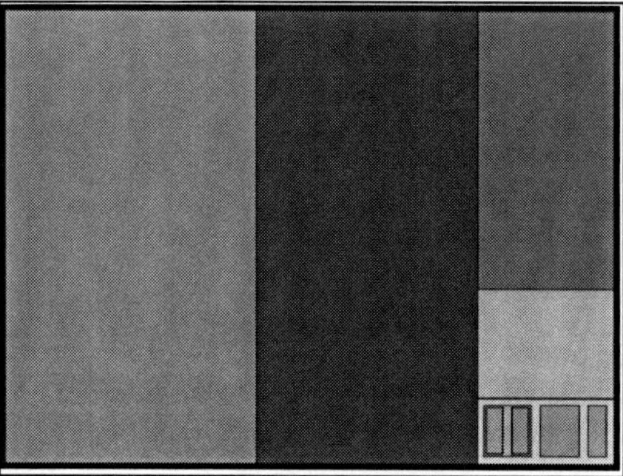

Getting ready

To get this sample right, you will need to start from our last recipe, *Tree maping and recursiveness*, and adjust it to work for this sample.

How to do it...

This is our first sample where we make our canvas area interactive. In the next few steps, we will add some logic from the last sample into our recipe, to enable the user to zoom into or out of it:

1. Add a new global variable,

   ```
   var currentDataset;
   ```

2. Store the current data that is sent to the tree mapping function.

   ```
   currentDataset = chartData;
   drawTreeMap(chartData,wid,hei,0,0,total);
   ```

3. Add a `click` event to our canvas area.

   ```
   can.addEventListener('click', onTreeClicked, false);
   ```

4. Create the `onTreeClick` event.

   ```
   function onTreeClick(e) {
     var box;
     for(var item in currentDataset){
       if(currentDataset[item].data){
         box = currentDataset[item].box;
   ```

```
        if(e.x>= box.x && e.y>= box.y &&
        e.x<= box.x2 && e.y<= box.y2){
          context.clearRect(0,0,wid,hei);
          drawTreeMap(currentDataset[item].data,wid,
          hei,0,0,currentDataset[item].total);
          currentDataset = currentDataset[item].data;

        break;
        }

      }
    }
  }
```

5. Draw a rectangle twice—within `drawTreemap`—for the first time in the first loop and again in the second loop. Let's replace it with an external function—replace both the `for` loop lines to draw a rectangle with:

   ```
   drawRect(cx+pad ,cy+pad ,wid*percent - pad2,hei-
   pad2,infoArray[i]);
   ```

6. Time to create the rectangle function.

   ```
   function drawRect(x,y,wid,hei,dataSource){
     context.fillRect(x,y,wid,hei);
     context.strokeRect(x,y,wid,hei);
     dataSource.box = {x:x,y:y,x2:x+wid,y2:y+hei};

   }
   ```

There you go! We have a fully functional, deep-level, endless interaction with the user (just dependent on how much data we have).

How it works...

The Canvas element doesn't currently support a smart way to interact with objects. As there are no objects in the canvas, as soon as you create the element it tunes into a bitmap and its information is removed from memory. Luckily for us, our sample is constructed out of rectangles, making it much easier to recognize when our element is clicked on. We will need to store in memory the current box location of each element that we draw.

As such, our first step of logic is the last thing that we did in our procedure (in step 6). We want to capture the points that construct our rectangles, so then in our `click` event we can figure out where our dot is in relation to the rectangle:

```
function onTreeClick(e) {
   var box;
  for(var item in currentDataset){
    if(currentDataset[item].data){
```

We loop through our data source (current one) and check to see whether the element we are currently in has a data source (that is, children); if it does, we continue, and if not, we will skip to the next element to test it as well.

Now that we know our element has children, we are ready to see if our dot is in the range of our element.

```
box = currentDataset[item].box;
if(e.x>= box.x && e.y>= box.y &&
   e.x<= box.x2 && e.y<= box.y2){
```

If it is, we are ready to redraw the tree map and replace our current dataset with the current deeper dataset.

```
context.clearRect(0,0,wid,hei);
drawTreeMap(currentDataset[item].data,wid,hei,0,0,currentDataset[it
em].total);
currentDataset = currentDataset[item].data;

break;
```

We then exit from the loop (by using a `break` statement). Please note that the last thing we do is update `currentDataset`, as we still need information from it to send the total data into `drawTreeMap`. When we have finished using it, we are ready to override it with the new dataset (what were the children before turn into our main players for the next round).

There's more...

Currently, there is just no way to get back without refreshing everything. So, let's add it to our logic that if the user clicks in an element with no children, we will revert to the original map.

Going back to the main treemap

Let's add the following code into the `click` event:

```
function onTreeClick(e) {
   var box;
  for(var item in currentDataset){
    if(currentDataset[item].data){
      box = currentDataset[item].box;
      if(e.x>= box.x && e.y>= box.y &&
      e.x<= box.x2 && e.y<= box.y2){
        context.clearRect(0,0,wid,hei);
        drawTreeMap(currentDataset[item].data,wid,
        hei,0,0,currentDataset[item].total);
        currentDataset = currentDataset[item].data;
```

```
            break;
            }

        }else{
            currentDataset = chartData;
            drawTreeMap(chartData,wid,hei,0,0,total);

        }
    }
}
```

Fantastically done! We have just finished creating a fully interactive experience for our users, and now it's in your hands to make this look a bit better. Add some rollover labels and all the visualization that will make your chart visually pleasing and will help understanding.

Making an interactive click meter

In this next example, we will focus on one more powerful feature of any client-side programming—the ability to interact with the user and the ability to update data dynamically. To keep it simple, let's revisit an old chart—the bar chart from *Chapter 3, Creating Cartesian-based Graphs*—and integrate a counter that will count how many times a user clicks on an HTML document in any given second and update the chart accordingly.

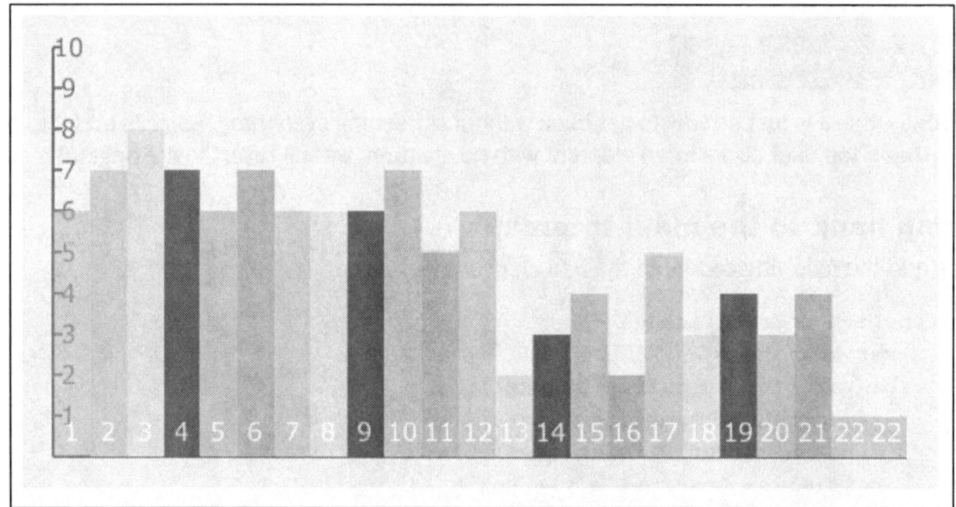

How to do it...

Most of the steps are going to be familiar, if you have worked on the bar chart from *Chapter 3, Creating Cartesian-based Graphs*. So, let's run through them and then focus on the new logic:

1. Let's create some helper variables.

   ```
   var currentObject = {label:1,
     value:0,
     style:"rgba(241, 178, 225, .5)"};
     var colorOptions = ["rgba(241, 178, 225,
     1)","#B1DDF3","#FFDE89","#E3675C","#C2D985"];

     var data = [];


   var context;
   var wid;
   var hei;
   ```

2. Follow this with our `init` function.

   ```
   function init(){

     var can = document.getElementById("bar");
     wid = can.width;
     hei = can.height;

     context = can.getContext("2d");


     document.addEventListener("click",onClick);
     interval = setInterval(onTimeReset,1000);
     refreshChart();
   }
   ```

3. Now it's time to create the `onTimeReset` function.

   ```
   function onTimeReset(){
     if(currentObject.value){
       data.push(currentObject);
       if(data.length>25) data = data.slice(1);
       refreshChart();
     }
     currentObject = {label:currentObject.label+1, value:0,
     style: colorOptions[currentObject.label%5]};

   }
   ```

4. The next step is to create the `onClick` listener.

```
function onClick(e){
  currentObject.value++;
  refreshChart();
}
```

5. Now create the `refreshChart` function.

```
function refreshChart(){
  var newData = data.slice(0);
  newData.push(currentObject);

  drawChart(newData);
}
```

6. Last but not least, let's create `drawChart` (most of its logic is the same as for the `init` function discussed in *Chapter 3, Creating Cartesian-based Graphs*).

```
function drawChart(data){
  context.fillStyle = "#eeeeee";
  context.strokeStyle = "#999999";
  context.fillRect(0,0,wid,hei);

  var CHART_PADDING = 20;

  context.font = "12pt Verdana, sans-serif";
  context.fillStyle = "#999999";


  context.moveTo(CHART_PADDING,CHART_PADDING);
  context.lineTo(CHART_PADDING,hei-CHART_PADDING);
  context.lineTo(wid-CHART_PADDING,hei-CHART_PADDING);

  var stepSize = (hei - CHART_PADDING*2)/10;
  for(var i=0; i<10; i++){
    context.moveTo(CHART_PADDING, CHART_PADDING + i*
    stepSize);
    context.lineTo(CHART_PADDING*1.3,CHART_PADDING + i*
    stepSize);
    context.fillText(10-i, CHART_PADDING*1.5,
    CHART_PADDING + i*     stepSize + 6);
  }
  context.stroke();
```

```
    var elementWidth =(wid-CHART_PADDING*2)/ data.length;
    context.textAlign = "center";
    for(i=0; i<data.length; i++){
      context.fillStyle = data[i].style;
      context.fillRect(CHART_PADDING +elementWidth*i ,hei-
      CHART_PADDING - data[i].value*stepSize,
      elementWidth,data[i].value*stepSize);
      context.fillStyle = "rgba(255, 255, 225, 0.8)";
      context.fillText(data[i].label, CHART_PADDING
      +elementWidth*(i+.5), hei-CHART_PADDING*1.5);

    }
  }
```

That's it! We have an interactive chart that will be updated every second, depending on how many times you manage to click your mouse in 1 second—I assume no one can click more than 10 times a second but I've managed to get there (when using two hands).

How it works...

Let's focus on the breakdown of the data variables in *Chapter 3, Creating Cartesian-based Graphs*. We had all our data ready inside our data object. This time around, we are keeping the data object empty, and instead, we have one data line in a separate variable.

```
var currentObject = {label:1,
  value:0,
  style:"rgba(241, 178, 225, .5)"};
var data = [];
```

Each time the user clicks, we update the counter for `currentObject` and refresh the chart thus making the user experience more dynamic and live.

```
function onClick(e){
  currentObject.value++;
  refreshChart();
}
```

We set the interval in the `init` function as follows:

```
interval = setInterval(onTimeReset,1000);
```

Every time a second passes, the function checks whether the user had any clicks in that time interval, and if they did, it ensures that we push `currentObject` into the dataset. If the size of the dataset is greater than `25`, we cut the first item out of it and we refresh the chart. No matter what we create, a new empty object is labeled with a new label showing the current time in seconds.

```
function onTimeReset(){
  if(currentObject.value){
    data.push(currentObject);
    if(data.length>25) data = data.slice(1);
    refreshChart();
}
  currentObject = {label:currentObject.label+1, value:0, style:
  colorOptions[currentObject.label%5]};

}
```

One last thing that you should look at before we wrap this sample up is:

```
function refreshChart(){
  var newData = data.slice(0);
  newData.push(currentObject);

  drawChart(newData);

}
```

This part of our logic is really the glue that makes it possible for us to update our data every time a user clicks a button. The idea is we want to have a new array that will store the new data, but we do not want to the current element to be affected, so for that we are duplicating this data source by adding the new data object into it and then sending it off to create the chart.

6
Bringing Static Things to Life

In this chapter, we will cover the following topics:

- Stacking graphical layers
- Moving to an OOP perspective
- Animating independent layers
- Adding an interactive legend
- Creating a context-aware legend

Introduction

Until now, the importance of keeping things organized and clean wasn't as great as that of getting our projects done as we had relatively small projects. This chapter will break us into a few new habits by first making everything dynamic followed by creating a more object-oriented program so it's easier for us to separate tasks and reduce our code footprint. After all this hard work, we will revisit our application and start adding extra logic geared at making our application animated layer by layer.

This chapter is a great resourse for refactoring practice. In the first half of this chapter, we will be focused on improving our code structure to make it possible for us to have the level of control we will need in the second half of the chapter.

Stacking graphical layers

Before we can do any real animations on our canvas we really need to rethink the concept of building everything on one canvas layer. Once a canvas element is drawn, it's incredibly hard to create subtle small changes to it, such as fade-ins for specific elements. We will revisit one of our famous charts, the bar chart, which we played around with and enhanced many times throughout the earlier chapters. In this chapter, our goal will be to break the logic apart and make it more modular. In this recipe we will separate layers. Each layer will give us more control later when we are ready to animate.

Getting ready

Start by grabbing the latest files from the previous chapter: `05.02.line-revisit.html` and `05.02.line-revisit.js`.

How to do it...

The following changes are made to the HTML file:

1. Update the HTML file to incorporate more canvas elements (one per drawn line):

```
<body onLoad="init();" style="background:#fafafa">
    <h1>Users Changed between within a year</h1>
    <div class="graphicLayers" >
      <canvas id="base" class="canvasLayer" width="550"
      height="400"> </canvas>

      <canvas id="i2011" class="canvasLayer" width="550"
      height="400"> </canvas>
      <canvas id="i2010" class="canvasLayer" width="550"
      height="400"> </canvas>
      <canvas id="i2009" class="canvasLayer" width="550"
      height="400"> </canvas>

  </div>
  <div class="controllers">
  2009 : <input type="radio" name="i2009" value="-1" /> off
        <input type="radio" name="i2009" value="0" /> line
        <input type="radio" name="i2009" value="1" select="1" />
full ||
    2010 : <input type="radio" name="i2010" value="-1" /> off
        <input type="radio" name="i2010" value="0" /> line
        <input type="radio" name="i2010" value="1" select="1" />
full ||
```

```
        2011 : <input type="radio" name="i2011" value="-1" /> off
            <input type="radio" name="i2011" value="0" /> line
            <input type="radio" name="i2011" value="1" select="1" />
full
  </div>
</body>
</html>
```

2. Add a CSS script so the layers will be stacked:

```
<head>
    <title>Line Chart</title>
    <meta charset="utf-8" />
    <style>
    .graphicLayers {
       position: relative;
       left:100px
    }

    .controllers {
      position: relative;
      left:100px;
      top:400px;

    }

    .canvasLayer{
      position: absolute;
      left: 0;
      top: 0;
    }
    </style>
  <script src="06.01.layers.js"></script>
  </head>
```

Let's move into the JavaScript file to update it.

3. Add a `window.onload` callback function (changes highlighted in the code snippet):

```
window.onload = init;

function init(){
```

4. Remove the variable `context` from global scope (delete the highlighted code snippet):

```
var CHART_PADDING = 20;
var wid;
var hei;
var context;
```

5. Consolidate all bar line information into one object for easier control (delete all the highlighted code snippets):

```
var a2011 = [38,65,85,111,131,160,187,180,205,146,64,212];
var a2010 = [212,146,205,180,187,131,291,42,98,61,74,69];
var a2009 = [17,46,75,60,97,131,71,52,38,21,84,39];


var chartInfo= { y:{min:0, max:300, steps:5,label:"users"},
        x:{min:1, max:12, steps:11,label:"months"}
      };


var HIDE_ELEMENT = -1;
var LINE_ELEMENT = 0;
var FILL_ELEMENT = 1;


var elementStatus={i2009:FILL_ELEMENT,i2010:FILL_
ELEMENT,i2011:FILL_ELEMENT};

var barData = {
        i2009:{
          status:   FILL_ELEMENT,
          style: "#E3675C",
          label: "/2009",
          data:[17,46,75,60,97,131,71,52,38,21,84,39]
        },
        i2010:{
          status:   FILL_ELEMENT,
          style: "#FFDE89",
          label: "/2010",
          data:[212,146,205,180,187,131,291,42,98,61,74,69]
        },
        i2011:{
          status:   FILL_ELEMENT,
          style: "#B1DDF3",
          label: "/2011",
          data:[38,65,85,111,131,160,187,180,205,146,64,212]
        }

      };
```

6. Remove all canvas logic from the `init` function and add it to the `drawChart` function:

```
function init(){
  var can = document.getElementById("bar");

  wid = can.width;
  hei = can.height;
  context = can.getContext("2d");

  drawChart();

  var radios ;
  for(var id in elementStatus){
    radios = document.getElementsByName(id);
    for (var rid in radios){
       radios[rid].onchange = onChangedRadio;
      if(radios[rid].value == elementStatus[id] ) radios[rid].
checked = true;
    }

  }

}

function drawChart(){
  var can = document.getElementById("base");

  wid = can.width;
  hei = can.height;
  var context = can.getContext("2d");
...
```

7. Update references to the new data object in the `init` function:

```
function init(){
  drawChart();

  var radios ;
  for(var id in barData){
    radios = document.getElementsByName(id);
    for (var rid in radios){
       radios[rid].onchange = onChangedRadio;
      if(radios[rid].value == barData[id].status ) radios[rid].
      checked = true;
    }

  }

}
```

8. In the `drawChart` function, extract the logic of line creation to an external function (delete the highlighted code snippets):

```
  if(elementStatus.i2011>-1) addLine(context,formatData(a2011, "/2
011","#B1DDF3"),"#B1DDF3",elementStatus.i2011==1);
  if(elementStatus.i2010>-1) addLine(context,formatData(a2010, "/2
010","#FFDE89"),"#FFDE89",elementStatus.i2010==1);
  if(elementStatus.i2009>-1) addLine(context,formatData(a2009, "/2
009","#E3675C"),"#E3675C",elementStatus.i2009==1);
  changeLineView("i2011",barData.i2011.status);
  changeLineView("i2010",barData.i2010.status);
  changeLineView("i2009",barData.i2009.status);
```

9. Change the logic in the `onChangedRadio` callback function. Instead of what it was doing so far let's have it trigger a call to the `changeLineView` function (we will create that function next):

```
function onChangedRadio(e){
  changeLineView(e.target.name,e.target.value);
}
```

10. Create the function `changeLineView`:

```
function changeLineView(id,value){
  barData[id].status = value;
  var dataSource = barData[id];

  can = document.getElementById(id);
  context = can.getContext("2d");
  context.clearRect(0,0,wid,hei);
  if( dataSource.status!=HIDE_ELEMENT){
    context.beginPath();
    addLine(context,formatData(dataSource.data, dataSource.
label,dataSource.style),dataSource.style,dataSource.status==1);
  }
}
```

When you run your HTML file after all these changes, you should see exactly the same thing as you did before we started making all these changes. If that's true then you are in a great place. However, we can't visually see any change yet.

How it works...

The heart of this recipe is our HTML file that enables us to layer canvas elements on top of each other, and as our canvas is by default transparent, we can see through to the elements that are under it. After our canvas is layered with four layers, it's time for us to separate our background from our lines and as such we want to put all of our chart background information right into the base canvas:

```
var can = document.getElementById("base");
```

With each line layer, we are using a preconfigured canvas element that is already set:

```
changeLineView("i2011",barData.i2011.status);
changeLineView("i2010",barData.i2010.status);
changeLineView("i2009",barData.i2009.status);
```

The first parameter is both the ID of our canvas and the key we are using in our new object that stores our line information (to keep our code simple):

```
var barData = {
        i2009:{...},
        i2010:{...},
        i2011:{...}

      };
```

In this data object we have exactly the same number of elements as we do in our canvas with the exact same names. This way we can very easily fetch information without using extra variables or conditions. This ties in to the logic of creating/updating lines:

```
function changeLineView(id,value){
  barData[id].status = value;
  var dataSource = barData[id];

  can = document.getElementById(id);
  context = can.getContext("2d");
  context.clearRect(0,0,wid,hei);
  if( dataSource.status!=HIDE_ELEMENT){
    context.beginPath();
    addLine(context,formatData(dataSource.data, dataSource.
    label,dataSource.style),dataSource.style,dataSource.status==1);
  }
}
```

We didn't change the core logic of our line but redirected the logic into the context of the current line:

```
can = document.getElementById(id);
```

This way we can extract any direct mention of a year or element without referring to element names directly. This way we can add or remove elements and we would only need to add another canvas in our HTML file, add new properties, and finish off by adding the line in our creating function. That is still a lot, so how about we continue and optimize this code before we move on to more creative lands?

There's more...

Our final goal is this recipe is to help minimize the number of changes the user needs to do to create lines. Currently to add more lines the user would need to make changes in three places. The next few optimization tricks will help us reduce the number of steps it takes to add/remove lines.

Optimizing the drawChart function

Our `drawChart` function has been through a facelift, but right now, when we are creating our lines we are still referring directly to our current elements:

```
changeLineView("i2011",barData.i2011.status);
changeLineView("i2010",barData.i2010.status);
changeLineView("i2009",barData.i2009.status);
```

Instead, let's take advantage of the `barData` object and use the data keys of this object. This way we can completely avoid the need to refer directly to our explicit elements and instead depend on our data source as the source of information:

```
for(var id in barData){
  changeLineView(id,barData[id].status);
}
```

Perfect! Now any change in our `barData` object will define the elements that will get rendered initially when the application starts. We just cut down the number of changes users will need to do to two.

Further streamlining our code

We are in much better shape now than when we started. Originally there where three places in our code that referred directly to hardcoded values for our chart information. With the last update we reduced it to two (once within the HTML file and once in our data source).

It's time for us to remove one more hardcoded instance. Let's remove our extra canvases and create them dynamically.

So let's start by removing our chart canvas elements from the HTML file and setting up an ID to our `<div>` tag (delete the highlighted code snippet):

```
<div id="chartContainer" class="graphicLayers" >
      <canvas id="base" class="canvasLayer" width="550" height="400">
      </canvas>

      <canvas id="i2011" class="canvasLayer" width="550" height="400">
      </canvas>
      <canvas id="i2010" class="canvasLayer" width="550" height="400">
      </canvas>
      <canvas id="i2009" class="canvasLayer" width="550" height="400">
      </canvas>

  </div>
```

By the way, we added an ID for our `<div>` containing the layers so we can easily access it and change things within JavaScript.

Now that there isn't any canvas for our layers, we want to dynamically create them only when we draw the chart for the first time (this happens in the `drawChart` function with the new `for` loop we just created in the *Optimizing the drawChart function* section in the previous recipe):

```
var chartContainer = document.getElementById("chartContainer");


  for(var id in barData){
    can = document.createElement("canvas");
    can.id=id;
        can.width=wid;
        can.height=hei;
    can.setAttribute("class","canvasLayer");
    chartContainer.appendChild(can);

    changeLineView(id,barData[id].status);

  }

}
```

Refresh your HTML file and you will find our canvas elements looking exactly the way they did before. We have one last thing to sort out to truly make this application dynamic, and that is our controllers that right now are hardcoded in the HTML file.

Creating the radio buttons dynamically

Yet another section that could be dynamic is our creation of radio buttons. So let's start with removing our radio buttons from the HTML file and adding an ID to our wrapper (delete the highlighted code snippet):

```
<div id="chartContainer" class="controllers">
  2009 : <input type="radio" name="i2009" value="-1" /> off
        <input type="radio" name="i2009" value="0" /> line
        <input type="radio" name="i2009" value="1" select="1" /> full
||
    2010 : <input type="radio" name="i2010" value="-1" /> off
        <input type="radio" name="i2010" value="0" /> line
        <input type="radio" name="i2010" value="1" select="1" /> full
||
    2011 : <input type="radio" name="i2011" value="-1" /> off
        <input type="radio" name="i2011" value="0" /> line
        <input type="radio" name="i2011" value="1" select="1" /> full
  </div>
```

Back into our HTML file let's create a function that creates new radio buttons. We will call it the `appendRadioButton` function:

```
function appendRadioButton(container, id,value,text){
  var radioButton = document.createElement("input");
  radioButton.setAttribute("type", "radio");
  radioButton.setAttribute("value", value);
  radioButton.setAttribute("name", id);

  container.appendChild(radioButton);

  container.innerHTML += text;
}
```

Last but not the least let's draw our new button right before we start interacting with it:

```
function init(){
  drawChart();

  var radContainer = document.getElementById("controllers");

  var hasLooped= false;
  for(var id in barData){

    radContainer.innerHTML += (hasLooped ? " || ":"") + barData[id].
    label +": " ;

    appendRadioButton(radContainer,id,-1," off ");
    appendRadioButton(radContainer,id,0," line ");
```

```
      appendRadioButton(radContainer,id,1," full ");
      hasLooped = true;

    }

    var radios ;
    for(id in barData){
      radios = document.getElementsByName(id);
      for (var i=0; i<radios.length; i++){
          radios[i].onchange = onChangedRadio;
        if(radios[i].value == barData[id].status ){
            radios[i].checked = true;
        }
      }
    }

  }
```

Notice that we are not integrating the two `for` loops together. Even though it might look like the same thing, the separation is needed. It takes JavaScript some time, a few nanoseconds, to actually render the elements to the screen, and as such by separating our loops we are giving the browser a chance to catch up. The separation between creating the elements and manipulating the elements is present mainly to give JavaScript a chance to render the HTML file before interacting with the created elements.

Great job! We just finished updating our content to make it totally dynamic. Now that everything is controlled through one location, that is the data source, we are ready to start exploring layered canvas logic in the following recipes.

Moving to an OOP perspective

Our application has been developing with a growing momentum. It's time for us to stop that by changing our chart to be more OOP conducive. In this recipe we will clean up our code some more and convert some of it into objects. We will continue from where we left off in our previous recipe, *Stacking graphical layers*.

Getting ready

The first step is to get our latest source files: `06.01.layers.optimized.html` and `06.01.layers.optimized.js`. We will rename them and add our animation logic. Beyond changing the references on our HTML file we will not change anything else in our HTML file but focus our attention into the JavaScript file.

One of the simplest ways of creating objects in JavaScript is by using functions. We can create a function and refer within the function name to `this` and by doing that we can treat the function as an object (more details in the *How it works...* section of this recipe).

How to do it...

Let's jump right in and start converting our code to be more OOP friendly:

1. We start our code changes in the JavaScript file. Create the `LineChart` constructor method:

```
function LineChart(chartInfo,barData){
  this.chartInfo = chartInfo;
  this.barData = barData;

  this.HIDE_ELEMENT = -1;
  this.LINE_ELEMENT = 0;
  this.FILL_ELEMENT = 1;
  this.CHART_PADDING = 20;

  this.wid;
  this.hei;

  drawChart();

  var radContainer = document.getElementById("controllers");

  var hasLooped= false;
  for(var id in barData){

    radContainer.innerHTML += (hasLooped ? " || ":"") +
barData[id].label +": " ;

    appendRadioButton(radContainer,id,-1," off ");
    appendRadioButton(radContainer,id,0," line ");
    appendRadioButton(radContainer,id,1," full ");
    hasLooped = true;

  }

  var radios ;
  for(id in barData){
    radios = document.getElementsByName(id);
    for (var i=0; i<radios.length; i++){
       radios[i].onchange = onChangedRadio;
      if(radios[i].value == barData[id].status ){
         radios[i].checked = true;
      }
    }
  }

}
```

2. Let's update all of our functions to be prototypes of the `LineChart` function (our pseudo class):

```
LineChart.prototype.drawChart =function(){...}
LineChart.prototype.appendRadioButton = function(container,
id,value,text){...}
LineChart.prototype.onChangedRadio = function (e){...}
LineChart.prototype.changeLineView = function(id,value){...}
LineChart.prototype.fillChart = function (context, chartInfo){...}
LineChart.prototype.addLine = function(context,data,style,isFill)
{ …}
LineChart.prototype.formatData = function(data , labelCopy ,
style){...}
```

3. Now let's take a look at the really difficult part. We need to refer to all functions and object variables with `this`. For a full list of changes please review the source files (as we don't want to take up too many pages just for this). Here is a small sample:

```
LineChart.prototype.drawChart =function(){
  var can = document.getElementById("base");

  this.wid = can.width;
  this.hei = can.height;
  var context = can.getContext("2d");

  context.lineWidth = 1;
  context.fillStyle = "#eeeeee";
  context.strokeStyle = "#999999";
  context.fillRect(0,0,this.wid,this.hei);

  context.font = "10pt Verdana, sans-serif";
  context.fillStyle = "#999999";

  context.moveTo(this.CHART_PADDING,this.CHART_PADDING);
  context.rect(this.CHART_PADDING,this.CHART_PADDING,this.wid-
  this.CHART_PADDING*2,this.hei-this.CHART_PADDING*2);
  context.stroke();
  context.strokeStyle = "#cccccc";
  this.fillChart(context,this.chartInfo);

  var chartContainer = document.getElementById("chartContainer");


  for(var id in this.barData){
    can = document.createElement("canvas");
    can.id=id;
```

```
        can.width=this.wid;
        can.height=this.hei;
       can.setAttribute("class","canvasLayer");
       chartContainer.appendChild(can);
       this.changeLineView(id,this.barData[id].status);

  }

}
//continue and update all methods of our new object
```

4. In our application so far, to deal with radio buttons we created only one callback function that is set to all the radio buttons. When the user clicks on our radio buttons, an event is triggered. One issue will arise as our scope inside the events will break because `this` will be a `this` reference of something else and not our main object. Radio buttons have their own scope (their own `this` reference). We want to force a scope change; to do that we will create a helper function:

```
LineChart.prototype.bind = function(scope, fun){
   return function () {
        fun.apply(scope, arguments);
    };

}
```

5. We will now rewrite the lines that trigger our event in our `LineChart` constructor:

```
for (var i=0; i<radios.length; i++){
    radios[i].onchange = this.bind(this, this.onChangedRadio);
      if(radios[i].value == barData[id].status ){
         radios[i].checked = true;
      }
    }
```

6. We will now rewrite our `init` function. We will create our data points in it:

```
window.onload = init;


function init(){
  var chartInfo= { y:{min:0, max:300, steps:5,label:"users"},
        x:{min:1, max:12, steps:11,label:"months"}
      };

  var barData = {
        i2011:{
          status:   FILL_ELEMENT,
```

```
            style: "#B1DDF3",
            label: "2011",
            data:[38,65,85,111,131,160,187,180,205,146,64,212]
          },
          i2010:{
            status:   FILL_ELEMENT,
            style: "#FFDE89",
            label: "2010",
            data:[212,146,205,180,187,131,291,42,98,61,74,69]
          },

          i2009:{
            status:   FILL_ELEMENT,
            style: "#E3675C",
            label: "2009",
            data:[17,46,75,60,97,131,71,52,38,21,84,39]
          }

        };

    chart = new LineChart(chartInfo,barData);
  }
```

7. Delete all global variables.

Surprising but that's it; you have just moved all of your logic into an object. We don't have any global variables left in our application, making it much easier to have more than one chart at the same time.

How it works...

We kept our changes at this stage to a minimum. JavaScript is an object-oriented programing language, and as such we can take advantage of that by wrapping all of our functions into a new class. We start by creating a constructor function. This function will be used as our object type/name:

```
function MyFirstObject(){
 //constructor code
}
```

To create object variables we will refer to the constructor variables with `this`. The `this` operator is a dynamic name that always refers to the current scope. The current scope within an object is the object itself; in our case the `MyFirstObject` function will look as follows:

```
function MyFirstObject(){
 this.a = "value";
}
```

You can still create variables using the regular variable definition inside of functions, but there, scope would not be an object scope but instead, the scope would be only within that function. As such whenever you want to create variables that are shared throughout an object you must create them and refer to them with a leading `this` reference.

The next step is to rename all of our functions to be prototypes of the new class (function) we created. This way our functions will belong to the new object we are creating. We want the transition of our global variables of the past to become object variables belonging to the current object. Each time we want to refer to an object variable (property), we need to explicitly let JavaScript know by directing JavaScript to our object using the `this` directive. For example, if we want to refer to the `sampleVar` variable we would approach it in the following way:

```
this.sampleVar;
```

We had only one problem and that was when we introduced other objects into our code. The directive `this` needs to know the scope of its location to know which object we are referring to. In the situation of using events, our expectations of `this` referring to our object will not be true. Actually when dealing with `this` within an event listener, the `this` directive would always refer to the element being listened to, also known as the one being manipulated. As such, adding events to a radio button will produce a result of breaking our scope. To solve this problem, we create a function that will bind our scope to the listener. The `bind` method binds our function to our current scope. Even though by default, a listener would have the scope of what it is listening to, we are forcing the scope to stay on our object making our code work better for us.

This leaves us with our last task. We need to create a new instance of our object. By creating a new instance we will activate all the work we did so far. The steps involved with creating a new object are the same as creating other base objects, only this time around we are using our constructor function name:

```
new LineChart(chartInfo,barData);
```

The real test of our object will be if we can create more than one instance of our chart. Right now we can't, so we will need to do a few more changes to our logic to make it work.

There's more...

Although right now we have a working OOP object, it's not really optimized and it can use some refining. As we are in one scope, we can revisit and rewire what can be sent and what can depend on internal variables. We will explore this next task in this section of the chapter.

Moving our base canvas element into our constructor

Let's start by moving from the `drawChart` function. The following logic will fetch the base canvas and create a global variable within our new constructor:

```
var can = document.getElementById("base");

  this.wid = can.width;
  this.hei = can.height;
  this.baseCanvas = can.getContext("2d");
```

This will be followed by replacing the associated lines in the `drawChart` method with a reference to our newly created `baseCanvas` object:

```
LineChart.prototype.drawChart =function(){
  var context = this.baseCanvas;
...
  this.fillChart();
```

Notice that we removed the function parameters from our `fillChart` method as we can pass them internally now within the method:

```
LineChart.prototype.fillChart = function (){
  var context = this.baseCanvas;
  var chartInfo = this.chartInfo;
```

I strongly encourage you to continue and optimize the rest of the functions in this same manner, but for our sample let's continue on to the next topic.

Creating all the HTML components dynamically

Why would we want to create our controllers and base canvas dynamically as well? Because we created some of our classes in advance, we are forced to have only one object in every HTML page. If we had dynamically created the controllers or passed the class information, we could enable the creation of more than one controller in our application. As we have so many elements that we are creating dynamically, it seems logical to continue in this path. Let's first create the remaining two elements dynamically.

Let's start by removing the inner canvas details from our HTML page (delete the highlighted code snippet):

```
<div id="chartContainer" class="graphicLayers" >
          <canvas id="base" class="canvasLayer" width="550"
height="400"> </canvas>

    </div>
    <div id="controllers" class="controllers">

    </div>
```

We are going to start inserting the controller class within our global <div> tag that will be used for our canvas. We need to update our CSS information for the controllers:

```
.controllers {
      position: absolute;
      left:0;
      top:400px;

    }
```

OK. We are now ready to do some code updates to our constructor. The highlighted code snippets are the updates that should be implemented next:

```
function LineChart(chartInfo,barData,divID){
  this.chartInfo = chartInfo;
  this.barData = barData;

  this.HIDE_ELEMENT = -1;
  this.LINE_ELEMENT = 0;
  this.FILL_ELEMENT = 1;
  this.CHART_PADDING = 20;
  this.BASE_ID = divID;


  var chartContainer = document.getElementById(divID);
  var     can = document.createElement("canvas");
    can.width=chartInfo.width;
      can.height=chartInfo.height;
    can.setAttribute("class","canvasLayer");
  chartContainer.appendChild(can);

  this.wid = can.width;
  this.hei = can.height;
  this.baseCanvas = can.getContext("2d");


  this.drawChart();


  var     div = document.createElement("div");
    div.setAttribute("class","controllers");
  chartContainer.appendChild(div);
  var radContainer = div;

  var hasLooped= false;
  for(var id in barData){
```

```
        radContainer.innerHTML += (hasLooped ? " || ":"") + barData[id].
label +": " ;

        this.appendRadioButton(radContainer,id,-1," off ");
        this.appendRadioButton(radContainer,id,0," line ");
        this.appendRadioButton(radContainer,id,1," full ");
        hasLooped = true;

      }

      var radios ;
      for(id in barData){
        radios = document.getElementsByName(id);
        for (var i=0; i<radios.length; i++){
           radios[i].onchange = this.bind(this, this.onChangedRadio);
          if(radios[i].value == barData[id].status ){
             radios[i].checked = true;
          }
        }
      }

    }
```

We want to start our `LineChart` object by sending into it the `<div>` tag ID:

```
new LineChart(chartInfo,barData,"chartContainer");
```

If you refresh your screen, all this hard work should be invisible. If everything is still working the way it did before we started to make changes, then well done, you've just completed the conversion of your chart to be smart and dynamic.

Removing the lose ends

Although we extracted all of our external canvas and controllers and everything is working, we still are referring to internal canvas elements and radio buttons in a way that can break them. If we try to create a mirror chart right next to them to solve this problem, we will need to look through all our new elements and append to their name a unique key (we can use the `div id` element as that key as there can only be one `<div>` tag with the same ID in any HTML application). To save us some pages, I'll just show you the basic logic here but grab the latest code bundle to find all the updates:

```
LineChart.prototype.extractID = function(str){
  return  str.split(this.BASE_ID + "_")[1];
}

LineChart.prototype.wrapID = function(str){
  return  this.BASE_ID + "_"+str;
}
```

I've created two helper functions and their role is simple: to rename `<div>` tag/class/radio buttons by adding the main `<div>` tag ID into their name. This way we won't have duplicate elements. All that is left is to locate all the areas where we are creating elements (we are creating canvas in the `drawChart` function and radio buttons in our constructor, but we interact with them in a few functions). Search for the changes where the `this.extractID` or `this.wrapID` methods are called and understand why they are being called.

Testing our work by creating two charts

To make life harder, we are going to create the same exact chart twice using the same data sources (as that is a good edge case, so if that works any chart would work). Update the HTML file and add two `<div>` tags and update the CSS:

```
<!DOCTYPE html>
<html>
  <head>
    <title>Line Chart</title>
    <meta charset="utf-8" />
    <style>
    #chartContainer {
      position: relative;
      left:100px
    }
    #chartContainer2{
      position: relative;
      left:700px
    }
    .controllers {
      position: absolute;
      left:0;
      top:400px;

    }
    .canvasLayer{
      position: absolute;
      left: 0;
      top: 0;
    }
    </style>
  <script src="06.02.objects.optimized.js"></script>
  </head>
  <body style="background:#fafafa">
    <h1>Users Changed between within a year</h1>
    <div id="chartContainer" class="graphicLayers" >

  </div>
```

```
<div id="chartContainer2" class="graphicLayers2" >

</div>
</body>
</html>
```

In our `init` function let's set up both charts:

```
new LineChart(chartInfo,barData,"chartContainer");
new LineChart(chartInfo,barData,"chartContainer2");
```

Yes! We have two interactive charts working at the same time based on the same code base. Good job! And don't worry, the rest of this chapter is going to be much easier.

Animating independent layers

After a few really hard recipes let's do something fun and easy; let's add some animation to our chart and add some fade-ins and delays.

Getting ready

The core logic of our application was built in the previous two recipes *Stacking graphical layers* and *Moving to an OPP perspective*. We are in great shape so it will be extremely easy for us to expand and create content and add it into our application. We will make few very slight updates to our latest HTML file, mainly deleting things we don't need and then it's all JavaScript.

Grab the latest files from our last sample (`06.02.objects.optimized.html` and `06.02.objects.optimized.js`) and let's continue.

How to do it...

Our goal in the next few steps is to remove the code that is not required and then build our layered animations. Perform the following steps:

1. Remove the HTML, CSS, and `<div>` tags that are not required (delete the highlighted code snippets):

```
<!DOCTYPE html>
<html>
  <head>
    <title>Line Chart</title>
    <meta charset="utf-8" />
    <style>
    #chartContainer {
```

```
        position: relative;
        left:100px
    }
    #chartContainer2{
      position: relative;
      left:700px
    }


    .controllers {
      position: absolute;
      left:0;
      top:400px;

    }

    .canvasLayer{
      position: absolute;
      left: 0;
      top: 0;
    }
    </style>
  <script src="06.02.objects.optimized.js"></script>
  </head>
  <body style="background:#fafafa">
    <h1>Users Changed between within a year</h1>
    <div id="chartContainer" class="graphicLayers" >

  </div>
  <div id="chartContainer2" class="graphicLayers2" >

  </div>
  </body>
</html>
```

2. Create the new `Animator` constructor:

```
function Animator(refreshRate){
  this.animQue = [];
  this.refreshRate = refreshRate || 50; //if nothing set 20 FPS
  this.interval = 0;
}
```

3. Create the `add` method:

```
Animator.prototype.add = function(obj,property,
from,to,time,delay){
  obj[property] = from;
```

```
  this.animQue.push({obj:obj,
            p:property,
            crt:from,
            to:to,
            stepSize: (to-from)/(time*1000/this.refreshRate),
            delay:delay*1000 || 0});


  if(!this.interval){ //only start interval if not running already
    this.interval = setInterval(this._animate,this.
refreshRate,this);
  }

}
```

4. Create the internal `_animate` method:

```
Animator.prototype._animate = function(scope){
  var obj;
  var data;

  for(var i=0; i<scope.animQue.length; i++){
      data = scope.animQue[i];

      if(data.delay>0){
        data.delay-=scope.refreshRate;
      }else{
        obj = data.obj;
        if(data.crt<data.to){
          data.crt +=data.stepSize;
          obj[data.p] = data.crt;
        }else{
          obj[data.p] = data.to;
          scope.animQue.splice(i,1);
          --i;
        }
      }

  }

  if(  scope.animQue.length==0){
    clearInterval(scope.interval);
    scope.interval = 0; //so when next animation starts we can
start over
  }
}
```

5. Create a new `Animate` object within the `LineChart` constructor method and animate key components:

```
function LineChart(chartInfo,barData,divID){
...
  this.animator = new Animator(50);

  var chartContainer =this.mainDiv;
  var  can = document.createElement("canvas");
    can.width=chartInfo.width;
      can.height=chartInfo.height;
    can.setAttribute("class","canvasLayer");
  chartContainer.appendChild(can);
  this.animator.add(can.style,"opacity",0,1,.5,.2);

...


  var  div = document.createElement("div");
    div.setAttribute("class","controllers");
  chartContainer.appendChild(div);

  this.animator.add(div.style,"opacity",0,1,.4,2.2);
...
```

6. Add animation to canvas elements in the `drawChart` method:

```
  var delay = .75;
  for(var id in this.barData){
    can = document.createElement("canvas");
    can.id=this.wrapID(id);
        can.width=this.wid;
        can.height=this.hei;
    can.setAttribute("class","canvasLayer");
    chartContainer.appendChild(can);
    this.changeLineView(id,this.barData[id].status);

    this.animator.add(can.style,"opacity",0,1,1,delay);
    delay+=.5;

  }
```

When you run the webpage again you will find a fade-in of the separate layers.

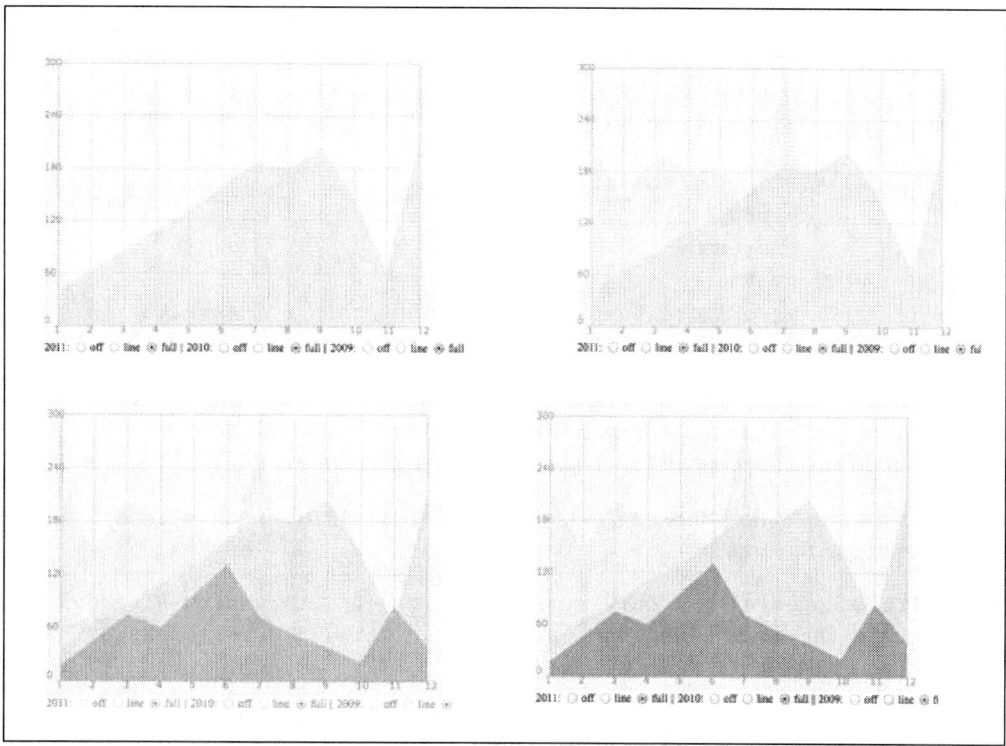

How it works...

Let's start by looking into our `Animator` constructor. We start with a few variables in our constructor:

```
function Animator(refreshRate){
  this.animQue = [];
  this.refreshRate = refreshRate || 50; //if nothing set 20 FPS
  this.interval = 0;
}
```

These variables are the key to everything else. The `animQue` array will store each new animation request we make. The `refreshRate` property will control how often our animation will update. The more often it updates the smoother our animation will be (the higher the value in the refresh rate the less stress on user's system). For example, if we want to have a few animations, one in a smoother setting and others with a lower refresh rate, we can set two separate `Animator` classes with different refresh rates.

Our add method takes in all the necessary information to animate a property:

```
Animator.prototype.add =
    function(obj,property, from,to,time,delay){}
```

Each element sent in to animate is then converted into a reference object that will be used when animations are running and pushed into our animQue array:

```
this.animQue.push({obj:obj,
            p:property,
            crt:from,
            to:to,
            stepSize: (to-from)/(time*1000/this.refreshRate),
            delay:delay*1000 || 0});
```

storing within the queue all the information we will need to animate an element, from the object's current status to how much of a change should be made each interval. On top of that we added a delay option enabling us to start the animation later.

We control the creation of intervals only in this function so until this function is called, there will be no interval running:

```
if(!this.interval){ //only start interval if not running already
    this.interval = setInterval(this._animate,this.refreshRate,this);
  }
```

Now it's time for the internal logic of our object. The _animate method is called internally for as long as there is something to animate. In other words, as long as there is something in the animQue array. It loops through all the animQue array elements and goes through a few tests per element:

1. If the element has a delay set, it will downgrade the delay value by the refreshRate property such that the delay will become smaller during each loop until it will be zero or less. When that happens the next step will trigger.
2. Now that the delay is complete, the _animate method changes gear. It starts to animate the objects within the animQue array for as long as the value of data.crt is lesser than data.to.
3. The interval will continue one more time before testing to remove our element from the array. The separate step here is to help us avoid adding an if statement within our core logic reducing the complexity of our for loop. As we only need to test this once, we can absorb the cost of one extra loop cycle. In this extra cycle, we force the exact final value to our object and remove it from the animation queue.

This is the only strange logic, where we force the value of our loop variable down:

```
}else{
  obj[data.p] = data.to;
  scope.animQue.splice(i,1);
  --i;
}
```

In this code we are removing our element. As soon as we remove our element our current value of `i` will be one value larger than it should be, as our object has shrunk. To solve this problem, we need to force down the value to reset it back to the new current index.

Last but not the least, at the end of each update we check to see if there is anything in our array. If the array is empty, it's time for us to remove the interval. We want to avoid having an interval running when it's not needed. Next time the `add` method is triggered, it will restart the interval:

```
if(      scope.animQue.length==0){
  clearInterval(scope.interval);
  scope.interval = 0; //reset interval variable
}
```

That's the core of our logic and now it's time to create a new `animator` object and start sending elements that we want to animate. Play around with it, animate other things, and find your favorite animation balance between speed, delay, and properties you want to animate. This `animator` class is the base of all animation libraries, although our sample is more minimal and has more chances of user overkill such as sending the same object multiple times.

Adding an interactive legend

Although we created a legend in the past, our legend was bound to be non-interactive as we had no way to move it around. In this sample, we will create a quick and easy legend that will update its position and fade in and fade out when a user rolls over our chart.

Getting ready

Grab the latest files from our previous recipe, `06.03.fade.html` and `06.03.fade.js`, and let's jump right in. We will hardcode our values in this example, but a more modular approach of extracting elements that would be dynamic is a great way to make this class reusable.

How to do it...

This time around we will create a method in the `LineChart` object that will create legends for us. Perform the following steps:

1. Create the `createLegend` method:

```
LineChart.prototype.createLegend = function (){
  var  can = document.createElement("canvas");
    can.width=70;
      can.height=100;
    can.setAttribute("class","canvasLayer");
  chartContainer.appendChild(can);



  this.legend = can;
  this.updateLegend();
  can.style.opacity = 0;
}
```

2. Create the `updateLegend` method:

```
LineChart.prototype.updateLegend = function(){
  var wid = this.legend.width;
  var hei = this.legend.height;
  var context = this.legend.getContext("2d");
  context.fillStyle = "rgba(255,255,255,.7)";
  context.strokeStyle = "rgba(150,150,150,.7)";
  context.fillRect(0,0,wid,hei);
  context.strokeRect(5,5,wid-10,hei-10);

  var nextY= 10;
  var space = (hei-10 - this.chartInfo.bars * nextY) / this.
chartInfo.bars;
  for(var id in this.barData){
    context.fillStyle = this.barData[id].style;
    context.fillRect(10,nextY,10,10);
    context.fillText(this.barData[id].label,25, nextY+9);
    nextY+=10+space;


  }
  this.legend.style.left = this.wid +"px";

}
```

3. The next step for us is to create a few methods that will be used as event listeners. Let's add a few listeners to control our animation:

```
LineChart.prototype.onMouseMoveArea = function(e){
  this.legend.style.top = (e.layerY) +"px";

}

LineChart.prototype.fadeInLegend = function(){
  this.animator.add(this.legend.style,"opacity",this.legend.style.
opacity,1,.5);
}


LineChart.prototype.fadeOutLegend = function(){
  this.animator.add(this.legend.style,"opacity",this.legend.style.
opacity,0,.5);
}
```

4. The methods we created just now are ready to be linked to a callback method such as an `onmouseover` or `onmouseout` event of our `mainDiv`. We will bind our scope back into our main object and trigger the methods we created earlier when the user triggers these built-in events. Let's register our listeners in the constructor:

```
      this.drawChart();

this.createLegend();
this.mainDiv.onmousemove = this.bind(this,this.onMouseMoveArea);
this.mainDiv.onmouseover = this.bind(this,this.fadeInLegend);
this.mainDiv.onmouseout = this.bind(this,this.fadeOutLegend);
```

5. Add into the code a variable that will count how many bars are there in the chart in the `drawChart` update code:

```
this.chartInfo.bars = 0;
  for(var id in this.barData){
    this.chartInfo.bars++;
    can = document.createElement("canvas");
    can.id=this.wrapID(id);
        can.width=this.wid;
        can.height=this.hei;
    can.setAttribute("class","canvasLayer");
    chartContainer.appendChild(can);
    this.changeLineView(id,this.barData[id].status);

    this.animator.add(can.style,"opacity",0,1,1,delay);
    delay+=.5;

  }
```

Well done! When you refresh your browser you will see a legend fading in/out and repositioning based on our mouse moves.

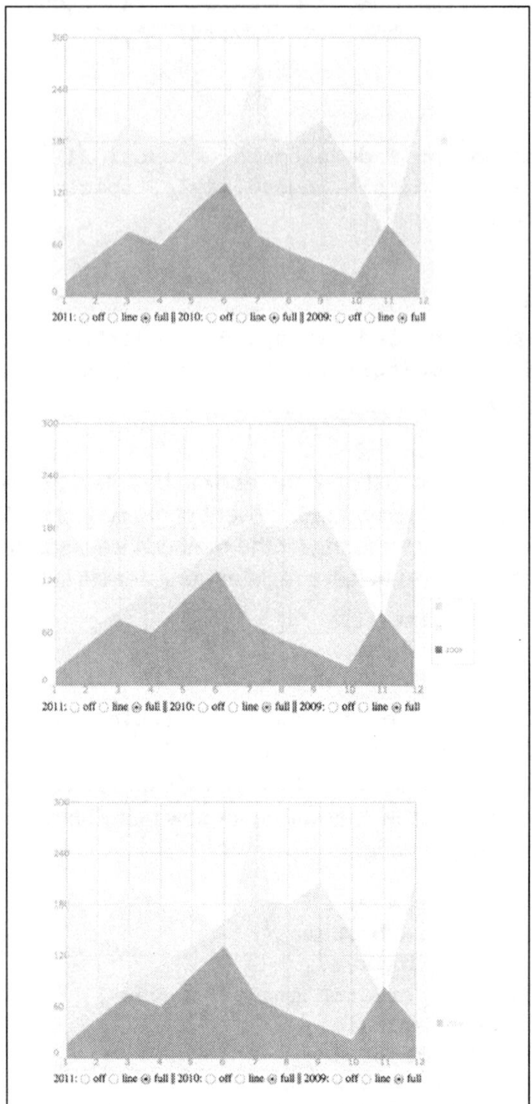

How it works...

The logic this time around is simple as our application already is nicely set and optimized. Our `createLegend` method creates for us a new canvas area that we can use for our legend. I've added some hardcoded values into it, but it would be a good idea to extract them into our `chartInfo` variable.

The only thing that requires explanation is the logic involved with the layout of the legend. We need to know how many items our chart contains to avoid looping through the data source again or asking the user to add this information. We can calculate this information the first time we loop through the user-generated data and thus update it to have our total items within it.

We set up our method in a way that would make it easy for us to actually put dynamic data directly into our chart. I've left that challenge open for you to explore and set up the ground work for it.

There's more...

One more thing to note is, if you search hard and stress test our `Animator` class in this example, you will find that its not hundred percent optimized. If we send to the `Animator` class the same object with conflicting instructions, it will not automatically terminate the conflict. Instead, it will run through both until completion (for example, it will fade-out and fade-in at the same time; it will not break our application but it will create unwanted outcomes). To solve problems such as this one, we would need to modify our `Animator` class to override animations that are in conflict.

Let's fix the animation conflicts by checking that our animation queue does not have the same object with the same property animating already. We will create a `find` function to help us find in the `animQue` property the index of a duplicate:

```
Animator.prototype.find= function(obj,property){
  for(var i=0; i<this.animQue.length; i++){
    if(this.animQue[i].obj == obj && this.animQue[i].p == property)
return i;

  }

  return -1;
}
```

The function will scan through our `animQue` array and locate duplications. If a match is found, the index value will be returned. If not, `-1` will be returned. Now it's time to update our `add` method to use this new `find` method:

```
Animator.prototype.add = function(obj,property, from,to,time,delay){
  obj[property] = from;

  var index = this.find(obj,property);
  if(index!=-1) this.animQue.splice(index,1);
  this.animQue.push({obj:obj,
           p:property,
           crt:from,
```

```
            to:to,
            stepSize: (to-from)/(time*1000/this.refreshRate),
            delay:delay*1000 || 0});


    if(!this.interval){ //only start interval if not running already
      this.interval = setInterval(this._animate,this.refreshRate,this);
    }

  }
```

Great! Problem solved! Although we have not addressed the dynamic legend in this example, we are going to create a new direction for our legend that will be just as dynamic and maybe a bit more in our next recipe, *Creating a context-aware legend*.

Creating a context-aware legend

Our goal will be to create a legend that updates based on what is under the user's mouse cursor as they roll over our application. Based on the mouse position of the user, we will update our legend to reflect the information that is under the user's mouse.

Getting ready

Grab the latest files from the previous recipe: `06.04.legend.html` and `06.04.legend.js`.

How to do it...

We aren't going to change anything in the HTML files so let's jump right into the JavaScript and build out our dynamic legend:

1. From the `ChartLine` constructor, remove rollover/rollout events as we want to keep our legend always visible:

   ```
   this.drawChart();

   this.createLegend();
   this.mainDiv.onmousemove = this.bind(this,this.onMouseMoveArea);
   this.mainDiv.onmouseover = this.bind(this,this.fadeInLegend);
   this.mainDiv.onmouseout = this.bind(this,this.fadeOutLegend);
   ```

2. Update the `createLegend` method:

```
LineChart.prototype.createLegend = function (){
  var  can = document.createElement("canvas");
    can.width=90;
      can.height=100;
    can.setAttribute("class","canvasLayer");
  chartContainer.appendChild(can);



  this.legend = can;
  this.updateLegend(null,-1);
  can.style.left = this.wid +"px";
}
```

3. Update the method `updateLegend`:

```
LineChart.prototype.updateLegend = function(ren,currentXIndex){
  var ren = ren || this.barData;
  var wid = this.legend.width;
  var hei = this.legend.height;
  var context = this.legend.getContext("2d");
  context.fillStyle = "rgba(255,255,255,.7)";
  context.strokeStyle = "rgba(150,150,150,.7)";
  context.fillRect(0,0,wid,hei);
  context.strokeRect(5,5,wid-10,hei-10);

  var nextY= 10;
  var space = (hei-10 - this.chartInfo.bars * nextY) / this.
chartInfo.bars;
  var isXIndex = currentXIndex !=-1;
  for(var id in ren){
    context.fillStyle = this.barData[id].style;
    context.fillRect(10,nextY,10,10);
    context.fillText(this.barData[id].label + (isXIndex ? (":"+
this.barData[id].data[currentXIndex] ):""),25, nextY+9);
    nextY+=10+space;


  }

}
```

4. Change the event listener `onMouseMoveArea`:

```
LineChart.prototype.onMouseMoveArea = function(e){
  var pixelData;
  var barCanvas;


  var chartX = e.layerX-this.CHART_PADDING;
  var chartWid =     this.wid -this.CHART_PADDING*2;
  var currentXIndex = -1;
  if(chartX>=0 && chartX<= chartWid){
    currentXIndex = Math.round(chartX/this.chartInfo.x.stepSize)
  }

  var renderList = {};
  var count = 0;
  for(var id in this.barData){
    barCanvas = this.barData[id].canvas;
    pixelData = barCanvas.getImageData(e.layerX, e.layerY, 1,
    1).data

    if( pixelData[3]){
       count++;
       renderList[id] = true; //there is content on this layer now
    }
  }

  if(!count) renderList = this.barData;

  this.updateLegend(renderList,currentXIndex);
}
```

5. We need to add the step size into our data. This variable should be calculated dynamically as there is no need for the user to know this information if we can calculate it. As such, we will add this calculation to our `chartInfo` object when we calculate the step size in the `fillChart` method:

```
stepSize = rangeLength/steps;
this.chartInfo.x.stepSize = chartWidth/steps;
```

6. Last but not the least, let's add our canvas information directly into our `barData` object so we can easily interact with it (added in the `drawChart` function):

```
for(var id in this.barData){
    this.chartInfo.bars++;
    can = document.createElement("canvas");
    can.id=this.wrapID(id);
        can.width=this.wid;
        can.height=this.hei;
```

```
        can.setAttribute("class","canvasLayer");
        chartContainer.appendChild(can);
        this.barData[id].canvas =can.getContext("2d");
        this.changeLineView(id,this.barData[id].status);

        this.animator.add(can.style,"opacity",0,1,1,delay);
        delay+=.5;

    }
```

We should be all set. When you run the page again, your mouse should be in control of the information provided by the legend based on the exact coordinate you are on.

How it works...

In the last two steps of the previous section of this recipe, we add a few helper variables to help us create our mouse move logic. This is an interesting part because in addition in this sample we are asking our canvas for pixel information for the first time. We will focus our attention mainly on the logic within the `onMouseMoveArea` event listener.

We start by establishing the boundaries of our canvas area:

```
var chartX = e.layerX-this.CHART_PADDING;
var chartWid =   this.wid -this.CHART_PADDING*2;
```

This will be followed by a quick calculation of the current area in the chart we are in:

```
var currentXIndex = -1;
    if(chartX>=0 && chartX<= chartWid){
            currentXIndex = Math.round(chartX/this.
chartInfo.x.stepSize);
    }
```

If we are out of the area, our `currentXIndex` variable will remain `-1`, while if we are in the area, we will get a value between `0` and the highest possible value based on the number of steps in the data source. We will send this value to our newly updated `updateLegend` method that will append the actual value of that index information from the data source into the rendering of the legend.

The next step is a `for` loop where we loop through our data to test our canvas elements to see if they are opaque or not:

```
var renderList = {};
  var count = 0;
  for(var id in this.barData){
    barCanvas = this.barData[id].canvas;
    pixelData = barCanvas.getImageData(e.layerX, e.layerY, 1, 1).data;
```

```
        if( pixelData[3]){
            count++;
            renderList[id] = true; //there is content on this layer now
        }
    }
```

Only if the data returned confirms that there is content under the mouse pointer, we will add that ID into the `renderList` object. The `renderList` object is going to be our hub; it will control the legend data fields to be sent to the `updateLegend` method. If our mouse is above an element that is drawn then we will showcase the legend information related to the user's rollover; if not, we won't.

We will update the way we call the `updateLegend` method, but right before we send it to our new parameters, we want to confirm we are really sending something. If our helper (linker object) is empty, we will send instead the original object. That way, everything will render if no chart is under our mouse pointer:

```
if(!count) renderList = this.barData;
this.updateLegend(renderList,currentXIndex);
```

Time to take a peek at the changes within the `updateLegend` method. The first new thing comes right in the first line:

```
var ren = ren || this.barData;
```

This is a nice coding trick that enables us to update our `ren` parameter. The way it works is very simple; the || operator will always return the first true value it sees. In our case if the `ren` parameter is empty, or zero, or false it would return the value in `this.barData`. The logic is simple, if the `ren` parameter has content, it will remain the same while if it's empty the `this.barData` property will be set within the `ren` variable.

```
var isXIndex = currentXIndex !=-1;
  for(var id in ren){
    context.fillStyle = this.barData[id].style;
    context.fillRect(10,nextY,10,10);
    context.fillText(this.barData[id].label + (isXIndex ?
    (":"+ this.barData[id].data[currentXIndex] ):""),25, nextY+9);
    nextY+=10+space;


  }
```

This is really the magic of this whole recipe. Instead of looping through the `this.barData` property we are looping through the key object that contains all the items we want to render. All that is left to do is to add the data when adding the text if there is a valid index listed.

There you go! We just added a really cool dynamic legend that changes as the user explores our chart.

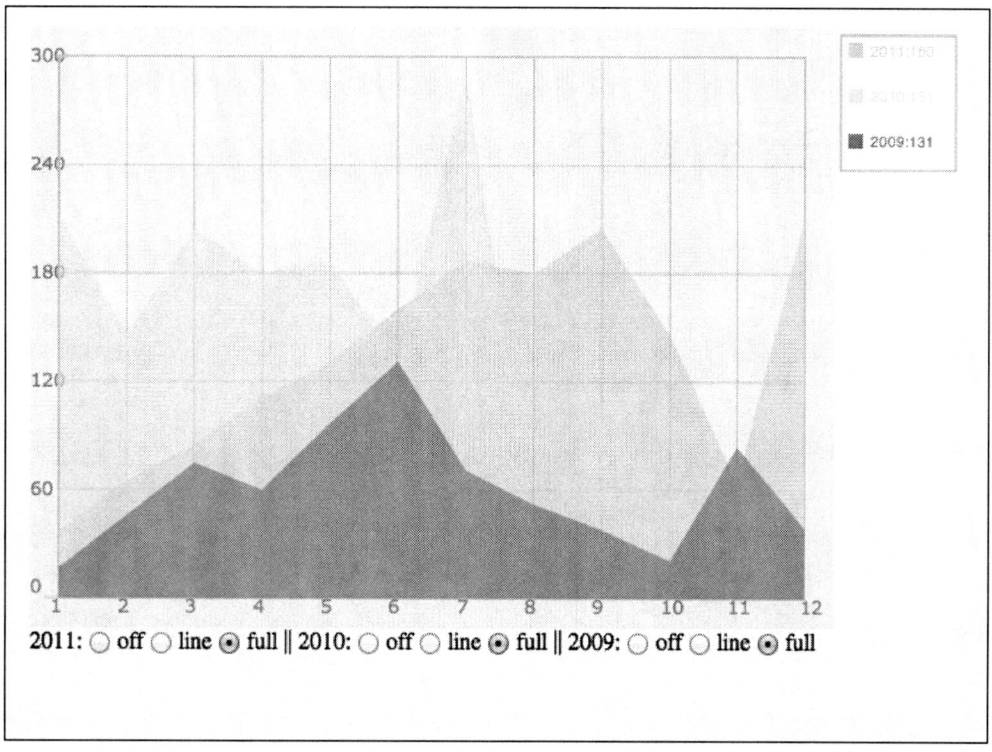

7

Depending on the Open Source Sphere

In this chapter we will cover:

- Animating a gauge meter (jqPlot)
- Creating an animated 3D chart (canvas3DGraph)
- Charting over time (flotJS)
- Building a clock with RaphaelJS
- Making a sunburst chart with InfoVis

Introduction

The open source data visualization community is extremely rich and detailed, with many options and some really amazing libraries. Each library has its strong points and its disadvantages. Some are standalone code while others depend on other platforms such as jQuery. Some are really big and some are really small; there isn't any one option that is perfect for all opportunities, but with such a rich amount of options, the most important thing is to figure out what library is the right one for you.

There is always a trade-off when working with open source libraries, mainly when it comes to file sizes and having just too many features that drag down the speed of your application, load time, and so on. But with the richness and creativeness of the community, it's hard to avoid really fantastic charts that can be created in minutes instead of hours.

In this chapter we will explore working with some of these options. Instead of using the libraries according to the documentation of the projects, our goal will be to find ways to override the built-in libraries to provide us with better control over our applications, in case we can't find a suitable solution in the documentation of an application. So the goal in this chapter is now double, namely to find ways to do things that aren't naturally set to work and to find ways to bypass problems.

One more important thing to note is that all of these open source libraries have copyrights. It is advised that you check the legal documentation of the project before you go ahead with it.

Animating a gauge meter (jqPlot)

In this recipe, we will be creating a really fun gauge meter and injecting some random animation into it to make it look like a real source of live data is connected to it, such as the speed of a car:

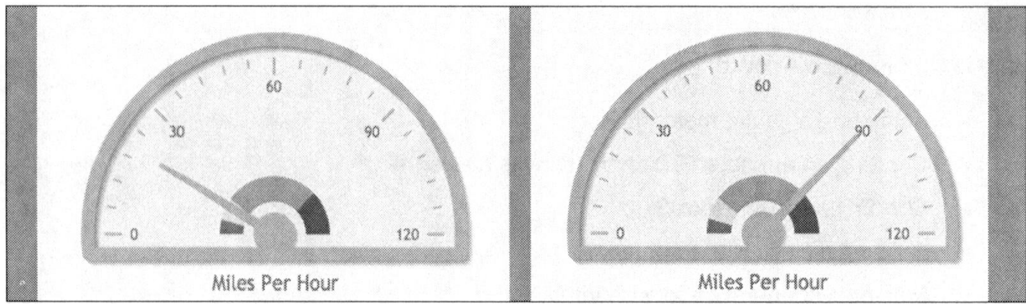

Getting ready

To get started you will need to use jQuery and jqPlot. This time around we will start from scratch.

To get the latest scripts, visit the creator site at `http://blog.everythingfla.com/?p=339`.

Download both jQuery and jqPlot, or download our source files to start with.

How to do it...

Let's list the steps required to complete the task:

1. Create an HTML page for our project:

```
<!DOCTYPE html>
<html>
  <head>
    <title>JQPlot Meter</title>
```

```
    <meta charset="utf-8" />
    <link rel="stylesheet"
    href="./external/jqplot/jquery.jqplot.min.css">
    <script src="http://ajax.googleapis.com/
    ajax/libs/jquery/1.7.2/jquery.min.js"></script>
    <script src="./external/jqplot/
    jquery.jqplot.js"></script>
    <script src="./external/jqplot/plugins/
    jqplot.meterGaugeRenderer.min.js"></script>

    <script src="./07.01.jqplot-meter.js"></script>
  </head>
  <body style="background:#fafafa">

  <div id="meter" style="height:400px;width:400px;
  "></div>
  </body>
</html>
```

2. Create the `07.01.jqplot-meter.js` file.
3. Let's add a few helper variables. We will use them when rendering our meter:

```
var meter;
var meterValue=0;
var startingSpeed = parseInt(Math.random()*60) + 30;
var isStarting = true;
var renderOptions= {
               label: 'Miles Per Hour',
               labelPosition: 'bottom',
               labelHeightAdjust: -10,
               intervalOuterRadius: 45,
               ticks: [0, 40, 80, 120],
               intervals:[25, 90, 120],
               intervalColors:[ '#E7E658','#66cc66',
               '#cc6666']
            };
```

4. Now it's time to create our meter. We will use jQuery to know when our document is being read and then create our chart.

```
$(document).ready(function(){

  meter = $.jqplot('meter',[[meterValue]],{
    seriesDefaults: {
      renderer: $.jqplot.MeterGaugeRenderer,
      rendererOptions:renderOptions
    }
  });

});
```

5. Now it's time to animate our chart. Let's add in the last line of our `ready` listener interval (it will run from now on until the end of the recipe):

```
$(document).ready(function(){

  meter = $.jqplot('meter',[[meterValue]],{
    seriesDefaults: {
      renderer: $.jqplot.MeterGaugeRenderer,
      rendererOptions:renderOptions
    }
  });

  setInterval(updateMeter,30);

});
```

6. Last but not least, it's time to create the `updateMeter` function:

```
function updateMeter(){
  meter.destroy();


  if(isStarting && meterValue<startingSpeed){
    ++meterValue
  }else{
    meterValue += 1- Math.random()*2;
    meterValue = Math.max(0,Math.min(meterValue,120)); //keep our
value in range no mater what
  }

  meter = $.jqplot('meter',[[meterValue]],{
    seriesDefaults: {
      renderer: $.jqplot.MeterGaugeRenderer,
      rendererOptions:renderOptions
    }
  });

}
```

Well done. Refresh your browser and you will find an animated speedometer that looks like that of a car driving around (if you only imagine it).

How it works...

This task was really easy as we didn't need to start everything from scratch. For the meter to run, we need to import the library `meterGaugeRenderer`. We do that by adding that into our JavaScript files that we are loading. But let's focus on our code. The first step in our JavaScript is to prepare a few global variables; we are using global variables as we want to re-use these variables in two different functions (when we are ready to reset our data).

```
var meter;
var meterValue=0;
var startingSpeed = parseInt(Math.random()*60) + 30;
var isStarting = true;
```

The `meter` variable will hold the meter that we will generate from our open source library. The `meterValue` will be our initial value when the application loads. Our `startingSpeed` variable is going to be a random value between `30` and `90`. The goal is to start from a different place each time to make it more interesting. As soon as our application starts, we will want our meter to quickly animate to its new base speed (the `startingSpeed` variable). Lastly, this connects to the `isStarting` variable as we will want to have one animation that will get us to our base speed. When we get there, we want to switch to a random driving speed that would cause the animation to change. Now that we have all the helper variables set, we are ready to create the `renderOptions` object:

```
var renderOptions= {
               label: 'Miles Per Hour',
               labelPosition: 'bottom',
               labelHeightAdjust: -10,
               intervalOuterRadius: 45,
               ticks: [0, 40, 80, 120],
               intervals:[25, 90, 120],
               intervalColors:[ '#E7E658','#66cc66', '#cc6666']
          };
```

This object is really the heart of the visuals for our application. (There are other options that you are welcome to explore in the jqPlot project home page documentation.) Now let's review a few of the key parameters.

`intervalOuterRadius` has a bit of a tricky name, but it's actually the internal radius. The actual size of our meter is controlled by the size of `div` that we set our application to be in. `intervalOuterRadius` controls the size of our internal shape in the speedometer's core.

```
var renderOptions= {
  label: 'Miles Per Hour',
  labelPosition: 'bottom',
  labelHeightAdjust: -10,
  intervalOuterRadius: 45,
```

```
    //ticks: [0, 40, 80, 120],
    intervals:[10,25, 90, 120],
    intervalColors:['#999999', '#E7E658','#66cc66', '#cc6666']
  };
```

The `ticks` function controls where the copy outlines would be. The default would take our top range and divide it by 4 (that is 30, 60, 90, and 120). The `intervals` and `intervalColors` functions let the meter know the ranges and the inner, internal, pie colors (separated from the ticks).

```
$(document).ready(function(){

  meter = $.jqplot('meter',[[meterValue]],{
    seriesDefaults: {
      renderer: $.jqplot.MeterGaugeRenderer,
      rendererOptions:renderOptions
    }
  });
  setInterval(updateMeter,30);

});
```

To create a new chart using the jqPlot library, we always call the `$.jqplot` function. The first parameter of the function is the `div` layer, which is where our work will live. The second parameter is a two-dimensional array containing the data of the chart (kind of looks odd for this example as it expects a 2D array and as our sample only includes one data entry at a time, we need to wrap it in two arrays). The third parameter defines the used renderer and `rendererOptions` (that we created earlier).

There's more...

Let's explore a few more functions.

Creating the updateMeter function

The `updateMeter` function gets called every 30 milliseconds. What we need to do is start by clearing our art every time that it is called:

```
meter.destroy();
```

This will clear everything related to our meter so we can recreate it.

If we are still in the intro part of our application where we want our speed to go up to the goal speed, we need to update our `meterValue` by `1`.

```
if(isStarting && meterValue<startingSpeed){
    ++meterValue;
}
```

If we are already passed this state and want our meter to go up and down randomly, making it look like variations in driving speed, we'll use the following code snippet:

```
}else{
    meterValue += 1- Math.random()*2;
    meterValue = Math.max(0,Math.min(meterValue,120)); //keep our
    value in range no mater what
}
```

We are randomly adding a value between `-1` and `1` to our meter value. A correction to our result can be achieved by keeping our value not lower than `0` and not higher than `120`, followed by redrawing our meter with our new `meterValue` value.

Creating an animated 3D chart (canvas3DGraph)

This recipe is real fun. It's based on the source files of Dragan Bajcic. It's not a full library of charts, but it's a great inspirational chart that can be modified and used to create your own 3D data visualizations.

Although our source files in our attached sample are modified from the original source (mainly `canvas3DGraph.js`), to get the original source for the open source projects used in this book, please visit our centralized list at `http://blog.everythingfla.com/?p=339`.

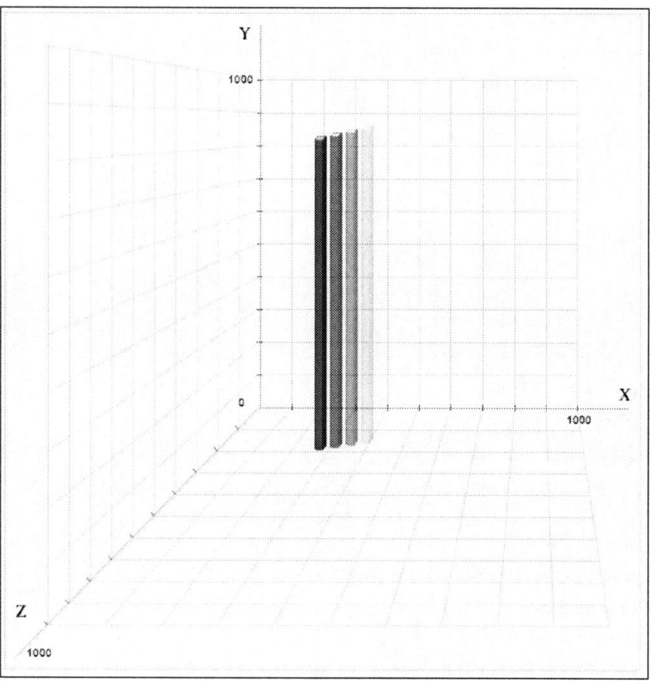

Getting ready

If you want to follow our updates, download the original source files from the provided link or review the changes that we make to Dragan's source files.

How to do it...

Let's jump right in as we have a lot of work to do:

1. Create the HTML file:

```
<!DOCTYPE html>
<html>
  <head>
    <title>canvas3DGraph.js</title>
    <meta charset="utf-8" />
    <link rel="stylesheet"
    href="./external/dragan/canvas3DGraph.css">
    <script src="./external/dragan/
    canvas3DGraph.js"></script>
    <script src="./07.02.3d.js"></script>

  </head>
  <body style="background:#fafafa">

    <div id="g-holder">
      <div id="canvasDiv">
        <canvas id="graph" width="600" height="600" >
        </canvas>
        <div id="gInfo"></div>
      </div>

    </div>
  </body>
</html>
```

2. Create the CSS file `canvas3DGraph.css`:

```
#g-holder {
    height:620px;
    position:relative;
}

#canvasDiv{
    border:solid 1px #e1e1e1;
    width:600px;
    height:600px;
    position:absolute;
```

```
        top:0px; left:0px;
        z-index:10;
    }
    #x-label{
        position:absolute;
        z-index:2;
        top:340px;
        left:580px;
    }

    #y-label{
        position:absolute;
        z-index:2;
        top:10px;
        left:220px;
    }

    #z-label{
        position:absolute;
        z-index:2;
        top:540px;
        left:10px;
    }

    #gInfo div.gText{
        position:absolute;
        z-index:-1;
        font:normal 10px Arial;
    }
```

3. Now it's time to move into the JavaScript file.
4. Let's add a few helper variables:

```
var gData = [];

var curIndex=0;
var trailCount = 5;
var g;
var trailingArray=[];
```

5. We need to create our chart when the document is ready:

```
window.onload=function(){
  //Initialize Graph
  g = new canvasGraph('graph');
  g.barStyle = {cap:'rgba(255,255,255,1)',main:
  'rgba(0,0,0,0.7)', shadow:'rgba(0,0,0,1)',
  outline:'rgba(0,0,0,0.7)',formater:styleFormater};
```

```
    for(i=0;i<100;i++){
      gData[i] = {x:(Math.cos((i/10)) * 400 + 400),
      y:(1000-(i*9.2)), z:(i*10)};
    }

  plotBar();
  setInterval(plotBar,40);



  }
```

6. Create the `plotBar` function:

```
function plotBar(){
  trailingArray.push(gData[curIndex]);

  if(trailingArray.length>=5) trailingArray.shift();

  g.drawGraph(trailingArray);//trailingArray);
  curIndex++
  if(curIndex>=gData.length) curIndex=0;
}
```

7. Create the formatter function `styleFormatter`:

```
function styleFormatter(styleColor,index,total){
  var clrs = styleColor.split(",");
  var alpha = parseFloat(clrs[3].split(")"));
  alpha *= index/total+.1;
  clrs[3] = alpha+")";
  return clrs.join(",");
}
```

Assuming that you are using our modified, open source JavaScript file, you should now see your chart animated. (In the *There's more...* section in this recipe, we will look deeper into the changes and why we made them.)

How it works...

Let's first look at our code in the way that we interact with the JavaScript library. After that we will dig deeper into the inner workings of this library.

```
var gData = [];
var trailingArray=[];
var trailCount = 5;
var curIndex=0;
```

The gData array will store all the possible points in the 3D space. A 3D bar will be created with these points (the points are the 3D points x, y, and z values that will be put into this array as objects). The trailingArray array will store the current bar elements in the view. The trailCount variable will define how many bars can be seen at the same time, and our current index (curIndex) will keep track of our latest addition into the chart.

When the window loads we create our graph element:

```
window.onload=function(){
  //Initialise Graph
  g = new canvasGraph('graph');
  g.barStyle = {cap:'rgba(255,255,255,1)',main:'rgba(0,0,0,0.7)',
  shadow:'rgba(0,0,0,1)',outline:'rgba(0,0,0,0.7)',
  formatter:styleFormatter};
  for(i=0;i<100;i++){
    gData[i] = {x:(Math.cos((i/10)) * 400 + 400), y:(1000-
    (i*9.2)), z:(i*10)};
  }

  plotBar();
  setInterval(plotBar,40);


}
```

After creating our graph, we update the barStyle property to reflect the colors that we want to use on our bar. In addition to this, we are sending a formatter function as we want to treat each bar separately (visually treat them differently). We then create our data feed—in our case it's a traveling Math.cos in our inner space. Feel free to play around with all the data points; it creates some really amazing content. In a real-life application, you would want to use live or real data. To ensure that our data will be stacked from back to front, we would need to sort our data so that the z value that is in the back would be rendered first. In our case sorting isn't needed as our loop is creating an order of z indexes that grow in order, so the array is already organized.

There's more...

Next we call plotBar and repeat the action every 40 milliseconds.

The logic behind plotBar

Let's review the logic within the plotBar function. This is the really cool part of our application, where we update the data feed to create an animation. We start by adding the current index element into the trailingArray array:

```
trailingArray.push(gData[curIndex]);
```

If our array length is 5 or more, we need to get rid of the first element in the array:

```
if(trailingArray.length>=5) trailingArray.shift();
```

We then draw our chart and push the value of `curIndex` up by one. If our `curIndex` is greater than our array elements, we reset it to 0.

```
g.drawGraph(trailingArray);//trailingArray);
curIndex++
if(curIndex>=gData.length) curIndex=0;
```

The logic behind styleFormatter

Our formatter function is called each time a bar is drawn to calculate the color to be used. It will get the index of the bar and the total length of the data feed in the chart being processed. In our example, we are only changing the `alpha` value of the bars based on their position. (The greater the number, the closer we are to the last entered data source.) In this way, we create our fade-out effect:

```
function styleFormatter(styleColor,index,total){
  var clrs = styleColor.split(",");
  var alpha = parseFloat(clrs[3].split(")"));
  alpha *= index/total+.1;
  clrs[3] = alpha+")";
  return clrs.join(",");
}
```

There is actually much more to this sample. Without going too deep into the code itself, I want to outline the changes.

To control the colors of our bars, line 66 of the third-party package has to be changed. As such, I introduced `this.barStyle` and replaced all the references of the hardcoded values during the creation of the bar elements (and set some default values):

```
this.barStyle = {cap:'rgba(255,255,255,1)',main:'rg
ba(189,189,243,0.7)', shadow:'rgba(77,77,180,0.7)',outline:'rgba(0,0,0
,0.7)',formatter:null};
```

I've created a style generator for our bars. This was done to help us redirect the logic between an external formatter and an internal style:

```
canvasGraph.prototype.getBarStyle= function(baseStyle,index,total){
  return this.barStyle.formatter?
  this.barStyle.formatter(baseStyle,index,total):baseStyle;
}
```

We have created a clear function to delete all the visuals from the graph so we can re-render the data each time we call it:

```
canvasGraph.prototype.getBarStyle= function(baseStyle,index,total){
  return this.barStyle.formatter?
  this.barStyle.formatter(baseStyle,index,total):baseStyle;
}
```

We moved the logic of drawing the chart to the `drawGraph` function, so I can delete the chart at the same time, making it easier for it to refresh all the data each time:

```
canvasGraph.prototype.drawGraph=function(gData){
  //moved this to the drawGraph so i can clear each time its
  called.
  this.clearCanvas();
  // Draw XYZ AXIS
  this.drawAxis();
  this.drawInfo();

  var len = gData.length;

  for(i=0;i<len;i++){
    this.drawBar(gData[i].x,gData[i].y,gData[i].z,i,len);
  }
}
```

The current index and length information now travel through `drawBar` until it gets to the formatter function.

Last but not least, I've deleted the drawing of the chart from the constructor, so our chart will be more conducive for our animation idea.

Charting over time (flotJS)

One of the more impressive features of this library is the ease with which one can update the chart information. It's very easy to see from the first moment when you review this library and its samples that the author loves math and loves charting. My favorite feature is the way the chart can update its x ranges dynamically based on the input added into it.

My second favorite feature is how easy it is to update the chart text info by using a `tickFormater` method:

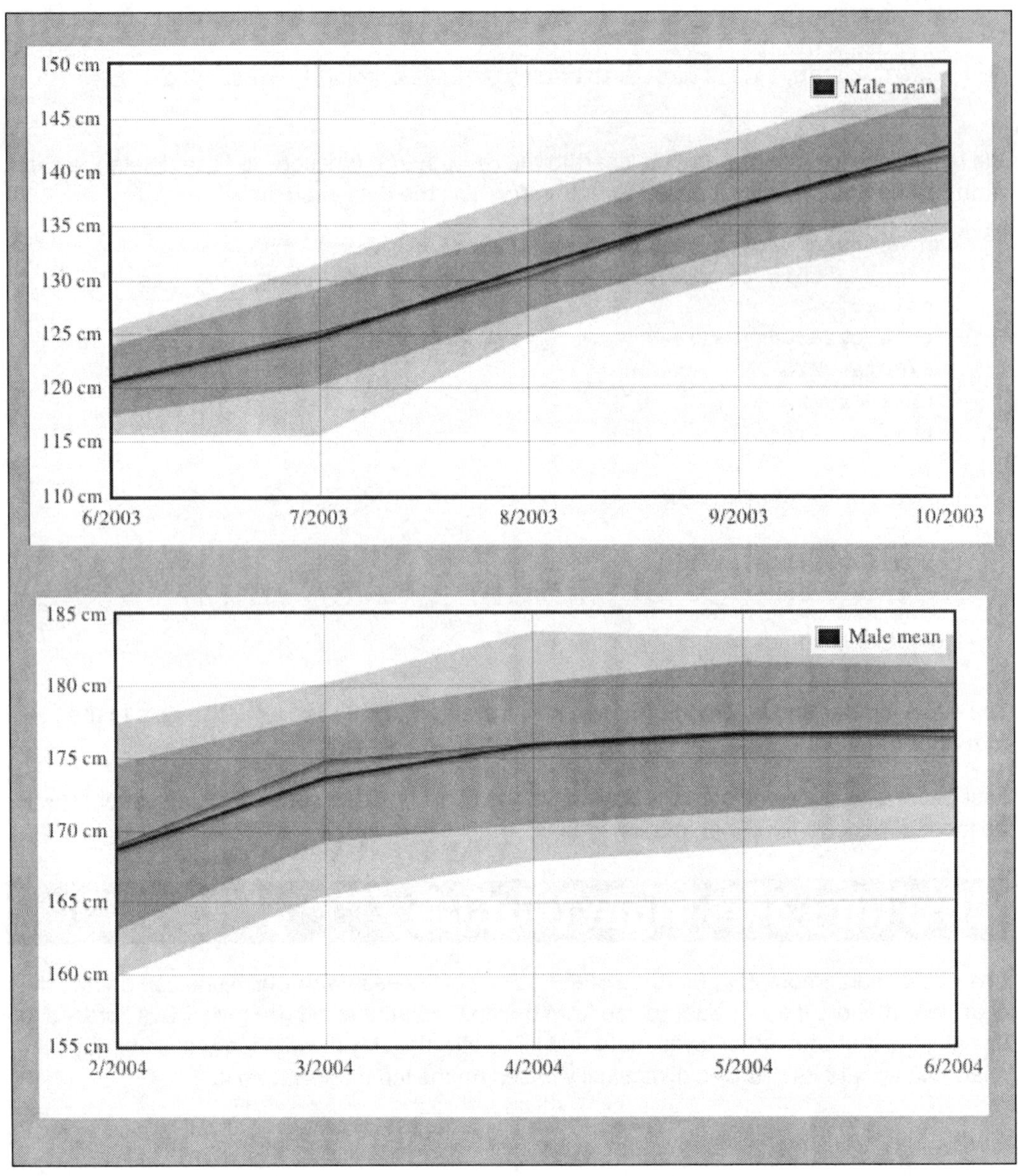

Getting ready

To get the latest builds of the `flotJS` library, please visit our link hub at `http://blog.everythingfla.com/?p=339` for charting open source libraries or download our book's source files where we include the latest build as of publication at `http://02geek.com/books/html5-graphics-and-data-visualization-cookbook.htm`.

How to do it...

Let's create our HTML and JavaScript files:

1. Create an HTML file:

```
<!DOCTYPE html>
<html>
  <head>
    <title>flot</title>
    <meta charset="utf-8" />
    <script src="http://ajax.googleapis.com/
    ajax/libs/jquery/1.7.2/jquery.min.js"></script>
    <script src="./external/flot/jquery.flot.js">
    </script>
    <script src="./external/flot/
    jquery.flot.fillbetween.js">
    </script>

    <script src="./07.03.flot.js"></script>

  </head>
  <body style="background:#fafafa">

    <div id="placeholder"
    style="width:600px;height:300px;"></div>
  </body>
</html>
```

2. Create a new JavaScript file (`07.03.flot.js`) and then create our data source:

```
var males = {

//...
//please grab from source files its a long list of numbers
};Create helper variables:
var VIEW_LENGTH = 5;
var index=0;
var plot;

var formattingData = {
```

```
  xaxis: { tickDecimals: 0, tickFormatter: function (v) {
  return v%12 + "/" + (2009+Math.floor(v/12)); } },
  yaxis: { tickFormatter: function (v) { return v + "
  cm"; } }
};
```

3. Create a `ready` event and trigger `updateChart`:

```
$(document).ready(updateChart);
```

4. Create `updateChart`:

```
function updateChart() {
  plot = $.plot($("#placeholder"), getData(),
  formattingData);

  if(index+5<males['mean'].length){
    setTimeout(updateChart,500);
  }
}
```

5. Create `getData`:

```
function getData(){
  var endIndex = index+5>=males.length?males.length-
  1:index+5;
  console.log(index,endIndex);
  var dataset = [
    { label: 'Male mean', data:
    males['mean'].slice(index,endIndex),
    lines: { show: true }, color: "rgb(50,50,255)" },
    { id: 'm15%', data:
    males['15%'].slice(index,endIndex),
    lines: { show: true, lineWidth: 0,
    fill: false }, color: "rgb(50,50,255)" },
    { id: 'm25%', data:
    males['25%'].slice(index,endIndex),
    lines: { show: true, lineWidth: 0, fill: 0.2 },
    color: "rgb(50,50,255)", fillBetween: 'm15%' },
    { id: 'm50%', data:
    males['50%'].slice(index,endIndex),
    lines: { show: true, lineWidth: 0.5, fill: 0.4,
    shadowSize: 0 }, color: "rgb(50,50,255)",
    fillBetween: 'm25%' },
    { id: 'm75%', data:
    males['75%'].slice(index,endIndex),
    lines: { show: true, lineWidth: 0, fill: 0.4 },
    color: "rgb(50,50,255)", fillBetween: 'm50%' },
    { id: 'm85%', data:
    males['85%'].slice(index,endIndex),
    lines: { show: true, lineWidth: 0, fill: 0.2 },
    color: "rgb(50,50,255)", fillBetween: 'm75%' }
```

```
    ];

    index++;
    return dataset;
  }
```

Now if you run the chart in your browser, you will see 6 months at a time, and at every half of a second, the chart will be updated by pushing the chart one month forward until the end of data source is reached.

How it works...

`flotJS` has a built-in logic to reset itself when its redrawn, and that's part of our magic. Our data source has been borrowed from one of the `flotJS` samples. We are actually using the data to represent a fictional situation. Originally this data was representing the average weight of people based on their age, broken down into percentiles. But our point in this example is not to showcase the data but instead show ways of visualizing the data. So in our case, we had to treat the data by keeping the percentiles as they are intended to be, but use the inner data to showcase the average over years instead of over ages, as follows:

```
{'15%': [[yearID, value], [yearID, value]...
```

The `yearID` values range from `2` through `19`. We want to showcase this information as if we started our data picking from 2006. Each `yearId` will represent a month (19 would be 1.5 years after 2006, instead of the age 19 as the data actually represents).

So let's start breaking it down. Now that we know how we are going to treat our dataset, we want to limit the number of months that we can see at any given time. As such we will add two helper parameters, one of which will keep track of our current index and the other will track the maximum number of visible elements at any given time:

```
var VIEW_LENGTH = 5;
var index=0;
```

We will create a global variable for our Flot graph and create a formatter to help us format the data that will be sent in.

```
var plot;
var formattingData = {
  xaxis: { tickDecimals: 0, tickFormatter: function (v) { return 
  v%12 + "/" + (2003+Math.floor(v/12)); } },
  yaxis: { tickFormatter: function (v) { return v + " cm"; } }
};
```

Note that `tickFormater` enables us to modify the way our tick will look in the chart. In the case of the x axis, the goal is to showcase the current date `2/2012...`, and in the y axis, we want to add `cm` to the numbers that will be printed out on the screen.

There's more...

There are still two more things to cover—the getData function and the updateChart function.

The GetData function

In flotJS every data point has an ID. In our case, we want to showcase six related content types. Play around with the parameters to see how they change the way the view is rendered. Before we send the created array back, we update the index ID by one, so the next time that the function is called it will send the next range.

One more thing we need to note is the actual data range. As we are not sending the full data range (but a maximum of 5), we need to validate that there are atleast five items after the index, and if not we will return the last element of the array, ensuring that we never slice more than the actual length:

```
var endIndex = index+5>=males.length?males.length-1:index+5;
```

The UpdateChart function

This part is probably the simplest one. The same code is used for the first render and all the following renders. If the dataset is valid, we create a timeout and call this function again until the animation completes.

Building a clock with RaphaelJS

Hands down this is my favorite sample in this chapter. It's based on a mix of two samples on Raphael's website (I strongly encourage you to explore it). Although Raphael isn't a graphing library, it's a really powerful animation and drawing library that is really worth playing with.

In this recipe, we will create a clock that is creative (I think). I planned to play with this library for a day or two, and ended up playing with it all weekend as I was just having so much fun. I ended up with a digit morphing clock (based on a sample that Raphael created on his site for letter morphing) and incorporated some arcing into it based on the polar clock example on his site. Let's see it in action:

Getting ready

As always in this chapter, you need the original library of Raphael. I've added it into our project. So just download the files and let's get rolling.

To grab the original library, visit our external source files hub for this chapter at `http://blog.everythingfla.com/?p=339`.

How to do it...

Let's build up our application:

1. Create the HTML file:

```
<!DOCTYPE html>
<html>
  <head>
    <title>Raphael</title>
    <meta charset="utf-8" />
    <script src="http://ajax.googleapis.com/ajax/
    libs/jquery/1.7.2/jquery.min.js"></script>
    <script src="./external/raphael/raphael-
    min.js"></script>
    <script src="./07.04.raphael.js"></script>
    <style>
```

```
        body {
          background: #333;
          color: #fff;
          font: 300 100.1% "Helvetica Neue", Helvetica,
          "Arial Unicode MS", Arial, sans-serif;
        }
        #holder {
          height: 600px;
          margin: -300px 0 0 -300px;
          width: 600px;
          left: 50%;
          position: absolute;
          top: 50%;
        }
      </style>

    </head>
    <body>

    <div id="holder"></div>
    </body>
  </html>
```

2. Now it's time to move into the JavaScript file `07.04.raphael.js`. Copy the path parameters to draw the digits `0` through `9` and the `:` sign into an object called `helveticaForClock`. It's really just a long list of numbers, so please copy them from our downloadable source files:

   ```
   var helveticaForClock = {…};
   ```

3. We are going to create an `onload` listener and put all of our code into it, to match it up with the style of code on Raphael's samples:

   ```
   window.onload = function () {
     //the rest of the code will be put in here from step 3
     and on
   };
   ```

4. Create a new `Raphael` object with a 600 x 600 size:

   ```
   var r = Raphael("holder", 600, 600);
   ```

5. Now we need to use a helper function to figure out the path to an arc. For that we are going to create an `arc` function as an extra attribute for our newly created `Raphael` object:

   ```
   r.customAttributes.arc = function (per,isClock) {
     var R = this.props.r,
     baseX = this.props.x,
     baseY = this.props.y;
   ```

```
    var degree = 360 *per;
    if(isClock) degree = 360-degree;

    var a = (90 - degree) * Math.PI / 180,
    x = baseX + R * Math.cos(a),
    y = baseY - R * Math.sin(a),
    path;

    if (per==1) {
      path = [["M", baseX, baseY - R], ["A", R, R, 0, 1, 1,
      baseX, baseY - R]];
    } else {
      path = [["M", baseX, baseY - R], ["A", R, R, 0,
      +(degree > 180), 1, x, y]];
    }

    var alpha=1;

    if(per<.1 || per>.9)
      alpha = 0;
    else
      alpha = 1;


    return {path: path,stroke: 'rgba(255,255,255,'+(1-
    per)+')'};
  };
```

6. Create our drawing of the hours of the clock (00:00):

```
var transPath;

var aTrans = ['T400,100','T320,100','T195,100','T115,100'];
var base0 = helveticaForClock[0];
var aLast = [0,0,0,0];
var aDigits = [];

var digit;
for(i=0; i<aLast.length; i++){
  digit = r.path("M0,0L0,0z").attr({fill: "#fff", stroke:
  "#fff", "fill-opacity": .3, "stroke-width": 1, "stroke-
  linecap": "round", translation: "100 100"});

  transPath = Raphael.
  transformPath(helveticaForClock[aLast[i]], aTrans[i]);
  digit.attr({path:transPath});
  aDigits.push(digit);
}
```

```
var dDot = r.path("M0,0L0,0z").attr({fill: "#fff", stroke: "#fff",
"fill-opacity": .3, "stroke-width": 1, "stroke-linecap": "round",
translation: "100 100"});
transPath = Raphael.transformPath(helveticaForClock[':'],
'T280,90');
dDot.attr({path:transPath});
```

7. Now it's time to create our art for our `seconds` animation:

```
var time;
var sec = r.path();
sec.props = {r:30,x:300,y:300}; //new mandatory params

var sec2 = r.path();
sec2.props = {r:60,x:300,y:300};

animateSeconds();
animateStrokeWidth(sec,10,60,1000*60);
```

8. Create the `animateSeconds` recursive function:

```
function animateSeconds(){ //will run forever
  time = new Date();

  sec.attr({arc: [1]});
  sec.animate({arc: [0]}, 1000, "=",animateSeconds);
  sec2.attr({arc: [1,true]});
  sec2.animate({arc: [0,true]}, 999, "=");

  var newDigits = [time.getMinutes()%10,
  parseInt(time.getMinutes()/10),
  time.getHours()%10,
  parseInt(time.getHours()/10)    ];
  var path;
  var transPath;
  for(var i=0; i<aLast.length; i++){
    if(aLast[i]!=newDigits[i]){
      path = aDigits[i];
      aLast[i] = newDigits[i];
      transPath = Raphael.transformPath
      (helveticaForClock[newDigits[i]], aTrans[i]);
      path.animate({path:transPath}, 500);
    }
  }

}
```

9. Create the `animateStrokeWidth` function:

```
function animateStrokeWidth(that,startWidth,endWidth,time){
  that.attr({'stroke-width':startWidth});
  that.animate({'stroke-width':endWidth},time,function(){
    animateStrokeWidth(that,startWidth,endWidth,time); //repeat
forever
  });
}
```

If you run the application now, you will see the outcome of my day of play with Raphael's library.

How it works...

There are a lot of elements to this project. Let's start focusing on the arc animation. Note that one of the elements that we are using in our code is when we are creating our new paths (we create two of them). We are adding some hardcoded parameters that will be used later when we draw the arcs in the `arc` method:

```
var sec = r.path();sec.props = {r:30,x:300,y:300}; //new mandatory
params

var sec2 = r.path();sec2.props = {r:60,x:300,y:300};
```

We are doing that to avoid sending these three properties into the arc each time, and to enable us to pick a radius and stick with it without it being integrated or hardcoded into the animations. We based our `arc` method on the `arc` method used for the polar clock in Raphael's examples, but changed it so the values can be positive or negative (making it easier to animate back and forth).

The `arc` method is then used to draw our arc when we are animating it inside the `animateSeconds` function:

```
sec.attr({arc: [1]});
sec.animate({arc: [0]}, 1000, "=",animateSeconds);
sec2.attr({arc: [1,true]});
sec2.animate({arc: [0,true]}, 999, "=");
```

The `attr` method will reset our `arc` attribute so that we can reanimate it.

By the way, note that in `animateStrokeWidth` we are animating the width of our stroke for 60 seconds from its lowest value to its highest value.

There's more...

Did you really think we are done? I know you didn't. Let's take a look at a few other critical steps.

Animating paths

One of the cooler things in this library is the capability to animate paths. If you have ever worked with Adobe Flash Shape Tweens, this will look very familiar—hands down, this is just really cool.

The idea is very simple. We have an object with a lot of path points. They create a shape together if we draw the line information through them. We have borrowed a list that Raphael created so we don't need to start from scratch, and literally all that we are changing in it is that we don't want our elements to be drawn in their current path. All we need to do is transform their location using the internal `Raphael.transformPath` method:

```
transPath = Raphael.transformPath(helveticaForClock[0], 'T400,100');
```

In other words, we are grabbing the path information for the digit 0 and then we are transforming, moving it 400 pixels to the right and 100 pixels down.

In our source code, it looks like we are executing the function in a loop (which is a bit more complicated but condensed):

```
for(i=0; i<aLast.length; i++){
  digit = r.path("M0,0L0,0z").attr({fill: "#fff", stroke: "#fff",
  "fill-opacity": .3, "stroke-width": 1, "stroke-linecap":
  "round", translation: "100 100"});

  transPath = Raphael.transformPath(helveticaForClock[aLast[i]],
  aTrans[i]);
  digit.attr({path:transPath});
  aDigits.push(digit);
}
```

We are basically looping through the `aLast` array (the list of digits that we want to create) and creating a new digit for each element. We then figure out the position of the digit based on the transforming information that is located in the `aTrans` array and then we draw it out by adding a new path into the attributes. Last but not least, we are saving our digit into our `aDigits` array that is to be used when we re-render the element later.

Each time the `animateSeconds` function gets called (once every second), we figure out if a digit has changed, and if it has then we are ready to update its information:

```
var newDigits = [time.getMinutes()%10,
  parseInt(time.getMinutes()/10),
  time.getHours()%10,
  parseInt(time.getHours()/10)];
var path;
var transPath;
  for(var i=0; i<aLast.length; i++){
    if(aLast[i]!=newDigits[i]){
    path = aDigits[i];
    aLast[i] = newDigits[i];
    transPath = Raphael.transformPath
    (helveticaForClock[newDigits[i]], aTrans[i]);
    path.animate({path:transPath}, 500);
  }
}
```

We start by gathering the current time `HH:MM` into an array (`[H,H,M,M]`) followed by looking to see if our digits have changed. If they have changed, we grab the new data needed from our `helveticaForClock` function and animate it in our new path information for our digit (path).

That covers the most important factors for following this recipe.

Making a sunburst chart with InfoVis

Another really cool library is `InfoVis`. If I had to categorize the library, I would say it's about connections. When you review the rich samples provided by Nicolas Garcia Belmonte, you will find a lot of relational datatypes that are very unique.

This library is distributed freely through Sencha legal owners. (The copyright is easy to follow, but please review the notes for this and any open source project that you encounter.)

We will start with one of his base samples—the sunburst example from the source files. I've made a few changes to give it a new personality. The basic idea of a sunburst chart is to showcase relationships between nodes. While a tree is an ordered parent-child relationship, the relationships in a sunbust chart are bidirectional. A node can have a relationship with any other node, and it can be a two-way or one-way relationship. A dataset that is perfect for this is the example of the total exports of a country—lines from one country to all the other countries that get exports from it.

We will keep it relatively simple by having only four elements (Ben, Packt Publishing, 02geek, and Nicolas the creator of InfoVis). I have a one-way relationship with each of them: as the owner of `02geek.com`, as a writer for Packt Publishing, and a user of InfoVis. While that is true about me, not all the others have a real in-depth relationship with me. Some of them have a relationship back with me, such as 02geek and Packt Publishing, while Nicolas for this example is a stranger that I've never interacted with. This can be depicted in a sunburst chart in the following way:

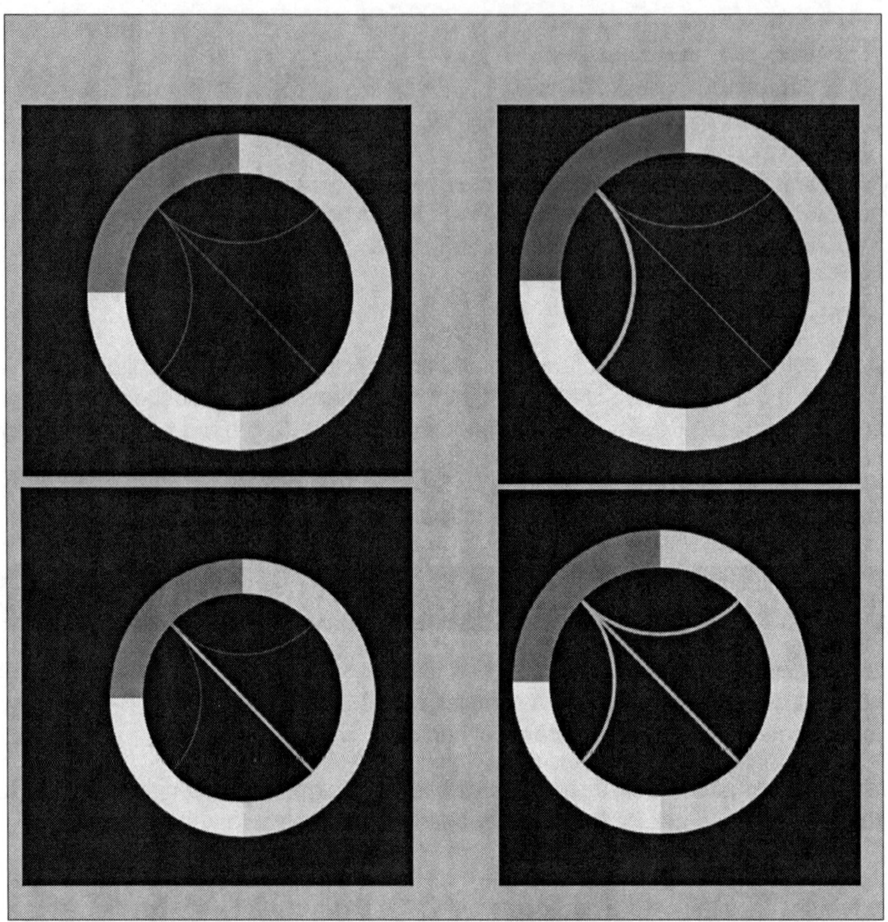

Getting ready

As always you will need the source files, you can either download our sample files or get the latest release by visiting our aggregated list at `http://blog.everythingfla.com/?p=339`.

How to do it...

Let's create some HTML and JavaScript magic:

1. Create an HTML file as follows:

```
<!DOCTYPE html>
<html>
  <head>
    <title>Sunberst - InfoVis</title>
    <meta charset="utf-8" />

    <style>
      #infovis {
        position:relative;
        width:600px;
        height:600px;
        margin:auto;
        overflow:hidden;
      }
    </style>

    <script  src="./external/jit/jit-yc.js"></script>
    <script src="./07.05.jit.js"></script>
  </head>

  <body onload="init();">
    <div id="infovis"></div>
  </body>
</html>
```

2. The rest of the code will be in `07.05.jit.js`. Create a base data source as follows:

```
var dataSource = [ {"id": "node0", "name": "","data": {"$type":
"none" },"adjacencies": []}]; //starting with invisible root
```

3. Let's create a function that will create the nodes needed for our chart system:

```
function createNode(id,name,wid,hei,clr){
  var obj = {id:id,name:name,data:{"$angularWidth":wid,
  "$height":hei,"$color":clr},adjacencies:[]};
  dataSource[0].adjacencies.push({"nodeTo": id,"data":
  {'$type': 'none'}});
  dataSource.push(obj);

  return obj;
}
```

4. To connect the dots, we will need to create a function that will create the relationships between the elements:

```
function relate(obj){
  for(var i=1; i<arguments.length; i++){
    obj.adjacencies.push({'nodeTo':arguments[i]});
  }
}
```

5. We want to be able to highlight the relationships. To do that we will need to have a way to rearrange the data and highlight the elements that we want highlighted:

```
function highlight(nodeid){
  var selectedIndex = 0;
  for(var i=1; i<dataSource.length; i++){
    if(nodeid!=     dataSource[i].id){
      for(var item in dataSource[i].adjacencies)
      delete dataSource[i].adjacencies[item].data;
    }else{
      selectedIndex = i;
      for(var item in dataSource[i].adjacencies)
      dataSource[i].adjacencies[item].data =  {"$color":
      "#ddaacc","$lineWidth": 4 };
      }

    }

    if(selectedIndex){ //move selected node to be first
    (so it will highlight everything)
    var node = dataSource.splice(selectedIndex,1)[0];
    dataSource.splice(1,0,node);
  }

}
```

6. Create an `init` function:

```
function init(){
/* or the remainder of the steps
all code showcased will be inside the init function  */
}
```

7. Let's start building up data sources and relationships:

```
function init(){
  var node =
  createNode('geek','02geek',100,40,"#B1DDF3");
  relate(node,'ben');
  node = createNode('packt','PacktBub',100,40,"#FFDE89");
```

```
    relate(node,'ben');
    node = createNode('ben','Ben',100,40,"#E3675C");
    relate(node,'geek','packt','nic');

    node = createNode('nic','Nicolas',100,40,"#C2D985");
    //no known relationships so far ;)
...
```

8. Create the actual sunburst and interact with the API (I've stripped it down to its bare bones; in the original samples it's much more detailed):

```
var sb = new $jit.Sunburst({
  injectInto: 'infovis', //id container
  Node: {
    overridable: true,
    type: 'multipie'
  },
  Edge: {
    overridable: true,
    type: 'hyperline',
    lineWidth: 1,
    color: '#777'
  },
  //Add animations when hovering and clicking nodes
  NodeStyles: {
    enable: true,
    type: 'Native',
    stylesClick: {
    'color': '#444444'
  },
  stylesHover: {
    'color': '#777777'
  },
    duration: 700
  },
  Events: {
    enable: true,
    type: 'Native',
    //List node connections onClick
    onClick: function(node, eventInfo, e){
      if (!node) return;

      highlight(node.id);
      sb.loadJSON(dataSource);
      sb.refresh()
    }
  },
  levelDistance: 120
});
```

9. Last but not least, we want to render our chart by providing its `dataSource` and refresh the render for the first time:

   ```
   sb.loadJSON(dataSource);
   sb.refresh();
   ```

That's it. If you run the application, you will find a chart that is clickable and fun, and just scratches the capabilities of this really cool data networking library.

How it works...

I'll avoid getting into the details of the actual API as that is fairly intuitive and has a really nice library of information and samples. So instead I will focus on the changes and enhancements that I've created in this application.

Before we do that we need to understand how the data structure of this chart works. Let's take a deeper look into how the data source object will look when filled with information:

```
{
        "id": "node0",
        "name": "",
        "data": {
          "$type": "none"
        },
        "adjacencies": [
            {"nodeTo": "node1","data": {'$type': 'none'}},
            {"nodeTo": "node2","data": {'$type': 'none'}},
            {"nodeTo": "node3","data": {'$type': 'none'}},
            {"nodeTo": "node4","data": {'$type': 'none'}}
                        ]
},

{
        "id": "node1",
        "name": "node 1",
        "data": {
          "$angularWidth": 300,
          "$color": "#B1DDF3",
          "$height": 40
        },
        "adjacencies": [
            {
              "nodeTo": "node3",
              "data": {
                "$color": "#ddaacc",
```

```
                    "$lineWidth": 4
                  }
                }
                        ]
    },
```

There are a few important factors to note. The first is that there is a base parent that is the parent of all the parentless nodes. In our case it's a flat chart. The relationships that are really thrilling are between nodes that are at an equal level. As such the main parent has a relationship with all the nodes that are to follow. The children elements, such as `node1` in this case, could have relationships. They are listed out in an array called `adjacencies` that holds objects. The only mandatory parameter is the `nodeTo` property. It lets the application know the one-way relationship list. There are optional layout parameters that we will add later only when we want to highlight a line. So let's see how we can create this type of data dynamically with the help of a few functions.

The `createNode` function helps us keep our code clean by wrapping up the dirty steps together. Every new element that we add needs to be added into our array and is needed to update our main parent (that is always going to be in position `0` of our array of new elements):

```
function createNode(id,name,wid,hei,clr){
  var obj = {id:id,name:name,data:{"$angularWidth":wid,
  "$height":hei,"$color":clr},adjacencies:[]};
  dataSource[0].adjacencies.push({"nodeTo": id,"data":
  {'$type': 'none'}});
  dataSource.push(obj);

  return obj;
}
```

We return the object as we want to continue and build up the relationship with this object. As soon as we create a new object (in our `init` function), we call the `relate` function and send to it all the relationships that our element will have to it. The logic of the `relate` function looks more complicated that it actually is. The function uses a hidden or often ignored feature in JavaScript that enables developers to send an open-ended number of parameters into a function with the use of the `arguments` array that is created automatically within every function. We can get these parameters as an array named `arguments`:

```
function relate(obj){
  for(var i=1; i<arguments.length; i++){
    obj.adjacencies.push({'nodeTo':arguments[i]});
  }
}
```

The `arguments` array is built into every function and stores all the actual information that has been sent into the function. As the first parameter is our object, we need to skip the first parameter and then add the new relationships into the `adjacencies` array.

Our last data-related function is our `highlight` function. The `highlight` function expects one parameter `nodeID` (that we created in `createNode`). The goal of the `highlight` function is to travel through all the data elements and de-highlight all the relationships limited to the one selected element and its relationships.

```
function highlight(nodeid){
  var selectedIndex = 0;
  for(var i=1; i<dataSource.length; i++){
    if(nodeid!=  dataSource[i].id){
      for(var item in dataSource[i].adjacencies)
      delete dataSource[i].adjacencies[item].data;
    }else{
      selectedIndex = i;
      for(var item in dataSource[i].adjacencies)
      dataSource[i].adjacencies[item].data =  {"$color":
      "#ddaacc","$lineWidth": 4 };
    }

  }
}
```

If we don't have `highlight`, we want to confirm and remove all the instances of the data object within the adjacencies of the node, while if it is selected, we need to add that same object by setting it with its own color and a thicker line.

We are almost done with the data. But when running the application, you will find an issue if we stop here. The issue is within the way the chart system works. If a line was drawn it will not redraw it again. In practical terms, if we select "Ben" while `ben` isn't the first element in the list, then not all the relationships that "Ben" has with the others will be visible. To fix this issue, we would want to push the selected node to be the first element right after position `0` (main parent), so it will render the selected relationships first:

```
if(selectedIndex){
  var node = dataSource.splice(selectedIndex,1)[0];
  dataSource.splice(1,0,node);
}
```

There's more...

One more thing left is that we need to be able to refresh our content when the user clicks on an element. To accomplish this task, we will need to add an event parameter into the initializing parameter object of jit.Sunburst:

```
var sb = new $jit.Sunburst({
  injectInto: 'infovis', //id container
     ...
  Events: {
    enable: true,
    type: 'Native',
    //List node connections onClick
    onClick: function(node, eventInfo, e){
      if (!node) return;

      highlight(node.id);
      sb.loadJSON(dataSource);
        sb.refresh();
    }
  },
  levelDistance: 120
});
```

One more thing to note in this sample is the levelDistance property that controls how close/far you are to/from the rendered element (making it bigger or smaller).

Where is the copy?

There is still one more issue. We don't have any copy in our chart enabling us to know what is actually being clicked on. I've removed it from the original sample as I just didn't like the positioning of the text and couldn't figure out how to get it up right, so instead I came up with a workaround. You can directly draw into the canvas by directly interacting with it. The canvas element will always be called by the same ID as our project (in our case infovis followed by -canvas):

```
var can = document.getElementById("infovis-canvas");
  var context = can.getContext("2d");
...
```

I'll leave the rest for you to explore. The rest of the logic is easy to follow as I've stripped it down. So if you enjoy this project as well, please visit the InfoVis Toolkit site and play more with their interface options.

8
Playing with Google Charts

In this chapter we will cover:

- Getting started with a pie chart
- Creating charts using the ChartWrapper
- Changing data source to Google Spreadsheet
- Customizing chart properties with an options object
- Adding a dashboard to charts

Introduction

In this chapter, we will explore the Google visualization API task by task. We will look at the steps involved in creating a chart and integrating it with the charting API.

To work with the Google APIs, you must comply with the Google terms of use and policies that can be located at `https://google-developers.appspot.com/readme/terms`.

Getting started with a pie chart

In this first recipe, we will start with Google Charts, covering the basic steps that you need to understand when working with Google Charts through an interactive dataset that is based on the CDC death rates in the USA (LCWK)—deaths, percent of total deaths, and death rates for the 15 leading causes of death in five-year age groups, by race and sex in the United States in 2008.

Getting ready

We will start from scratch with an empty HTML file and an empty JavaScript file named `08.01.getting-started.html` and `08.01.getting-started.js`.

How to do it...

Let's list the steps required to complete the task starting with the HTML file:

1. Let's start by creating a `head` and linking it to the Google `jsapi` and our local JavaScript file:

   ```
   <!DOCTYPE html>
   <html>
     <head>
       <title>Google Charts Getting Started</title>
       <meta charset="utf-8" />
       <script src="https://www.google.com/jsapi"></script>
       <script src="./08.01.getting-started.js"></script>
     </head>
   ```

2. Then create an empty `div` with `id chart`:

   ```
     <body style="background:#fafafa">
       <div id="chart"></div>
     </body>
   </html>
   ```

   Now, it's time to move into the `08.01.getting-started.js` file.

3. Lets request the visualization API from the Google `jsapi`:

   ```
   google.load('visualization', '1.0', {'packages':['corechart']});
   ```

4. We want to add a `callback` that will be triggered when the library is ready:

   ```
   google.setOnLoadCallback(init);
   ```

5. Create an `init` function as follows:

   ```
   function init(){
   ..

   }
   ```

   From now on we will break down the code added within the `init` function:

6. Create a new Google data object and provide data sources as shown in the following code snippet:

```
data.addColumn('string', 'Type of Death');
data.addColumn('number', 'Deaths');
data.addRows([
        ['Diseases of heart', 616828],
        ['Malignant neoplasms', 565469],
        ['Chronic lower respiratory diseases', 141090],
        ['Cerebrovascular diseases', 134148],
        ['Accidents', 121902],
        ['Alzheimer\'s disease', 82435],
        ['Diabetes mellitus', 70553],
        ['Influenza and pneumonia', 56284],
        ['Suicide', 36035],
        ['Septicemia', 35927],
        ['Chronic liver disease and cirrhosis', 29963],
        ['Essential hypertension and hypertensive renal
        disease', 25742],
        ['Parkinson\'s disease', 20483],
        ['Homicide', 17826],
        ['All other causes', 469062]

]);
```

7. Create an `options` object for the chart:

```
var options = {'title':'Deaths, for the 15 leading causes of
death: United States, 2008',
                     'width':800,
                     'height':600};
```

8. Create and draw the chart by using the following code snippet:

```
var chart = new google.visualization.PieChart(document.
getElementById('chart'));
    chart.draw(data, options);
```

Load the HTML file. You will find a working, interactive chart as shown in the following screenshot:

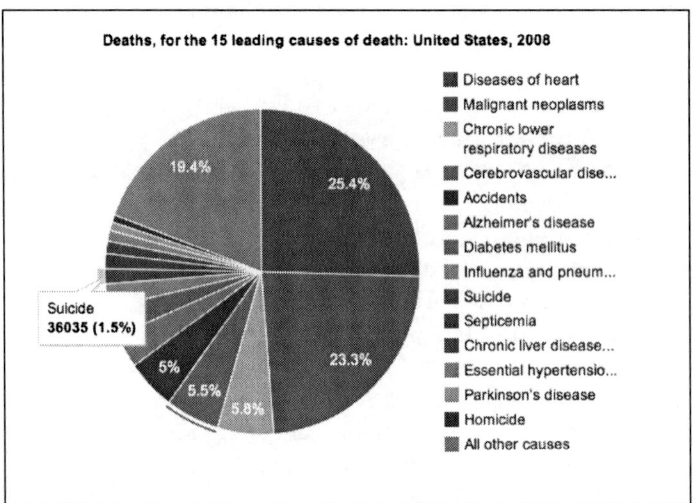

How it works...

Let's explore the steps involved in working with Google Charts. The first step we establish when working with the Google API's is adding Google's API link into our HTML file:

```
<script src="https://www.google.com/jsapi"></script>
```

Now that the Google API is loaded into our application, we can request the library we wish to work with. In our case, we want to work with the visualization API and the `corechart` package:

```
google.load('visualization', '1.0', {'packages':['corechart']});
```

Notice that we are requesting version 1.0; this might be confusing but we are actually asking for the production chart, 1.0 is always the current production version. As such if you wanted to lock into a build, you would need to discover what its code version is and send it instead of the 1.0 stable build.

The `corechart` library in the example defines most basic charts. For charts that are not included, you would need to pass in the extra packages needed, such as the table chart:

```
google.load('visualization', '1.0', {'packages':['corechart','tab
le']});
```

This covers the basics of how to load the API. But before we can finish our loading process, we need a way to have a callback so that we can know when the library is available for us to manipulate:

```
google.setOnLoadCallback(init);
```

We are asking the Google API to let us know when the package has loaded in a similar way to how we added a callback to our document. When the API is loaded, it is time for us to start interacting with the charting API.

There are three components that you will probably want to explore in each Google Chart:

- Creating the data source
- Adding options to your chart
- Creating the chart

Let's explore all these options.

All Google Charts need a data source. The data source format is based on an internal object created through the charting API:

```
var data = new google.visualization.DataTable();
```

Data tables are 2D arrays (or tables). They have columns and rows just like databases. Our next step will be to define the data columns:

```
data.addColumn('string', 'Type of Death');
data.addColumn('number', 'Deaths');
```

In our case, as we are working with a pie chart, only two rows are needed—one to name our elements and the other to provide them with a value. There is only one mandatory parameter to the `addColumn` method to define the datatype . The datatype can be one of the following:

- `string`
- `number`
- `boolean`
- `date`
- `datetime`
- `timeofday`

The second parameter is an optional descriptor of the type of data and it is used for visualization such as in our case `10 Deaths`. There are other parameters too, but as long as we provide the elements in an ordered list, we do not need to explore them.

Last but not least, we will call the `addRows` method. We can call the `addRows` method and send a one-dimensional array (again in the same order of data as we set our `addColumn`). In our case, we are using the `addRows` method that expects a two-dimensional array:

```
data.addRows([
        ['Diseases of heart', 616828],
....
]);
```

This covers our datasets. As long as we set our columns in the order of our data and send our information via arrays, we are set and don't need to dig any deeper into the data API.

The `options` object enables us to create and modify the elements of our chart. The elements we control in our application are width, height, and our title.

After creating the data sources and setting the options for our array, it's time for the easy part. To create the chart our first step is to pick our chart type and define where it will be created. Then we render it with the data source and options:

```
var chart = new google.visualization.PieChart(document.
getElementById('chart'));
chart.draw(data, options);
```

There's more...

Let's explore a few more tips, tricks, and advanced features of Google Charts. Using the option `Objectto create 3D chartsTo`, we can turn our chart into 3D. We can very quickly and simply add a new parameter into the options object:

```
var options = {'title':'Deaths, for the 15 leading causes of death:
United States, 2008',
                     'width':800,
                     'height':600,
                     "is3D": true};
```

The outcome would be a chart that is tilted in a 3D space.

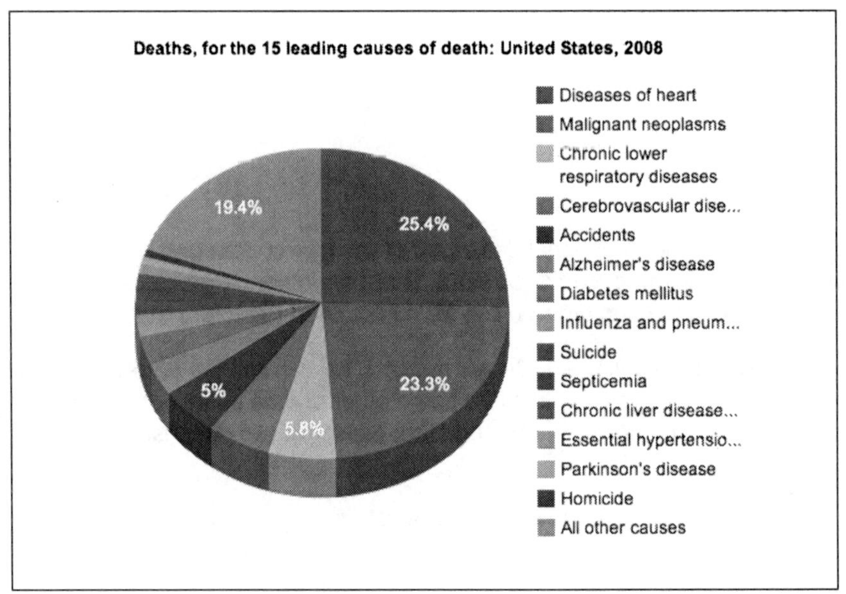

Changing the chart type

Changing a chart type isn't something complicated. As long as the chart types share the same number of data entries the change is usually one word from the actual constructor object of the chart. For example, we can very quickly switch our chart type by changing the method in the visualization library that is called:

```
var chart = new google.visualization.LineChart(document.
getElementById('chart'));
    chart.draw(data, options);
```

That would take the same data only rendered into a line chart (the `LineChart` object).

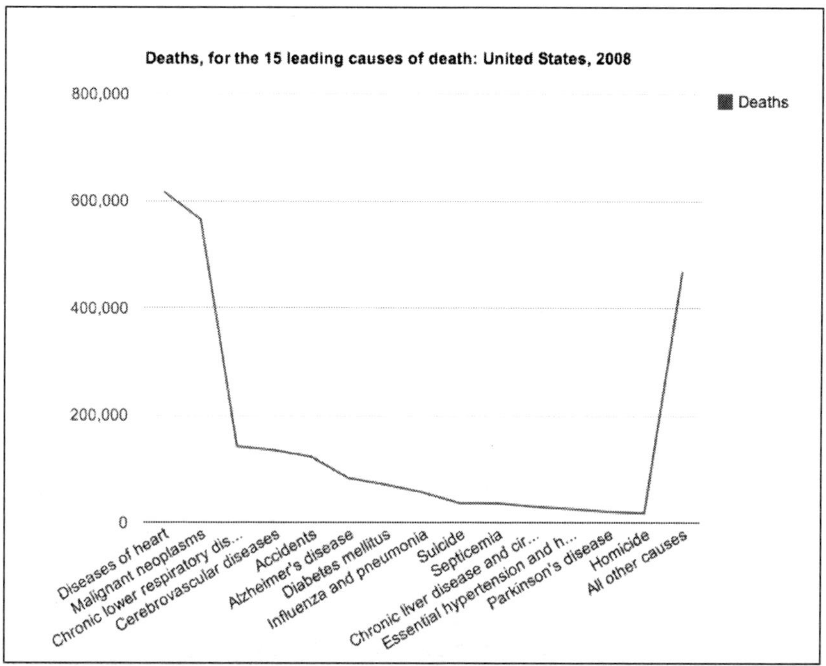

Creating charts using the ChartWrapper

There are two ways to create charts with Google Charts. One is the way we did it in the recipe *Getting started with a pie chart* and the second will be covered in this recipe. The goal of the ChartWrapper object is to enable you to cut down the amount of code needed to create a chart.

Its main advantages are less code and more flexibility of data sources. Its disadvantage is less control over the steps of graph creation.

Getting ready

Grab the HTML file from the last recipe (*Getting started with pie charts*). We will only modify the file path of the external JavaScript file and the rest of the code will remain the same.

How to do it...

After changing the path of the HTML file source to the JavaScript file, it's time to go into the JavaScript file and start over:

1. Load Google API (you do not need to mention what you want to load any more) and add a callback:

   ```
   google.load('visualization', '1.0');
   google.setOnLoadCallback(init);
   ```

2. Create the `init` function:

   ```
   function init(){
   ...
   }
   ```

3. Build a 2D array with the data source:

   ```
   var dataTable = [
           ['Type of Death','Deaths'],
           ['Diseases of heart', 616828],
           ['Malignant neoplasms', 565469],
           ['Chronic lower respiratory diseases', 141090],
           ['Cerebrovascular diseases', 134148],
           ['Accidents ', 121902],
           ['Alzheimer\'s disease ', 82435],
           ['Diabetes mellitus', 70553],
           ['Influenza and pneumonia', 56284],
           ['Suicide', 36035],
           ['Septicemia', 35927],
           ['Chronic liver disease and cirrhosis', 29963],
           ['Essential hypertension and hypertensive renal
           disease', 25742],
           ['Parkinson\'s disease', 20483],
           ['Homicide', 17826],
           ['All other causes', 469062]
         ];
   ```

4. Create the `options` object:

```
var options = {'title':'Deaths, for the 15 leading causes of
death: United States, 2008',
                     'width':800,
                     'height':600,
                     "is3D": true};
```

5. Build and render the chart:

```
var chart = new google.visualization.ChartWrapper({
  chartType:'PieChart',
  dataTable:dataTable,
  options:options,
  containerId:'chart'

});
chart.draw();
```

You've completed the creation of this chart type. Refresh your screen and you will see the same chart as in the last example, only using less code.

How it works...

The nice thing about this example is you don't need to know much more about how it works. The `ChartWrapper` function itself deals with all the information that you've had to deal with in the last recipe. With that said, it doesn't mean this way is always the better way—if you need more control over the steps, the last example would work better.

There's more...

As this recipe was very easy, let's add an extra pointer.

Changing a chart in one line

It's really easy changing between the types of views of the Google Chart API. All you need to do is switch the type. Let's change our chart to a `BarChart`:

```
var chart = new google.visualization.ChartWrapper({
  chartType:'BarChart',
  dataTable:dataTable,
  options:options,
  containerId:'chart'

});
```

Refresh your window and you will find a bar chart.

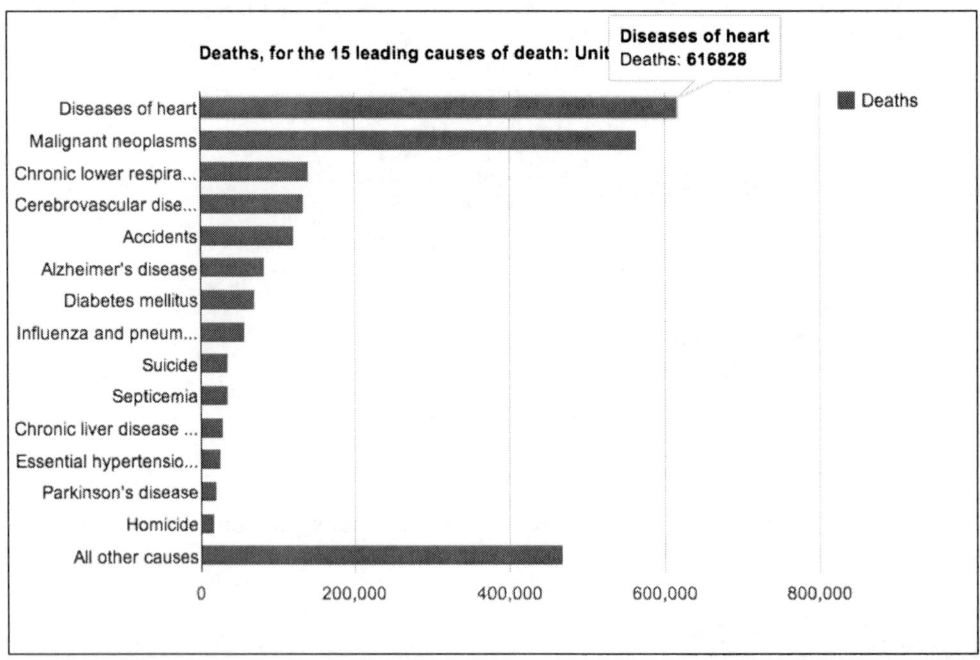

Changing data source to Google Spreadsheet

One of the powerful features of working with the Google API is the deep relationship between the product lines. In this recipe, based on the last recipe, we will create a Google Spreadsheet and then integrate it into our application.

Getting ready

Have a copy around you of the source files from the last recipe (*Creating charts using the ChartWrapper*).

How to do it...

The steps involved with creating a new Google document are simple, but are needed to be able to integrate our work; as such we will run through them quickly.

1. Go to `http://drive.google.com/` (formally known as Google Docs) and register/login.

2. Create a new spreadsheet.
3. Add data to the spreadsheet.

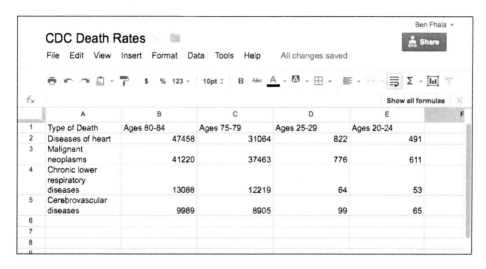

CDC Death Rates

	A	B	C	D	E
1	Type of Death	Ages 80-84	Ages 75-79	Ages 25-29	Ages 20-24
2	Diseases of heart	47458	31064	822	491
3	Malignant neoplasms	41220	37463	776	611
4	Chronic lower respiratory diseases	13088	12219	64	53
5	Cerebrovascular diseases	9989	8905	99	65

4. Click on the **Share** button and set the view to public:

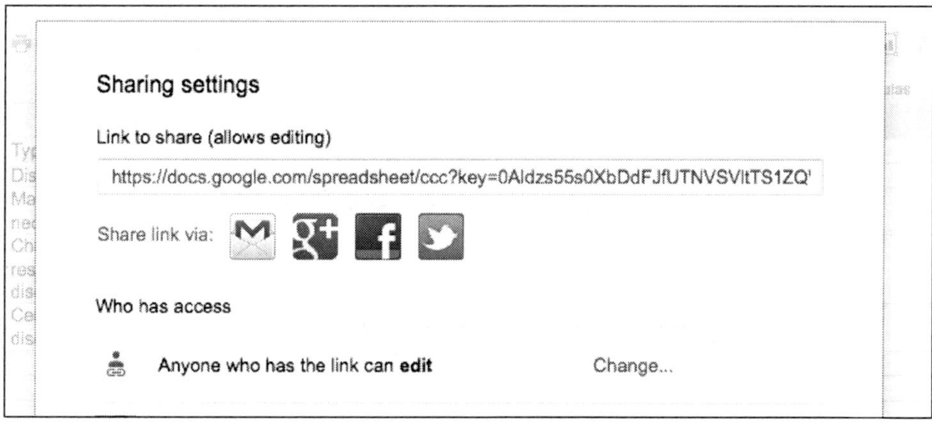

5. Create an API URL based on the document ID:
   - **Document link**:

     `https://docs.google.com/spreadsheet/ccc?key=0Aldzs55s0XbDdFJfUTNVSVltTS1ZQWQ0bWNsX2xSbVE`

   - **API link**:

     `https://spreadsheets.google.com/tq?key=0Aldzs55s0XbDdFJfUTNVSVltTS1ZQWQ0bWNsX2xSbVE`

6. Now, it's time to get into our JavaScript file, and delete the current data source and replace it with a URL feed:

```
google.load('visualization', '1.0');

google.setOnLoadCallback(init);

function init(){
  var options = {'title':'Deaths, for the 15 leading
  causes of death: United States, 2008',
                   'width':800,
                   'height':600};
  var chart = new google.visualization.ChartWrapper({
    chartType:'BarChart',
    dataSourceUrl:"https://spreadsheets.google.com/
    tq?key=0Aldzs55s0XbDdFJfUTNVSVltTS1ZQWQ0bWNsX2xSbVE",
    options:options,
    containerId:'chart'

  });
  chart.draw();
}
```

Amazing! See how little code we needed to create a rich and fully interactive chart:

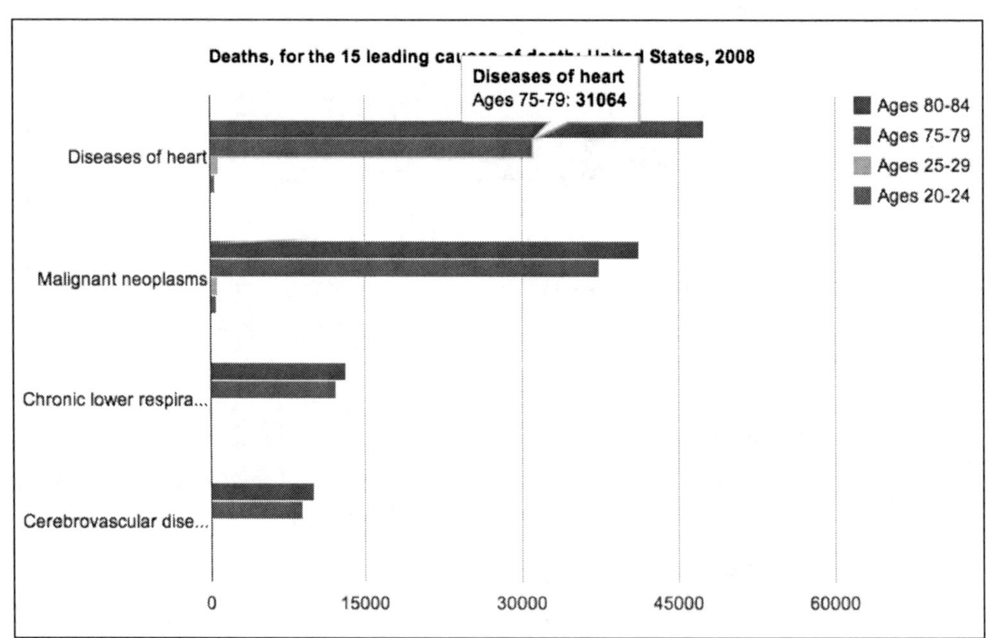

How it works...

This is really the amazing part about it. You just don't need to understand how it works, all you need to do is create your chart and use the steps provided in the preceding section, and you can convert any of your own spreadsheets into a Google Spreadsheet.

The most important step in the preceding steps is step 4. Notice that the URL that is generated through the Google Documents (Google Drive) is not the same as the URL that we need to hit when working in code. This is because the first URL is intended to be rendered as a visual page, while the second link generates a new Google data object. Don't forget that every page has its own unique ID.

There's more...

If you have a bit of a background with working with databases, you can send simple SQL queries into the data source and only get the items that you want to view. Let's say in our example we want to get the items in a different order, exclude column B, and sort based on column D (by age):

```
SELECT A,E,D,C ORDER BY D
```

Our `Select` statement is listing out what we want to select. The `ORDER BY` statement is self-explanatory. Let's add it to our code:

```
var chart = new google.visualization.ChartWrapper({
  chartType:'BarChart',
  dataSourceUrl:"https://spreadsheets.google.com/
  tq?key=0Aldzs55s0XbDdFJfUTNVSVltTS1ZQWQ0bWNsX2xSbVE",
  query: 'SELECT A,E,D,C ORDER BY D',
  options:options,
  containerId:'chart'

});
```

When you refresh your code, column B will be missing and the data will be organized based on column D.

Last but not least, add this to your code:

```
var chart = new google.visualization.ChartWrapper({
  chartType:'BarChart',
  dataSourceUrl:"https://spreadsheets.google.com/
  tq?key=0Aldzs55s0XbDdFJfUTNVSVltTS1ZQWQ0bWNsX2xSbVE",
  query: 'SELECT A,E,D,C ORDER BY D',
  refreshInterval: 1,
```

```
    options:options,
    containerId:'chart'

  });
  chart.draw();
```

Now go back to the public chart and change the data in it. You will see that it will automatically update the chart.

Customizing the chart properties with an options object

In this recipe, we will create a new chart with Google Charts API—a candlestick chart—and we will incorporate a variety of configurations into it.

Getting ready

We will start with a clean slate by creating a fresh new JavaScript and an HTML file.

How to do it...

Most of the steps will look almost identical to the past recipes in this chapter. Our main focus will be on our `options` parameters:

1. Create an HTML file and link it to a JavaScript file (in our case `08.04.candlestick.js`):

```
<!DOCTYPE html>
<html>
  <head>
    <title>Google Charts Getting Started</title>
    <meta charset="utf-8" />
    <script src="https://www.google.com/jsapi"></script>
    <script src="./08.04.candlestick.js"></script>
  </head>
  <body style="background:#fafafa">
    <div id="chart"></div>
  </body>
</html>
```

2. In the `08.04.candlestick.js` file, add the API `load` and `callback` functions:

```
google.load('visualization', '1', {packages: ['corechart']});
google.setOnLoadCallback(init);

function init(){
```

3. In the `init` function (from now until the end of this recipe we will remain in the `init` function), create a new `DataTable` object by using the `google.visualization.arrayToDataTable` method:

```
var data = google.visualization.arrayToDataTable([
  ['Mon', 10, 24, 18, 21],
  ['Tue', 31, 38, 55, 74],
  ['Wed', 50, 55, 20, 103],
  ['Thu', 77, 77, 77, 77],
  ['Fri', 68, 66, 22, 15]
], true);
```

4. Create an `options` object (a configuration object) for the chart:

```
var options = {
  legend:'none',
  backgroundColor:{fill:'#eeeeee',strokeWidth:2},
  bar:{groupWidth:17},
  candlestick:{hollowIsRising:true,
    fallingColor:{stroke:'red',fill:'#ffaaaa'},
    risingColor: {stroke:'blue',fill:'#aaaaff'}
  },
  enableInteractivity:false

};
```

5. Draw the chart by using the following code snippet:

```
var chart = new google.visualization.CandlestickChart
(document.getElementById('chart'));
chart.draw(data, options);
```

```
}
```

When you load the HTML file, you will discover a customized candlestick chart, as shown in the following screenshot:

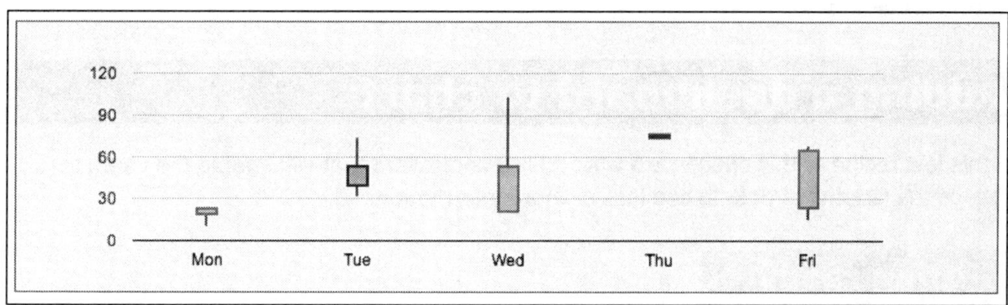

How it works...

This is the first time that we have used the method `google.visualization.arrayToDataTable`. This method takes in an array and returns a data table. When the second parameter of this method is set to `true`, it will treat the first row in the array as part of the data; and otherwise it will be treated as header data.

There are many options and for a full list of them, review Google Charts documentation. We will focus on the items that we have picked to modify our view. The Google charts enable you to send an object with parameters. Each chart type has a different set of options. In our case, we have many options that enable us to control the details of how our chart looks. Most of the options are style related:

```
backgroundColor:{fill:'#eeeeee',strokeWidth:2},
  bar:{groupWidth:17},
  candlestick:{hollowIsRising:true,
   fallingColor:{stroke:'red',fill:'#ffaaaa'},
  risingColor: {stroke:'blue',fill:'#aaaaff'}
  },
```

Some options directly relate to the function such as disabling the legend:

```
legend:'none',
```

Or disabling interactive elements:

```
enableInteractivity:false
```

There's more...

The main goal of highlighting this element is not because it's difficult, but because it's easy, and it is the main place where you would find yourself making changes to the charts. One point to note is that it is really important to check that you can do what you need by using Google Charts before working with them, as contrary to other chart systems, you can't go into their source files and change them, as we did in the recipes in *Chapter 7, Depending on the Open Source Sphere*.

Adding a dashboard to charts

In this last recipe of this chapter we will add live controllers that will enable the users to change the filtering of data to see less or more information.

Getting ready

We will start from scratch so nothing to worry about.

How to do it...

The following are the steps needed to create a basic dashboard controller:

1. Create an HTML file and link it to an external JavaScript file (in our case we will use the file `08.05.slider.js`):

```
<!DOCTYPE html>
<html>
  <head>
    <title>Google Charts DASHBOARD</title>
    <meta charset="utf-8" />
    <script src="https://www.google.com/jsapi"></script>
    <script src="./08.05.slider.js"></script>
  </head>
  <body style="background:#fafafa">
    <div id="chart"></div>
    <div id="dashboard"></div>
    <div id="filter"></div>
  </body>
</html>
```

2. Now, it's time to get into `08.05.slider.js` and to load the Google Visualization API. This time around we will load in the controller package:

```
google.load('visualization', '1', {packages: ['controls']});
```

3. Now, it's time to add a callback:

```
google.setOnLoadCallback(init);
function init(){
```

4. Let's create our data source. We will base it on CDC death rates for 2008:

```
var data = google.visualization.arrayToDataTable([
    ['Age (+- 2 Years)', 'Deaths'],
        [2, 4730],
        [7, 2502],
        [12, 3149],
        [17, 12407],
        [22, 19791],
        [27,20786],
        [32,21489],
        [37,29864],
        [42,46506],
        [47,77417],
```

```
            [52, 109125],
            [57,134708],
            [62,161474],
            [67,183450],
            [72,218129],
            [77,287370],
            [82,366190],
            [87,372552],
            [92,251381],
             [100,20892],
        ]);
```

5. Then create a new dashboard:

```
var dashboard = new google.visualization.Dashboard(document.
getElementById('dashboard'));
```

6. Let's create a slider and provide it with the information it needs to connect to the data source:

```
  var slider = new google.visualization.ControlWrapper({
    containerId: 'filter',
    controlType: 'NumberRangeFilter',
    options: {
    filterColumnLabel: 'Age (+- 2 Years)'
  }
});
```

7. Create a chart:

```
var chart = new google.visualization.ChartWrapper({
  chartType: 'ScatterChart',
  containerId: 'chart',
  options: {
    legend: 'left',
    title:'Deaths, for the 15 leading causes of death:
    United States, 2008',
    width: 800,
    height: 600

  }
});
```

8. Last but not least, it's time to bind and draw our controller:

```
dashboard.bind(slider, chart).draw(data);
}
```

Load the HTML file and you will discover a scatter chart with a controller that enables you to select the age range that you want to dig deeper into.

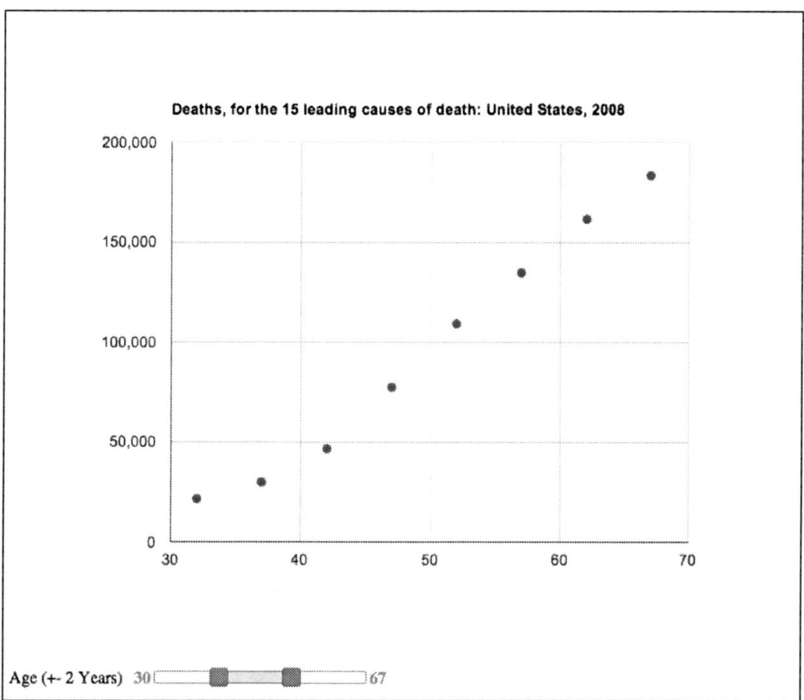

How it works...

This is probably one of the smoothest parts of working with the Google Charting API. So let's break down and figure out the steps involved in creating controllers for your chart. We will showcase one controller, but the same logic flow would work for all components.

First in our HTML file, we need to have a `div` layer with an ID associated for our dashboard and a `div` for each following controller. To add controllers we assign them to the dashboard. We start with creating a dashboard:

```
var dashboard = new google.visualization.Dashboard(document.
getElementById('dashboard'));
```

This dashboard is now going to be our hub where we connect all of our controllers (in our case, one controller). Then, we will create the next controller; in our case, we want to use a slider:

```
var slider = new google.visualization.ControlWrapper({
  containerId: 'filter',
  controlType: 'NumberRangeFilter',
  options: {
    filterColumnLabel: 'Age (+- 2 Years)'
  }
});
```

Notice that we are adding a control type to get our range slider and we are linking it to a column by giving it the column ID (the label in the first row).

We continue and create a chart in the same way as before. In this case we picked a scatter chart. The order here isn't important, but the most important part left is to link between our controller and the chart. We do that by using the `dashboard.bind` method:

```
dashboard.bind(slider, chart);
```

Then, we draw our element as our dashboard returns itself when a `bind` function is created:

```
dashboard.bind(slider, chart).draw(data);
```

If we want, we can split this into separate lines as follows:

```
dashboard.bind(slider, chart);
dashboard.draw(data);
```

And there you go! Now you know how to work with dashboards. These steps are critical, but you can now add any controller. The rest of the documentation for this product is self-explanatory.

9
Using Google Maps

In this chapter we will cover:

- Creating a geographic chart with the Google Visualization API
- Obtaining a Google API key
- Building a Google map
- Adding markers and events
- Customizing controls and overlapping maps
- Redesigning maps using styles

Introduction

This chapter will be dedicated to exploring some of the features available on Google Maps to get us ready to work with mapping in general. Mapping on its own isn't data visualization, but after we establish our base by understanding how to work with maps, we will have a very stable background that will enable us to create many cutting-edge, cool projects by integrating data and data visualization.

In this chapter, we will explore the main ways to create maps in the Google sphere.

Creating a geographic chart with Google Visualization API

In our first recipe for this chapter, we will start working with a vector-based map of the world. We will use it to highlight countries based on a data feed. In our case, we will use Wikipedia's list of countries as per the intentional homicide rate (latest numbers).

To view this raw data go to `http://en.wikipedia.org/wiki/List_of_countries_by_intentional_homicide_rate`.

Our goal will be to have a map of the world highlighted with a range of colors according to the number of intentional homicides per 100,000 people. As of the latest data in 2012 according to Wikipedia, it sounds like the most unsafe place to live in is Honduras—if you don't want to be intentionally killed—while you should feel really safe from intentional killing in Japan. How is your country doing? Mine is not that bad. I should probably avoid my local news stations that make me feel like I'm living in a war zone.

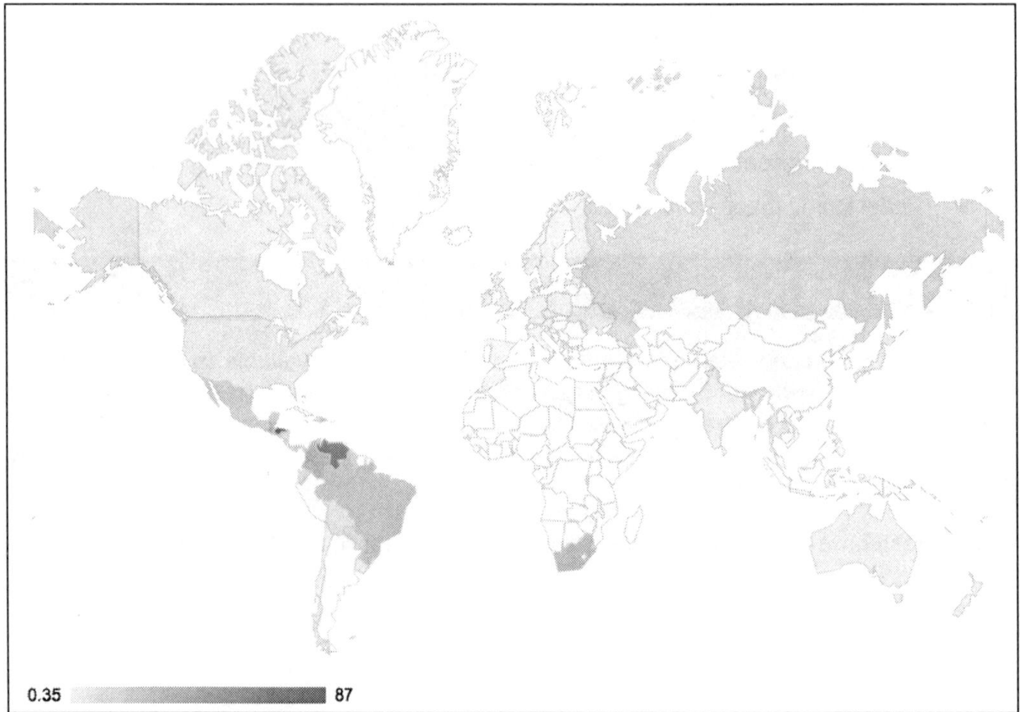

Getting ready

There isn't much that you need to do. We will be using the Google Visualization API for creating a geographic chart.

How to do it...

We will create a new HTML and a new JavaScript file and call them `08.01.geo-chart.html` and `08.01.geo-chart.js`. Follow these steps:

1. In the HTML file add the following code:

```
<!DOCTYPE html>
<html>
  <head>
    <title>Geo Charts</title>
    <meta charset="utf-8" />
    <script src="http://www.google.com/jsapi"></script>
    <script src="./08.01.geo-chart.js"></script>
  </head>
  <body style="background:#fafafa">
    <div id="chart"></div>
  </body>
</html>
```

2. Let's move to the `js` file. This time around we will want to request from the Google Visualization package the `geochart` functionality. To do that we will start our code, as follows:

```
google.load('visualization','1',{'packages': ['geochart']});
```

3. We'll then add a callback that will trigger the `init` function when the package is ready:

```
google.setOnLoadCallback(init);
function init(){
 //...
}
```

4. Now it's time to add the logic within the `init` function. In the first step, we will format the data from Wikipedia to another format that will work for the Google Visualization API:

```
var data = google.visualization.arrayToDataTable([
    ['Country','Intentional Homicide Rate per 100,000'],
    ['Honduras',87],['El Salvador',71],['Saint Kitts and
    Nevis',68],
    ['Venezuela',67],['Belize',39],['Guatemala',39],
    ['Jamaica',39],
    ['Bahamas',36],['Colombia',33],['South Africa', 32],
    ['Dominican Republic',31],['Trinidad and
    Tobago',28],['Brazil',26],
    ['Dominica', 22],['Saint Lucia',22],
    ['Saint Vincent and the Grenadines',22],
```

```
        ['Panama',20],['Guyana',18],['Mexico',18],
        ['Ecuador',16],
        ['Nicaragua',13],['Grenada',12],
        ['Paraguay',12],['Russia',12],
        ['Barbados',11],['Costa Rica',10 ],['Bolivia',8.9],
        ['Estonia',7.5],['Moldova',7.4],['Haiti',6.9],
        ['Antigua and
        Barbuda',6.8],['Uruguay',6.1],['Thailand',5.3],
        ['Ukraine',5.2],['United States',4.7 ],
        ['Georgia',4.1],['Latvia',4.1 ],
        ['India',3.2],['Taiwan',3.0 ],['Bangladesh',2.4 ],
        ['Lebanon',2.2],
        ['Finland',2.1 ],['Israel', 2.1],
        ['Macedonia',1.94 ],['Canada',1.7],
        ['Czech Republic',1.67],
        ['New Zealand',1.41],['Morocco',1.40 ],
        ['Chile',1.33],
        ['United Kingdom',1.23 ],['Australia',1.16],
        ['Poland',1.1 ],['Ireland',0.96 ],
        ['Italy',.87 ],['Netherlands',.86 ],
        ['Sweden',.86],
        ['Denmark',.85],['Germany',.81 ],['Spain',0.72],
        ['Norway',0.68],['Austria',0.56],['Japan',.35]
]);
```

5. Let's configure our chart options:

```
var options = {width:800,height:600};
```

6. Last but definitely not the least, let's create our chart:

```
 var chart = new google.visualization.GeoChart(document.
getElementById('chart'));
  chart.draw(data,options);
}//end of init function
```

When you load the HTML file, you will find the countries of the world with highlighted colors that reflect the homicide rate. (We don't have a full list of all the countries of the world, and some countries are so small that it will be hard to find them.)

How it works...

The logic of this recipe is very simple, so let's quickly dash through it and add some extra features. As in all the other visualization charts, there are three separate steps:

- Defining the data source
- Setting up the chart
- Drawing the chart

Not all countries are alike. If you are having issues while working with a country that is outlined, search through the latest Google documents on the supported countries. For the full list, you can check the sheet available at `http://gmaps-samples.googlecode.com/svn/trunk/mapcoverage_filtered.html`.

There's more...

Let's add some extra customization to our chart. As with all Google Visualization library elements, we can control many visuals through the `options` object.

The green color highlighted in our map just seems wrong. You would think that the less the killings the greener a country would be, so where the killings are more, a darker shade of red would be more appropriate. So let's change the colors by updating the `options` object:

```
var options = {width:800,height:600,
  colorAxis: {colors: ['#eeffee', 'red']}
    };
```

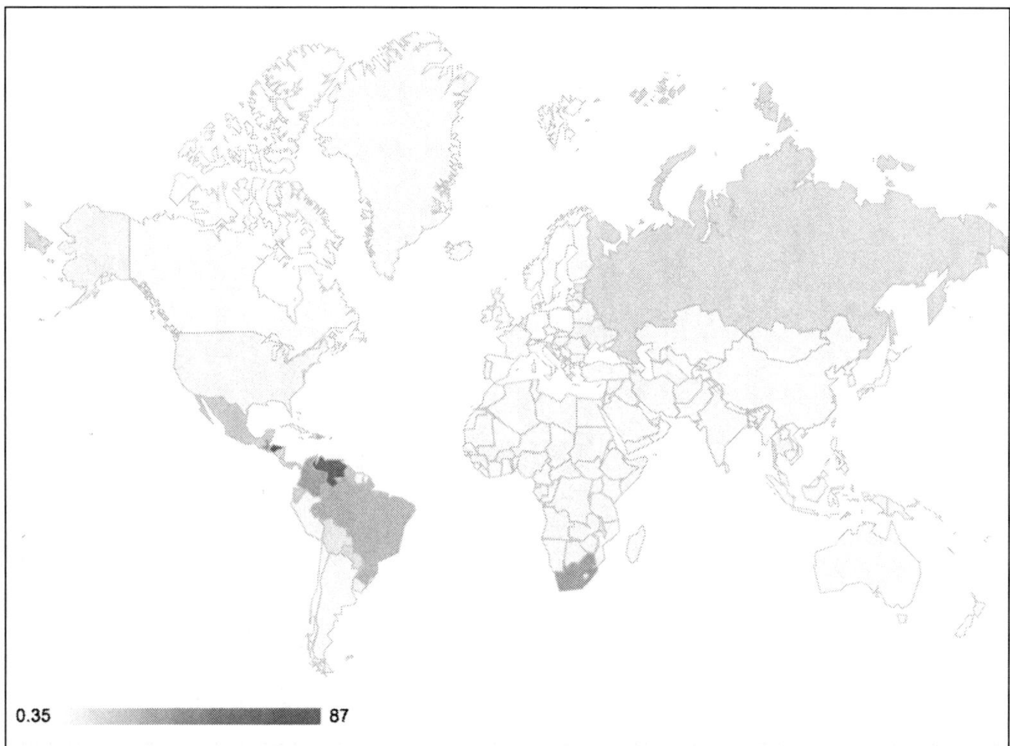

Making smaller areas more visible

To solve the problem of really small invisible countries, we can switch our rendering to be marker based. Instead of highlighting the land itself, we can switch to a marker-based rendering mode:

```
var options = {width:800,height:600,
    displayMode: 'markers',
        colorAxis: {colors: ['#22ff22', 'red']}
      };
```

By default when rendering visualization maps with markers, when you roll over condensed areas, a highlight zoom view will help create a clearer view:

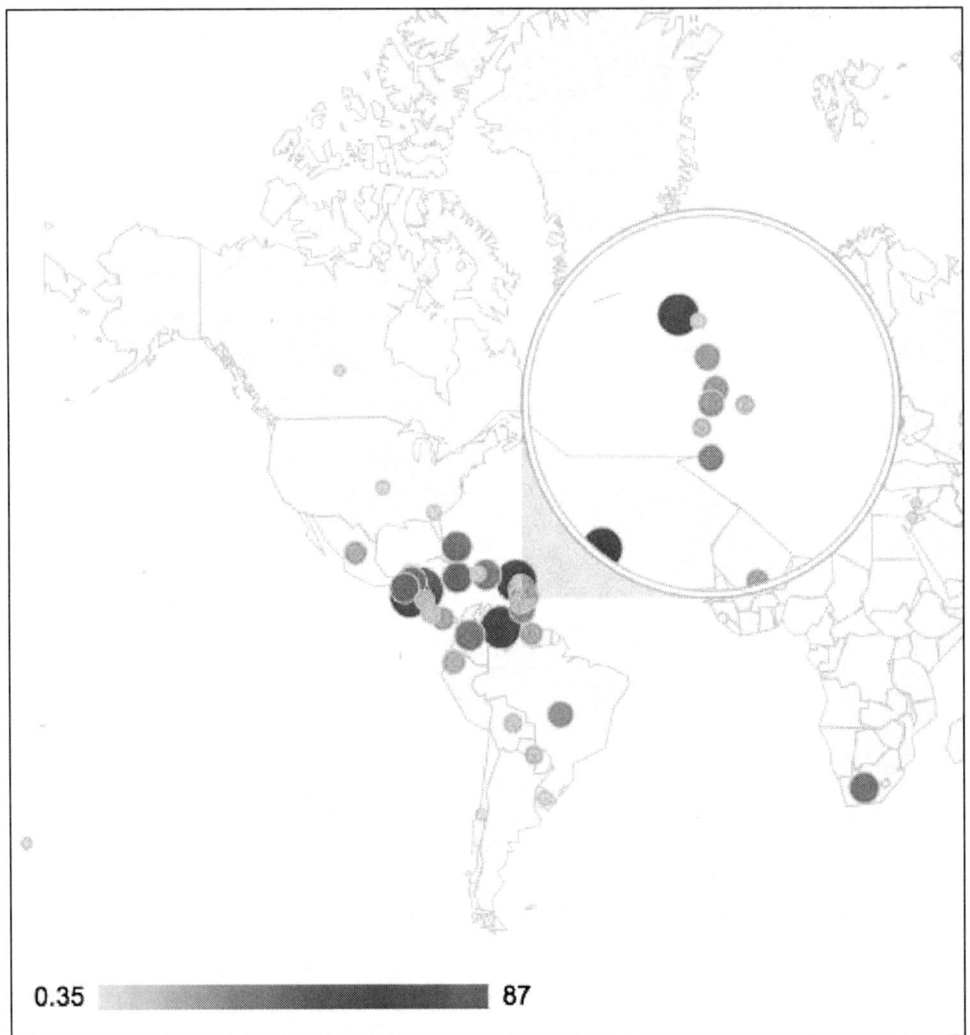

Another option instead would be to zoom into the area (we can do both or just zoom in). To zoom into an area we will use this code:

```
var options = {width:800,height:600,
  region:'MX',
     colorAxis: {colors: ['#22ff22', 'red']}
   };
```

To find out the list of possible values, refer back to the list of countries from earlier in this chapter. In this case we are zooming into the `MX` region:

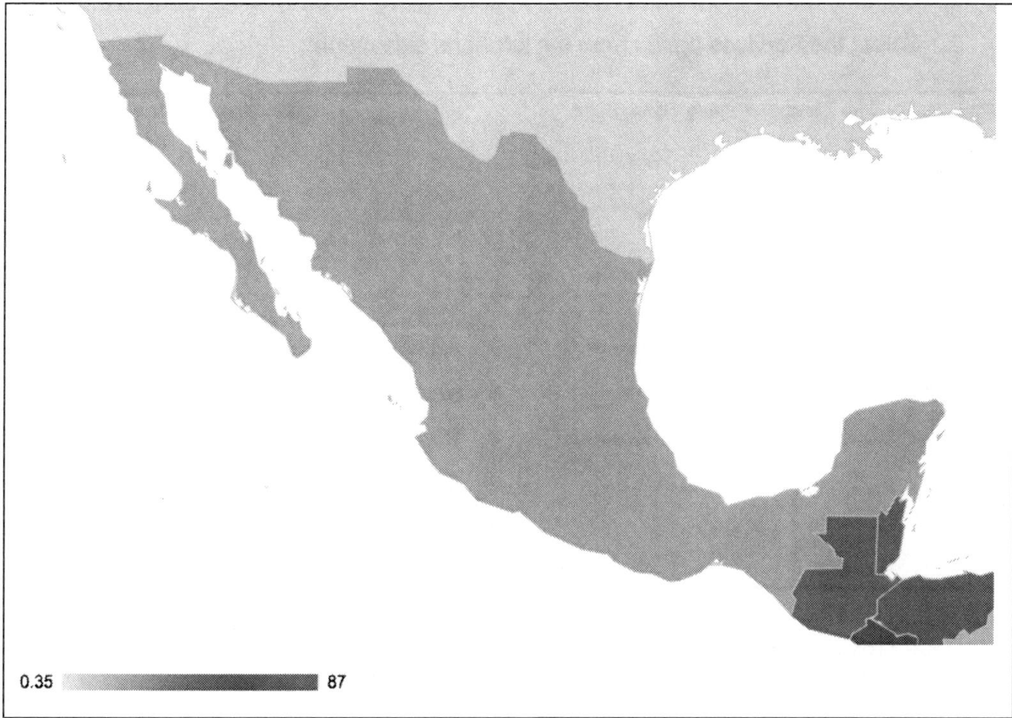

That covers the basics of working with a geographical chart. For more information on working with the Google Visualization API, please refer back to *Chapter 8, Playing with Google Charts*.

Obtaining a Google API key

To work with most of the Google APIs, you must have a Google API key. As such we will go through the steps involved in getting a Google API key.

Google API has certain limitations and constraints. Although most of the APIs are free to use for small- to medium-sized sites, you are bound by some rules. Please refer to each library for its rules and regulations.

Getting ready

To get through this recipe you must have a Google ID; if you do not have one, you will need to create one.

How to do it...

Let's list the steps required to gain access to the Google API:

1. Log in to the API console at `https://code.google.com/apis/console`.
2. Select the **Services** option from the left-hand side menu:

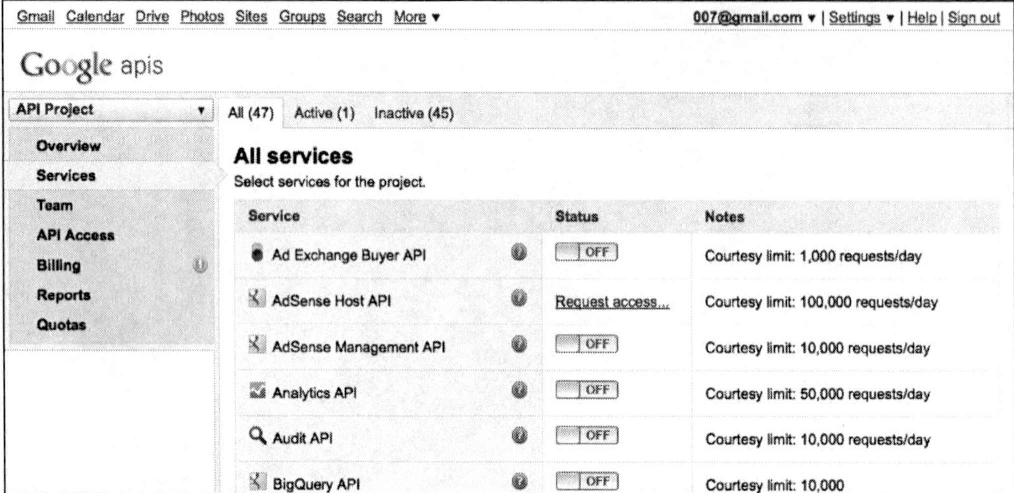

3. Activate the API that you want to use (for example, in the next recipe *Building a Google map* we will use the Google Maps API v3 service):

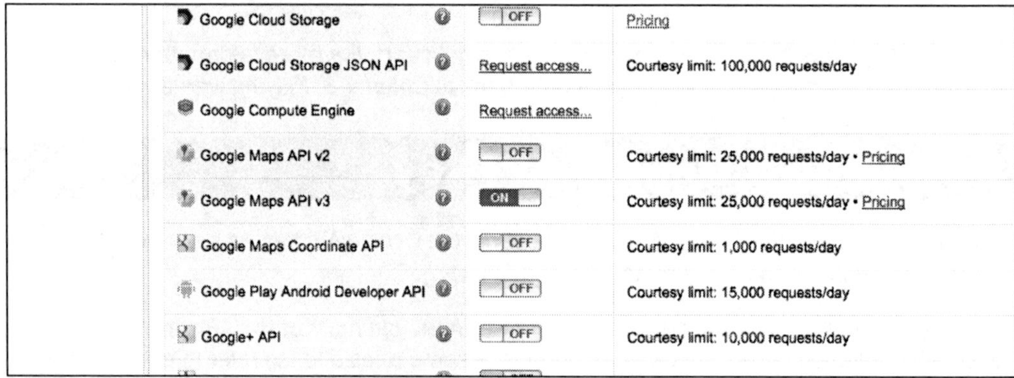

4. Again in the left-hand side menu select the **API Access** option. You will have to copy the **API key** and replace it in future Google API projects:

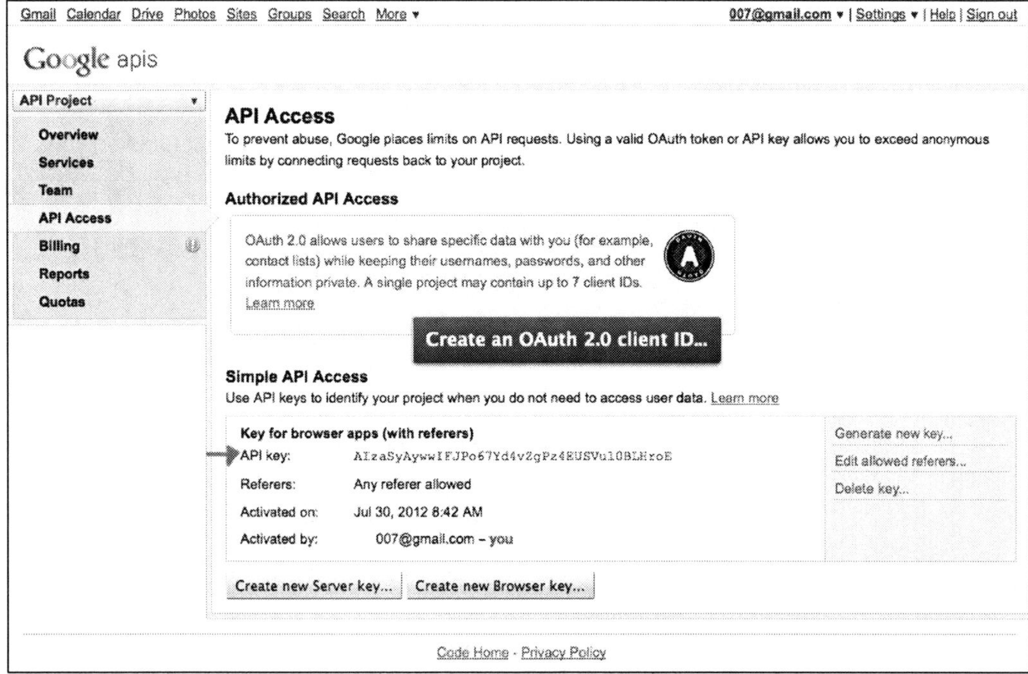

This is the only time we will be talking about keys and permissions for working with the Google API platforms. Please validate that you have activated a key and also set the right libraries to be accessible to you.

How it works...

It's not hard to understand how this works. You just need to remember the steps as they will be the baseline of the future Google API interactions that we create.

As you must have noticed, there are many more API's in the Google library than we could even go through, but I do recommend that you scan through them and explore your options. In the next few recipes, we will be using the Google API to perform some mapping-related tasks.

Building a Google map

Data and geography have a very natural relation. Data has more meaning when it's on a map. Using live maps is a very good option as it would enable the users to interact with a UI that is integrated with your own data presentations within the geographic area. In this recipe, we will integrate our first, real live map.

Getting ready

To get through this recipe, you must have a Google ID. If you do not have one, you will need to create one. Beyond that you will need to activate the Google Maps API v3 service in the API Console. For more information on this, please review the recipe *Obtaining a Google API key* discussed earlier in this chapter.

Our goal will be to create a full-screen Google map that will be zoomed in and focused on France:

How to do it...

Let's list the steps to create this sample. To create this sample we will create two files—a `.html` file and a `.js` file:

1. Let's start with the HTML file. We'll create a basic HTML file baseline for our project:

```
<!DOCTYPE html>
<html>
  <head>
    <title>Google Maps Hello world</title>
    <meta charset="utf-8" />
  </head>
  <body>
    <div id="jsmap"></div>
  </body>
</html>
```

2. We will add to the HTML viewport information. This is the direction for mobile devices on how to render the page (this step can be skipped if you don't care about accessing the maps in mobile devices):

```
<head>
  <title>Google Maps Hello world</title>
  <meta charset="utf-8" />
  <meta name="viewport" content="initial-scale=1.0,
  user-scalable=no" />
</head>
```

3. Add the style information into the header:

```
<style>
  html { height: 100% }
  body { height: 100%; margin: 0; padding: 0 }
  #jsmap { height: 100%; width:100% }
</style>
```

4. Load in Google Maps v3 API (replace the bolded text with your API key):

```
<script src="http://maps.googleapis.com/maps/api/js?key=ADD_YOUR_
KEY&sensor=true">
```

5. Add the script source for our `09.03.googleJSmaps.js` JavaScript file:

```
<script src="./09.03.googleJSmaps.js"></script>
```

6. Add an `onload` trigger that will call the `init` function (this is to be created in the next step):

```
<body onload="init();">
```

7. In the `09.03.googleJSmaps.js` JavaScript file, add the `init` function:

```
function init() {
  var mapOptions = {
    center: new google.maps.LatLng(45.52, 0),
    zoom: 7,
    mapTypeId: google.maps.MapTypeId.ROADMAP
  };
  var map = new
  google.maps.Map(document.getElementById("jsmap"),
  mapOptions);
}
```

8. Load the HTML file, and you should find a full-screen roadmap zoomed into France.

How it works...

The most important and first step is loading the `maps` API. For Google to honor your request, you must have a valid API key. As such, don't forget to replace the bolded text with your key:

```
<script src="http://maps.googleapis.com/maps/api/js?key=YOUR_
KEY&sensor=true">
```

Don't forget to use your own key. You might find yourself with a site that has a broken map. The `sensor` parameter in the URL is mandatory and must be set to `true` or `false`. If your map needs to know where the user location is, you must set it to `true`, and if not you may set it to `false`.

Another interesting thing to note in our application is that it's the first time we have used the viewport in our samples. As this topic is out of the scope of this book, I wanted to leave it. I know that many of you will end up using maps in mobile devices and will want to have the map default to a vertical/horizontal view. To learn more on how viewports work, check out the article available at: `https://developer.mozilla.org/en/Mobile/Viewport_meta_tag/`.

You must have noticed that we set many things in our CSS to be 100 percent, and as you probably guessed, it was for backward compatibility and validating that the map will fill the entire screen. If you just want to create a hard-set width/height, you may do so by replacing the CSS with the following code:

```
<style>
    #jsmap { height: 200px; width:300px; }
</style>
```

That covers the main things we need to do in the HTML file.

There's more...

We haven't yet covered the details of how the `init` function works. The basics of the `init` function are very simple. There are only two steps involved with creating a map. We need to know what `div` layer we want the map to be in and what options we want sent to our map:

```
var map = new google.maps.Map(div,options);
```

Contrary to the Google Visualization API that had three steps in the last recipe, we can see that the Google `maps` API has only one step and within it we send the two options directly to be rendered (there is no step between creating and rendering).

Let's take a deeper look into the options as they are what will change the majority of the visuals and functionality of the map.

Working with latitude and longitude

Latitude and longitude (**lat/long**) is a coordinate system that divides the Earth into a grid-like pattern, making it easy to locate points on the Earth. The lat represents the vertical space while the long represents the horizontal space. It's important to note that Google uses the World Geodetic System WGS84 standard. There are other standards out there, so if you don't use the same standard with your lat/long, you will find yourself at a different location from what you were originally looking for.

The easiest way to locate areas based on lat/long is through a helper tool on our map or through searching for the lat/long information of major cities.

`http://www.gorissen.info/Pierre/maps/googleMapLocation.php` will help you locate a dot by clicking on the Google map directly. Another option in this category is to turn on the labs feature in the main Google Map site (`http://maps.google.com/`). In the main Google Map site on the bottom-left side of the screen, you will find **Map Labs**. In there you will find a few lat/long helpers.

Or you can search the data per city by visiting `http://www.realestate3d.com/gps/latlong.htm`.

In our case when we are ready to make our pick, we will update the `options center` property to reflect where we want the map to be centered and adjust the zoom level until it feels right:

```
var mapOptions = {
    center: new google.maps.LatLng(45.52, 0),
    zoom: 7,
    mapTypeId: google.maps.MapTypeId.ROADMAP
};
```

Map types

There are many map types, and you can even create your own custom ones, but for our needs we will focus on the basic ones that are used most often:

- `google.maps.MapTypeId.ROADMAP`: Displays the normal, default 2D tiles of Google maps
- `google.maps.MapTypeId.SATELLITE`: Displays the photographic tiles
- `google.maps.MapTypeId.HYBRID`: Displays a mix of photographic tiles and a tile layer for prominent features (roads, city names, and so on)
- `google.maps.MapTypeId.TERRAIN`: Displays physical relief tiles for displaying elevation and water features (mountains, rivers, and so on)

This covers the basics that you need to know to get rolling with integrating maps onto a site.

Adding markers and events

It's great that we have a map on our screen (assuming that you have followed the last recipe *Building a Google map*), but what about connecting data and integrating it into our map. I'm glad you asked about that, as this recipe will be our first step into adding data in the form of markers and events.

In this sample, our goal is to place four markers in New York City. When the markers are clicked, we will zoom into that area and switch the map view type.

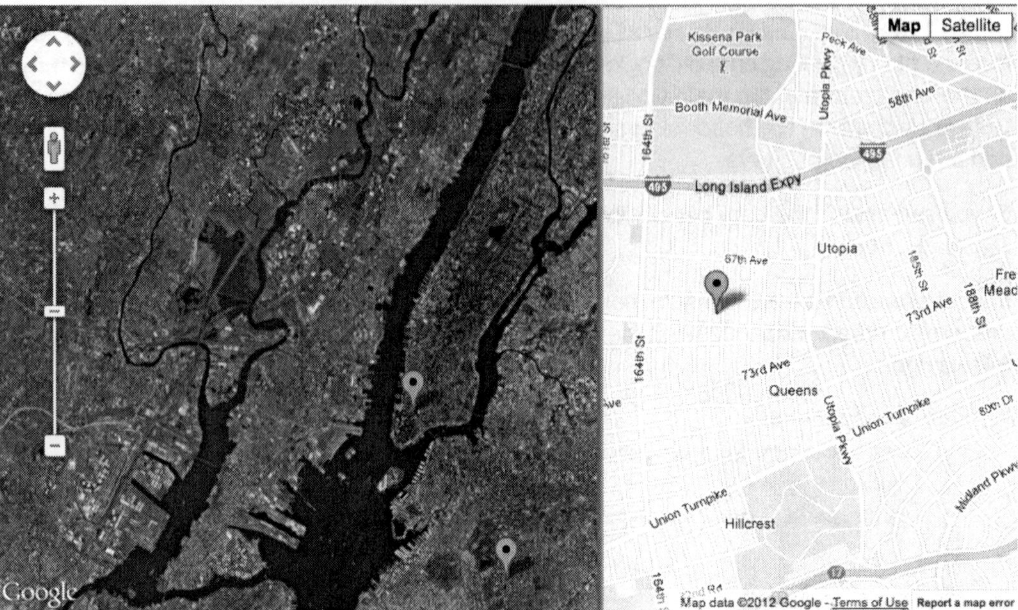

Getting ready

At this stage, you should have created (at least once) a Google map by using the JS API; if you haven't, please revert back to the *Building a Google map* recipe.

How to do it...

We are not making any further changes in the HTML page created in the last recipe *Building a Google map*; as such we will focus our attention on the JavaScript file:

1. Create an `init` function:

```
function init(){
//all the rest of logic in here
}
```

2. Create map constants in the `base` state and then zoom in on the state:

```
function init() {
  var BASE_CENTER = new google.maps.LatLng(40.7142,-
  74.0064 );
  var BASE_ZOOM = 11;
  var BASE_MAP_TYPE = google.maps.MapTypeId.SATELLITE;
  var INNER_ZOOM = 14;
  var INNER_MAP_TYPE = google.maps.MapTypeId.ROADMAP;
```

3. Create the default map options:

```
//40.7142° N, -74.0064 E NYC
var mapOptions = {
  center: BASE_CENTER,
  zoom: BASE_ZOOM,
  mapTypeId: BASE_MAP_TYPE
};
var map = new google.maps.Map(document.getElementById("jsmap"),
mapOptions);
```

4. Create a data source for our points:

```
var aMarkers = [
  {label:'New York City',
  local: map.getCenter()},
  {label:'Brooklyn',
  local: new google.maps.LatLng(40.648, -73.957)},
  {label:'Queens',
  local: new google.maps.LatLng(40.732, -73.800)},
  {label:'Bronx',
  local: new google.maps.LatLng(40.851, -73.871)},

];
```

5. Loop through each array element and create a marker with an event that will zoom to the location, switch the view and pan to the correct location:

```
var marker;

for(var i=0; i<aMarkers.length; i++){
  marker = new google.maps.Marker({
    position: aMarkers[i].local,
    map: map,
    title: aMarkers[i].label
  });
  google.maps.event.addListener(marker, 'click',
  function(ev) {
```

```
            map.setZoom(INNER_ZOOM);
            map.panTo(ev.latLng);
            map.setMapTypeId(INNER_MAP_TYPE);
          });

        }
```

6. Last but not the least, make the map clickable. So when the user clicks on the map, it should reset to its original state:

    ```
    google.maps.event.addListener(map, 'click', function() {
            map.setZoom(BASE_ZOOM);
        map.panTo(BASE_CENTER);
        map.setMapTypeId(BASE_MAP_TYPE);

    });
    ```

When you run the application, you will find four markers on the screen. When you click on them, you will jump into a deeper zoom view. When you click on an empty area, it will take you back to the original view.

How it works...

Working with events and Google Maps is very easy. The steps involved always start from calling the static method `google.maps.event.addListener`. This function takes in three parameters, namely the item to be listened to, the event type (as a string), and a function.

For example, in our `for` loop we create markers and then add events to them:

```
google.maps.event.addListener(marker, 'click', function(ev) {
   map.setZoom(INNER_ZOOM);
   map.panTo(ev.latLng);
   map.setMapTypeId(INNER_MAP_TYPE);
 });
```

Instead we can create the event and then do not need to recreate a new anonymous function each time we loop through:

```
for(var i=0; i<aMarkers.length; i++){
  marker = new google.maps.Marker({
    position: aMarkers[i].local,
    map: map,
    title: aMarkers[i].label
  });

  google.maps.event.addListener(marker, 'click', onMarkerClicked);
```

```
    }

    function onMarkerClicked(ev){
      map.setZoom(INNER_ZOOM);
      map.panTo(ev.latLng);
      map.setMapTypeId(INNER_MAP_TYPE);
    }
```

The advantage is really big. Instead of creating a function for each loop, we are using the same function throughout (smarter and smaller memory footprint). In our code, we are not mentioning any hardcoded values. Instead we are using the event information to get the `latLng` property. We can re-use the same function without any issue. By the way, you might have noticed that this is the first time that we put a named function inside another named function (`init` function). This isn't a problem and it works exactly the same way as the variable scopes work. In other words, this function that we created will have visibility only within the `init` function scope.

The creation of a marker is very simple; all we need to do is create a new `google.maps.Marker` and assign a position and a map to it. All other options are optional. (For a full list, please review the Google API documentation available at `https://developers.google.com/maps/documentation/javascript/reference#MarkerOptions`.)

There's more...

You might have noticed that we use the method `map.panTo`, but no panning actually happens and everything snaps to place. If you run the map, you will discover that we don't actually see any panning; that is because we are switching the map type, zooming out, and panning at the same time. Only panning can actually animate without a few tricks and bypasses, but all these steps make our application a lot more complex and the actual control over animation is very limited. We will come up with a solution to that in the next recipe as we use two maps instead of one in *Customizing controls and overlapping maps*. If we wanted we could add in a delay and do each step separately and animate the pan, but if we want to create a smooth transition, I would think about the idea of having two separate maps, one on top of each other instead, and fading in and out the main world map.

Customizing controls and overlapping maps

The goal of this recipe is to practice working with Google Maps. We will integrate what we learned about working with Google Maps in this chapter and incorporate our control over the user behaviors, such as what controllers the user can use, into it. We will start digging into creating our own unsupported undocumented behaviors, such as locking the users' pan area.

Our main task in this recipe will be to take our work from the previous recipe, and instead of having the map zoom in and move around, create clean transitions between the zoomed in and zoomed out options; but as that isn't supported in a clean way through the interface, we will use external focuses. The idea is simple; we will stack up two maps on top of each other and fade in and out the top map, giving us total control over the fluidity of the transitions.

Getting ready

Even though we are starting from scratch, a lot of the work that we did in the last recipe is being re-used, so I strongly encourage you to go through the last recipe *Adding markers and events* before moving into this one.

In this recipe, we will be integrating jQuery into our work as well, to save us time on creating our own animator tool (or re-using the one that we created in the *Animating independent layers* recipe in *Chapter 6, Bringing Static Things to Life*), as it would take us away from our main topic.

How to do it...

In this recipe we will be creating two files. An HTML file and a JS file. Let's look into it, starting with the HTML file:

1. Create an HTML file and import the Google `maps` API and jQuery:

```
<!DOCTYPE html>
<html>
  <head>
    <title>Google Maps Markers and Events</title>
    <meta charset="utf-8" />
    <meta name="viewport" content="initial-scale=1.0,
    user-scalable=no" />
    <script src="http://ajax.googleapis.com/
    ajax/libs/jquery/1.7.2/jquery.min.js"></script>
    <script
    src="http://maps.googleapis.com/maps/api/js?key=
    AIzaSyAywwIFJPo67Yd4vZgPz4EUSVu10BLHroE&sensor=true">
    </script>
    <script src="./09.05.controls.js"></script>
  </head>
  <body onload="init();">
    <div id="mapIn"></div>
  <div id="mapOut"></div>
  </body>
</html>
```

2. Use CSS to stack the map's layers on top of each other:

```
<style>
    html { height: 100% }
    body { height: 100%; margin: 0; padding: 0 }
    #mapIn, #mapOut { height: 100%; width:100%;
    position:absolute; top:0px; left:0px }
</style>
```

3. Create the `09.05.controls.js` JS file and create an `init` function in it (from this point onwards the rest of the code will be in the `init` function):

```
function init(){
  //rest of code in here
}
```

4. Create the two maps with their custom information:

```
var BASE_CENTER = new google.maps.LatLng(40.7142,-74.0064 );

//40.7142¬∞ N, -74.0064 E NYC
var mapOut = new google.maps.Map(document.
getElementById("mapOut"),{
  center: BASE_CENTER,
  zoom: 11,
  mapTypeId: google.maps.MapTypeId.SATELLITE,
  disableDefaultUI: true
});
var mapIn = new google.maps.Map(document.getElementById("mapIn"),{
  center: BASE_CENTER,
  zoom: 14,
  mapTypeId: google.maps.MapTypeId.ROADMAP,
  disableDefaultUI: true,
  panControl:true
});
```

5. Add the markers to the upper layer map:

```
var aMarkers = [
  {label:'New York City',
  local: mapOut.getCenter()},
  {label:'Brooklyn',
  local: new google.maps.LatLng(40.648, -73.957)},
  {label:'Queens',
  local: new google.maps.LatLng(40.732, -73.800)},
  {label:'Bronx',
  local: new google.maps.LatLng(40.851, -73.871)},

];
var marker;
```

```
    for(var i=0; i<aMarkers.length; i++){
      marker = new google.maps.Marker({
        position: aMarkers[i].local,
        map: mapOut,
        title: aMarkers[i].label
      });

    google.maps.event.addListener(marker, 'click',
    onMarkerClicked);

    }

    function onMarkerClicked(ev){
      mapIn.panTo(ev.latLng);
      $("#mapOut").fadeOut(1000);
    }
```

6. Add the `click` event to the internal map, and when you have clicked on it, you will be returned to the upper map:

   ```
   google.maps.event.addListener(mapIn, 'click', function() {
     mapIn.panTo(BASE_CENTER);
     $("#mapOut").fadeIn(1000);
     });
   ```

7. Force the user to disable `pan` in the upper map using the `center_changed` event:

   ```
   google.maps.event.addListener(mapOut, 'center_changed', function()
   {
           mapOut.panTo(BASE_CENTER);
   //always force users back to center point in external map
   });
   ```

When you load the HTML file, you will find a fullscreen map that cannot be dragged. When you click on a marker, it will fade into the selected area. You can now drag the cursor around the map. The next time you click in the internal map (regular click on any area), the map will fade back to the original upper layer.

How it works...

Our biggest step is the creation of two maps, one overlapping the other. We did that with some CSS magic by layering the elements and putting our top layer at the last position in the stack (we could probably use the z-index to validate it, but it worked so I didn't add that to the CSS). After that we created our two `div` layers and set their CSS code. In the JavaScript code, contrary to the way we did in the last recipe, we hardcoded the values that we wanted into both the maps.

In our options for both the maps, we set the default controllers not to take effect by setting the property `disableDefaultUI` to be `true`, while in `mapIn` we set `panControl` to be `true` to showcase that the map can be panned through:

```
var mapOut = new google.maps.Map(document.getElementById("mapOut"),{
  center: BASE_CENTER,
  zoom: 11,
  mapTypeId: google.maps.MapTypeId.SATELLITE,
  disableDefaultUI: true
});
var mapIn = new google.maps.Map(document.getElementById("mapIn"),{
  center: BASE_CENTER,
  zoom: 14,
  mapTypeId: google.maps.MapTypeId.ROADMAP,
  disableDefaultUI: true,
  panControl:true
});
```

We can manually set all the controllers by setting a Boolean value to any of the following options:

- `panControl`
- `zoomControl`
- `mapTypeControl`
- `streetViewControl`
- `overviewMapControl`

Our `event` logic works in the exact same way that it did in the last recipe. The only change is within the actual listeners where we switch between the maps using jQuery:

```
function onMarkerClicked(ev){
  mapIn.panTo(ev.latLng);
  $("#mapOut").fadeOut(1000);
}

google.maps.event.addListener(mapIn, 'click', function() {
  mapIn.panTo(BASE_CENTER);
  $("#mapOut").fadeIn(1000);
});
```

In both the event for the markers and the `click` event of the map, we are using the `fadeIn` and `fadeOut` methods of jQuery to animate our external maps visibility.

There's more...

When you try to drag around the higher-level map (the first visible map), you will notice that the map cannot move—it's not pannable. Google API v3 doesn't support the capability to disable the panning, but it does support the capability to get updated every time the map center point changes.

As such we listen in to the following change:

```
google.maps.event.addListener(mapOut, 'center_changed', function() {
        mapOut.panTo(BASE_CENTER);
});
```

All we are doing is that each time the map position changes, we force it back to its original position, making it impossible to move our map around.

Redesigning maps using styles

Many a time when creating more advanced applications by using Google Maps, you will want to create your own custom, skinned maps. This is really useful when you want to have a foreground content and don't want to have it compete with the background content.

In this recipe we will create a few styled maps. By the end of this recipe, you will know how to create global customization, individual styles, and last, but not least, add new map types.

Here is one style that we will create:

And here is a second style that we will create:

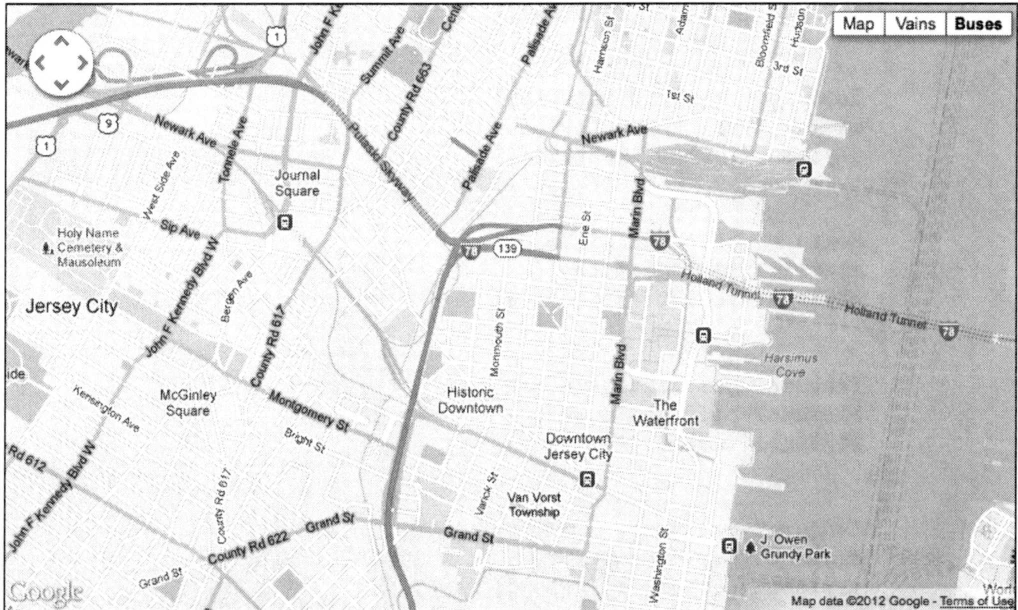

Getting ready

To complete this recipe, you will have to start from a copy of the previous recipe. We will only describe the new steps that differ from the last example in this recipe. To view and understand all the steps, please read the *Customizing controls and overlapping maps* recipe.

As such, we will skip the HTML code as it's exactly the same as in the previous recipe.

How to do it...

Open up your JavaScript file (`09.05.controls.js`) from the last recipe and follow these steps:

1. Within the `init` function create a `aVeinStyle` array. This array contains all the visual guides for skinning the map in the vein style:

```
var aVeinStyle =  [
  {
    featureType:'water',
    elementType: "geometry",
    stylers:[{color:'#E398BF'}]
  },
  {
```

```
      featureType:'road',
      elementType: "geometry",
      stylers:[{color:'#C26580'}]
    },
    {
      featureType:'road.arterial',
      elementType: "geometry",
      stylers:[{color:'#9B2559'}]
    },
    {
      featureType:'road.highway',
      elementType: "geometry",
      stylers:[{color:'#75000D'}]
    },
    {
      featureType:'landscape.man_made',
      elementType: "geometry",
      stylers:[{color:'#F2D2E0'}]
    },
    {
      featureType:'poi',
      elementType: "geometry",
      stylers:[{color:'#C96FB9'}]
    },
    {
      elementType: "labels",
      stylers:[{visibility:'off'}]
    }
  ];
```

2. Create a new `google.maps.StyledMapType` map with the name `Veins`:

```
var veinStyle = new google.maps.StyledMapType(aveinStyle,{name:
"Veins"});
```

3. Create a bus style:

```
var aBusStyle =  [
  {
    stylers: [{saturation: -100}]
  },
  {
    featureType:'transit.station.rail',
    stylers:[{ saturation:
    60},{hue:'#0044ff'},{visibility:'on'}]

  }
];

var busStyle = new google.maps.StyledMapType(aBusStyle,{name:
"Buses"});
```

4. For the internal map, make the map-type controller visible and include in it the IDs for our new map styles:

```
var mapIn = new google.maps.Map(document.getElementById("mapIn"),{
  center: BASE_CENTER,
  zoom: 14,
  mapTypeId: google.maps.MapTypeId.ROADMAP,
  disableDefaultUI: true,
  panControl:true,
  mapTypeControl:true,
  mapTypeControlOptions: {
    mapTypeIds: [google.maps.MapTypeId.ROADMAP,
    'veinStyle', 'busStyle']
  }

});
```

5. Add the map style information into the `mapIn` object:

```
mapIn.mapTypes.set('veinStyle', veinStyle);
mapIn.mapTypes.set('busStyle', busStyle);
```

6. Set a default map type:

```
mapIn.setMapTypeId('busStyle');
```

When you restart the HTML file in the internal map (after clicking on one of the markers), you will find a controller menu that enables you to switch between custom map types.

How it works...

Working with Google styles is fun, and they work in a way that is very similar to the way CSS works. The style we set has a few steps; the first step is to create the rules of the style, the next one is to define a Google-style object (`google.maps.StyledMapType`), and the last step is to define what map this style information is relevant to. Styles can only be applied to the maps of the `google.maps.MapTypeId.ROADMAP` type.

The first example is the creation of the bus style. The goal of this style is to make the map black and white and only highlight the public transportation stations:

```
var aBusStyle =  [
  {
    stylers: [{saturation: -100}]
  },
  {
    featureType:'transit.station.rail',
    stylers:[{ saturation:
    60},{hue:'#0044ff'},{visibility:'on'}]
```

```
    }
  ];

  var busStyle = new google.maps.StyledMapType(aBusStyle,{name:
  "Buses"});
```

The first variable is a regular array. We can add into it as many styles as we want; each time we want to define the rules (the search terms) that would apply before we actually list out the styles. Let's take a deeper look at one style rule:

```
{stylers: [{saturation: -100}]}
```

This example is the most basic. We have no rule, or in other words we want to apply this style to everything. As in this example we are setting the saturation to `-100`, we are making everything black and white (saturation values by default are `0` and can take values between `-100` and `100`).

The possible style properties are as follows:

- `visibility`: This is a string value (`no`, `off`, or `simplified`). This adds or removes elements from the map; for the most part, it would be used to remove text such as labels and details out of the elements depending on the information provided.
- `gamma`: This is a number value between `0.01` and `10` (`1.0` is the default). This option controls how much light is within the view. While lower values (lower than `1`) would sharpen the difference between lighter and darker colors, higher numbers (more than `1`) would have a more global effect, making everything glow more as the value goes up.
- `hue`: This is a hexadecimal color value wrapped into a string (such as #`222222`). For the best way to describe what the hue does, imagine putting on sunglasses that have tinted glass that matches the provided hexadecimal value. The way the tinted glass affects the colors around you and changes them is the same way that the hue colors of the map change.
- `lightness`: This is a value between `-100` and `100` (the default is `0`). This effect is really simple if you provide a value lower than `0`. It's the same effect as putting a black rectangle on top of your map and changing its opacity (that is, `-30` would match up to the opacity of 30 percent). You might have guessed the result of positive values—for positive values the idea is the same, but only with a white rectangle.
- `saturation`: This is a value between `-100` and `100` (the default is `0`). This effect focuses on a pixel-by-pixel value of `-100`. It would create grayscale image values that are nearer to `100`. It would remove all gray colors from the image, making everything more vivid.

This is all the style information that is available, and with it we can control every style element within the map. Each style property's information needs to be sent as a separate object within the `stylers` array; for example, if we wanted to add a `hue` to our snippet, it would look like this:

```
{stylers: [{saturation: -40},{hue:60}]}
```

Now that we know all the different ways in which we can change the visuals of the map, it's time to understand how we'll define what should be selected. In the last code snippet we've controlled the full map, but we can filter out what we want to control by adding filtering logic:

```
{elementType: "geometry",
  stylers:[{color:'#E398BF'}]
```

In this snippet, we are filtering out that we want to change the color of all the `geometry` elements, which means that whatever isn't a `geometry` element will not be affected. There are three types of element-type options:

- `all` (the default option)
- `geometry`
- `labels`

There is one more way to filter information, by using the `featureType` property. For example:

```
{
  featureType:'landscape.man_made',
  elementType: "geometry",
  stylers:[{color:'#F2D2E0'}]
}
```

In this case, we are listing out exactly what we want to focus on. We want to focus on both the type of feature and the element type. If we were to extract the `elementType` property, our color effect would affect both `geometry` and `labels`. Whereas if we were to extract `featureType`, it would affect all the `geometry` elements in the map.

For the full list of the `featureType` property options, please visit `http://goo.gl/H7HSO`.

There's more...

Now that we have under our belts how to create the styles we want to use, the next critical step is to actually connect our style to the map. The easiest way to do it (if we only have one style) is to connect it directly to the map:

```
inMap.setOptions({styles: styles});
```

This can be done by calling the `setOptions` function or by adding the `style` property when we create our map. Styles can only be added to road maps, and as such if you add this style to a map that isn't a road map, it would not be applied.

As we want to add more than one style option, we have to list out the map types. Before we can do that, we need to create a new map type object by using the following code:

```
var busStyle = new google.maps.StyledMapType(aBusStyle,{name:
"Buses"});
```

While creating the new map, we provided a name that will be used as our name in a controller—if we choose to create a controller (in our example we do). It's important to note that this name is not the ID of our element but just the label of the element, and we still need to create an ID for our element before sending it into the map. To do that we will first add the IDs into our controller and make our controller visible:

```
var mapIn = new google.maps.Map(document.getElementById("mapIn"),{
  center: BASE_CENTER,
  zoom: 14,
  mapTypeId: google.maps.MapTypeId.ROADMAP,
  disableDefaultUI: true,
  panControl:true,
  mapTypeControl:true,
  mapTypeControlOptions: {
    mapTypeIds: [google.maps.MapTypeId.ROADMAP, 'veinStyle',
    'busStyle']
  }

});
```

Following this, we will add the set instructions connecting our new map types to their style objects:

```
mapIn.mapTypes.set('veinStyle', veinStyle);
mapIn.mapTypes.set('busStyle', busStyle);
```

Last but not least, we can change our default map to be one of our styled maps:

```
mapIn.setMapTypeId('busStyle');
```

There you go. You now know everything that you need to know about how to work with styles in Google Maps.

10
Maps in Action

In this chapter we will cover the following topics:

- Connecting a Twitter feed to a Google map
- Building an advanced interactive marker
- Adding multiple tweets into an InfoWindow bubble
- Customizing the look and feel of markers
- Final project: building a live itinerary

Introduction

In this chapter on mapping, we will tie in more deeply to our topic of data visualization. One of the most popular ways to visualize data these days is by using maps. In this chapter, we will explore a few ideas on how to integrate data into maps, using the Google Maps platform.

Connecting a Twitter feed to a Google map

This is the start of a very fun experiment with Google Maps. The goal of the task is to create a link between Twitter posts and a Google map. It will take us a few recipes to get to our final goal. By the end of this recipe, we will have a Google map. This Google map will be clickable in any area of the screen. When the user clicks on the map, they will connect to the Twitter API and search for tweets in that area that have the word "HTML5" in them. When the result comes back, it will pop a new marker onto the area that was clicked and add the most recent tweet on that topic originating from that location. At this stage, it would just be a marker with a rollover that shows us the actual tweet without more information.

Getting ready

If you haven't read through *Chapter 9, Using Google Maps*, you might find this chapter a little difficult, so I encourage you to read it before starting with this recipe. At this stage you should have a Google API set up (see the *Obtaining a Google API key* recipe in *Chapter 9*).

How to do it...

We will create new HTML and JavaScript files and call them `10.01.socielmap.html` and `10.01.socielmap.js`, respectively, and then perform the following steps:

1. Add the following code in the HTML file using your own API key:

```
<!DOCTYPE html>
<html>
  <head>
    <title>Google Maps Markers and Events</title>
    <meta charset="utf-8" />
```

```
    <meta name="viewport" content="initial-scale=1.0, user-
scalable=no" />
    <style>
      html { height: 100% }
      body { height: 100%; margin: 0; padding: 0 }
      #map { height: 100%; width:100%; position:absolute; top:0px;
left:0px }
    </style>
  <script src="http://ajax.googleapis.com/ajax/libs/jquery/1.7.2/
jquery.min.js"></script>
    <script src="http://maps.googleapis.com/maps/api/js?key=AIzaSy
AywwIFJPo67Yd4vZgPz4EUSVu10BLHroE&sensor=true">
    </script>
    <script src="./10.01.socielmap.js"></script>
  </head>
  <body onload="init();">
    <div id="map"></div>
  </body>
</html>
```

2. Let's move into the JavaScript file. As we have an `init()` function being called when the `onload` event triggers, we will place all of our code within a new `init` function.

```
function init(){
 //all code here
}
```

3. We will start by setting our center point of the map. So far, we were extremely focused on my home state, New York, so let's change our focus to Europe.

```
var BASE_CENTER = new google.maps.LatL
ng(48.516817734860105,13.005318750000015 );
```

4. Next, let's create a black-and-white style for our map so it's easier to focus on the markers we are about to create.

```
var aGray =  [
    {
      stylers: [{saturation: -100}]
    }
  ];

  var grayStyle = new google.maps.StyledMapType(aGray,{name:
"Black & White"});
```

5. Create a new Google map.

```
var map = new google.maps.Map(document.getElementById("map"),{
    center: BASE_CENTER,
    zoom: 6,
```

```
    mapTypeId: google.maps.MapTypeId.ROADMAP,
    disableDefaultUI: true,

  });
```

6. Set up the `grayStyle` styling object to be our default style.

   ```
   map.mapTypes.set('grayStyle', grayStyle);
   map.setMapTypeId('grayStyle');
   ```

7. Our next step is going to use Google's API to create a new `click` event for the map. When the map is clicked we want to trigger a `listener` function. When a click happens, we want to start our Twitter search as we will connect to the Twitter API and search for the submission of the keyword `html5` within a 50 kilometer radius from where our click on the map was. Let's create a new mouse event and start up the Twitter search.

   ```
   google.maps.event.addListener(map, 'click', function(e) {
       //console.log(e.latLng);
         var searchKeyWord = 'html5';
         var geocode=e.latLng.lat() + "," + e.latLng.lng()+",50km";
         var searchLink = 'http://search.twitter.com/search.json?q='+
   searchKeyWord+ '&geocode=' + geocode +"&result_type=recent&rpp=1";


         $.getJSON(searchLink, function(data) {
           showTweet(data.results[0],e.latLng);
       });

       });
   ```

8. When the Twitter search value is returned, it is time to show our new tweet; if no tweet is found, we will put in default content letting the user know that nothing could be found.

   ```
   function showTweet(obj,latLng){
         if(!obj) obj = {text:'No tweet found in this area for this
   topic'};
         console.log(obj);

         var marker = new google.maps.Marker({
               map: map,
               position: latLng,
               title:obj.text     });


     }
   ```

When you load the map again, you will find a map of Europe waiting to be clicked on. Each click will trigger a new Twitter search and will generate a new result based on the location you clicked on. To read the tweet, roll over the marker after it returns.

How it works...

We live in an age when data about almost anything increasingly overlaps with geolocation data and maps. It's almost impossible to write a book about data without talking about maps, and it's not possible to write a book about data visualization without at least opening the Pandora's box of the world of mapping and its possibilities, either.

Twitter lately has been trying more and more to capture the location of users. For most of the time, the location is still void. That having been said, Twitter always knows the base location of users based on their information, and more so when users tweet through their cell phones. As such, Twitter always has a rough idea of where users are when they send a message, and in the coming years this accuracy is expected to only get better. In the future, more and more Twitter results will have such an accurate location for users that we will be able to pinpoint them directly on a map.

After creating the map, the first step is that, as soon as a user clicks on any area of the map, we start building out a search query to be used on the Twitter API:

```
google.maps.event.addListener(map, 'click', function(e) {
    //console.log(e.latLng);
      var searchKeyWord = 'html5';
      var geocode=e.latLng.lat() + "," + e.latLng.lng()+",50km";
      var searchLink = 'http://search.twitter.com/search.json?q='+
searchKeyWord+ '&geocode=' + geocode +"&result_type=recent&rpp=1";
```

We don't cover all the possibilities with search, but instead we are focusing on two main points: the search query, in our case HTML5, and the location of the query. We get the location information directly from the event that is passed into a marker. We reformat the information from our Google returned event and format it into a string, adding to it the range; in our case we set this to 50 kilometers (you can choose `ml` for miles as well). As we are taking a look at the map of Europe now, I thought it would be appropriate to work in kilometers and not miles.

We want to get our search values back as **JavaScript Object Notation** (**JSON**) values. JSON is a very minimal shorthand way to pass object information as strings between servers. For the most part, you will usually work with automatic converters so you will be sending objects and getting objects, but under the hood there is a JSON encoder and decoder that will process the request.

If you don't know what JSON is, don't worry about it; it's all done in the background and it's not critical to understand how JSON works in order to work with it.

We want to get our data in JSON format; to do that we will send our URL parameters to the following URL:

`http://search.twitter.com/search.json`

Append to it our `q` values and `geocode` values. If you want to explore options and possibilities with the Twitter search API more deeply, visit the following page:

`https://dev.twitter.com/docs/api/1/get/search`

The next step is to send our information to this service and get our results back. To do that, we will use the `$.getJSON` function in jQuery. This function will take care of all our needs: sending our request, getting it back, and then decoding the information into a regular JavaScript object.

```
$.getJSON(searchLink, function(data) {
        showTweet(data.results[0],e.latLng);
    });
```

The two parameters we need to send in are the search link and the return function. In our case, we will grab our data and send it to an external function, `showTweet`. We will send only the first result from the data to return and the `e.latLng` object information we got from our click event.

Time to create the marker. In the `showTweet` function, our first task will be to check whether there is actually any data in the returned first element. If there is no value it means Twitter didn't find anything.

```
if(!obj) obj = {text:'No tweet found in this area for this topic'};
```

If no object was returned, we will create a new object with placeholder information to replace the regular result information. This is a great way to avoid complexities in your code: by building the exceptions into the regular user experience. We are done; all that is left is for us to create the marker.

```
var marker = new google.maps.Marker({
            map: map,
            position: latLng,
            title:obj.text    });
```

Although we got what we had our minds set on, the `latLng` information we have is for our click and not the exact location of our tweet. Currently there is a property called geo that is returned in the object returned from Twitter. At the time of writing this book, it always comes back empty. Currently it looks like it's a feature that is about to be released or is partially implemented, so by the time you read this book try to check and see if there is a value being returned from the `obj.geo` property and use it to make your point more accurate when this information is available.

Building an advanced interactive marker

The next step in our social map project is to add more details for our Twitter search result. We would like to open up an information panel automatically when the Twitter result comes in. In the process, we will create a subclass of Google Marker and extend it and add a new InfoWindow to enable us to add live HTML data right into our map.

Getting ready

It will be really hard to join in, if you haven't started from the start of this chapter. As this recipe is in continuation of the previous recipe, we will not create a new HTML file or a new JavaScript file but will instead continue from where we left off.

How to do it...

Grab your latest JavaScript file and let's continue to the next steps:

1. In the function `showTweet`, replace the new marker with a new `TwitterMarker` marker.

```
function showTweet(obj,latLng){
      if(!obj) obj = {text:'No tweet found in this area for this
topic'};
      console.log(obj);

      var marker = new TwitterMarker({
            map: map,
            position: latLng,
            tweet: obj,
            title:obj.text    });

   }
```

2. Now that we are not using the regular built-in marker, it's time for us to create our own marker. Let's start with the constructor.

```
function TwitterMarker(opt){
  var strTweet = this.buildTwitterHTML(opt.tweet);
  this.infoWindow = new google.maps.InfoWindow({
      maxWidth:300,
      content:strTweet
  });


  this.setValues(opt);
  this.infoWindow.open(this.map,this);
  google.maps.event.addListener(this, 'click', this.
onMarkerClick);
}
```

3. We will want to extend our new object from the `google.maps.Marker` marker so we can have all the features of the regular marker.

```
TwitterMarker.prototype = new google.maps.Marker();
```

4. Let's create a toggle button in our marker event listener. When the event is called, it will open or close our InfoWindow:

```
TwitterMarker.prototype.onMarkerClick=function(evt){
  this.isOpen=!this.isOpen;
  if(this.isOpen)
    this.infoWindow.close();
  else
    this.infoWindow.open(this.map,this);

}
```

5. It is time to create the Twitter message by creating an HTML string.

```
TwitterMarker.prototype.buildTwitterHTML = function(twt){
  var str;
  if(twt.from_user_name){
   str =        "<span><img style='float: left' src='"+twt.profile_
image_url+"' />"+
          "<b>" +twt.from_user_name + "</b><br/><a href ='http://
twitter.com/"
         + twt.from_user + "'>@"+twt.from_user+"</a><br/> "
         + twt.location + "</span>"
         + "<p>"+twt.text+"</p>";
  }else{
```

```
        str="The 50 Kilometer radius around this point did not message
this value";
    }
    return str;
}
```

If you reload your HTML file, you will find it interactive in any area of the world; if it can find a tweet, it will output it on the map within an InfoWindow.

How it works...

Although there are not many lines, a lot of logic is condensed into this code. Let's start by looking at our new marker. This is the first time in this book that we use inheritance. Inheritance, as its name implies, enables us to extend the features of an object in JavaScript without affecting the original object. In our case, we want to take all the features of the marker (methods, properties, and so on) and add to them some custom behaviors.

The inheritance is done in JavaScript by defining a prototype. Until now, we have used the prototype without talking about it much, but we used it mainly to create new methods. If we assign a full object to the prototype, all of the properties and methods of that object will be copied into our new object as well.

```
TwitterMarker.prototype = new google.maps.Marker();
```

Always start first with extending of the object you want to extend, before any other additions. This is because if you've placed any new prototype methods before this line of code, they will silently be deleted and thus will not work.

The `buildTwitterHTML` method takes in the Twitter object returned and converts some of its data into HTML. We use this method once per marker. When we create a new marker, we create a new `InfoWindow` object as well. We place an InfoWindow on top of the marker and showcase the tweet information.

```
function TwitterMarker(opt){
 var strTweet = this.buildTwitterHTML(opt.tweet)
 this.infoWindow = new google.maps.InfoWindow({
     maxWidth:300,
     content:strTweet
 });
```

We are setting the width as well, to avoid having a really big panel. We send our newly created `strTweet` string into the `infoWindow` object.

We wanted our marker to be a toggle button that controls the InfoWindow status. To do that we add a newly dynamically created property called `isOpen`. Even though we open up the InfoWindow earlier in the constructor, we don't set the value of `isOpen` there. We can fix that issue in the first action we perform in our click event listener of the marker.

```
TwitterMarker.prototype.onMarkerClick=function(evt){
  this.isOpen=!this.isOpen;
```

When the marker is clicked, we automatically change the state of the `isOpen` variable. As it was not set before, it will now be set to `true`. The `!` operator is a `boolean` operator that switches a value between `true` and `false`. Its actual meaning is `not`. In other words, we are saying:

```
this.isOpen = is not this.isOpen
```

The interesting fact here is that undefined (the value of a variable that wasn't defined) for the not (`!`) operator is the same as `false`, `null`, or even `0`. Any other value would be considered true. This way, each time the marker is clicked, the value of the variable `this.isOpen` switches. And *that* is the heart of the logic of our toggle button. All that is left is to decide whether to open or close the InfoWindow.

```
  if(this.isOpen)
    this.infoWindow.close();
  else
    this.infoWindow.open(this.map,this);
}
```

This leads us to our final step of figuring out what will be our Twitter text. We will edit this method in the next few recipes. You can play around with it and ideally personalize it to what you prefer it to look like. We have two possible outcomes: *no Twitter messages in the search area* and *Twitter messages in the search area*. If there is a message, we will use some of the returned object properties to build up an HTML outline that will be used inside the `infoWindow` object that is associated with this marker. If there isn't a result, we will create one.

```
TwitterMarker.prototype.buildTwitterHTML = function(twt){
  var str;
  if(twt.from_user_name){
   //build custom message
   /*notice we are validating based on checking if the twitter has a
property (any of the properties would work) */
  }else{
    //the error message
    str="The 50 Kilometer radius around this point did not message
this value";
  }
  return str;
}
```

There you go! Our social map is starting to be much more interesting. It still is missing some features. It would be really nice if we could see more than one message in the InfoWindow result. In the next recipe we will try to solve that issue.

Adding multiple tweets into an InfoWindow bubble

So far, in our interactive social map, we added markers in each location that we clicked on and opened up an InfoWindow with the tweet information. Our next step will be to enable multiple tweets to live inside our InfoWindow by adding a pagination system into our window.

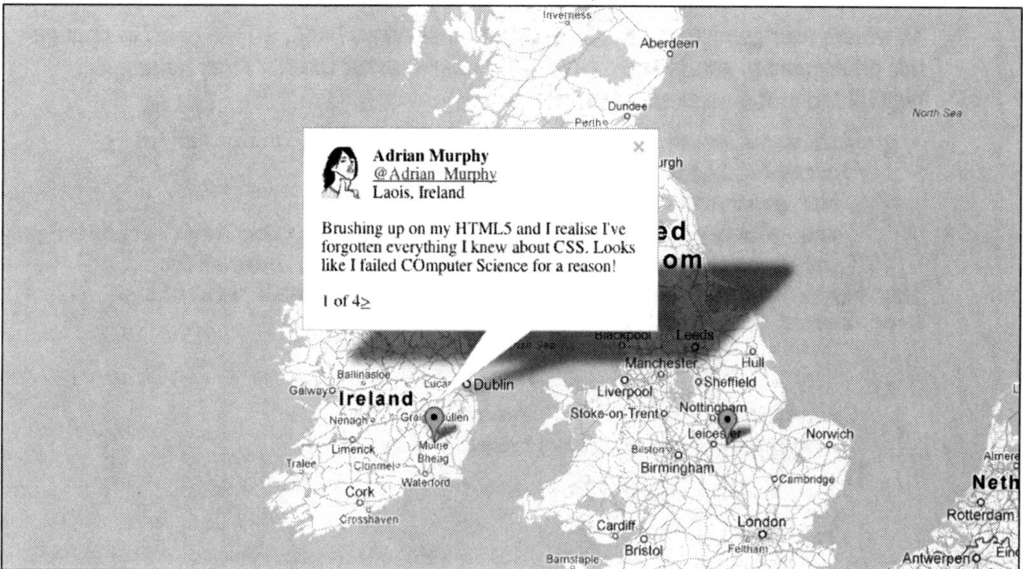

Getting ready

To get through this recipe you must be knee deep into our holistic chapter. If you dropped in just now, it would be a good idea to go back to the start of this chapter as we are going to continue from where we left off in the previous recipe.

How to do it...

We are still in our JavaScript file and we will continue to add code and adjust our code to get multiple Twitter posts into our social map.

1. Let's start by changing our Twitter search to return up to 100 values per search. We are doing this because there is a limit on how many times we can call the Twitter API. So, we will try to grab as much as we can in one hit (this code should be around line 30).

```
var searchLink = 'http://search.twitter.com/search.
json?q='+ searchKeyWord+ '&geocode=' + geocode +"&result_
type=recent&rpp=100";
```

2. As we are now going to treat all the tweets that come back, we will need to change our references to send to our `TwitterMaker` marker the full array (changes highlighted in the code snippet).

```
  google.maps.event.addListener(map, 'click', function(e) {
    //console.log(e.latLng);
      var searchKeyWord = 'html5';
      var geocode=e.latLng.lat() + "," + e.latLng.lng()+",50km";
      var searchLink = 'http://search.twitter.com/search.
json?q='+ searchKeyWord+ '&geocode=' + geocode +"&result_
type=recent&rpp=100";


      $.getJSON(searchLink, function(data) {
        showTweet(data.results,e.latLng);
    });

    });


  function showTweet(a,latLng){
      if(!a) a = [{text:'No tweet found in this area for this
topic'}];
      //console.log(obj);

      var marker = new TwitterMarker({
            map: map,
            position: latLng,
            tweet: a,
            title:a[0].text     });

  }
}
```

3. We want to update the `TwitterMarker` constructor to include our array and quick information on it, such as the total tweets and the current tweet we are in. We will need a way to identify our object, and as such, we will give it an ID as well (more on that in a few steps).

```
function TwitterMarker(opt){
  this.count = opt.tweet.length;
  this.crnt = 0;
  this.id = TwitterMarker.aMarkers.push(this);
  this.aTweets = opt.tweet;
  var strTweet = this.buildTwitterHTML(opt.tweet[0])
  this.infoWindow = new google.maps.InfoWindow({
      maxWidth:300,
      content:strTweet
  });


  this.setValues(opt);
  this.infoWindow.open(this.map,this);
  google.maps.event.addListener(this, 'click', this.
onMarkerClick);
}
```

4. We want to store, in a static array that can be accessed from any place in our code, all the markers created. To do that, we will add a new status array to our `TwitterMarker` class:

```
TwitterMarker.prototype = new google.maps.Marker();
TwitterMarker.aMarkers= [];
```

5. In the `buildTwitterHTML` method, we want to add in back/next links that will be visible to users from InfoWindow:

```
TwitterMarker.prototype.buildTwitterHTML = function(twt){
  var str;
  if(twt.from_user_name){
   str =       "<span><img style='float: left' src='"+twt.profile_
image_url+"' />"+
         "<b>" +twt.from_user_name + "</b><br/><a href ='http://
twitter.com/"
        + twt.from_user + "'>@"+twt.from_user+"</a><br/> "
        + twt.location + "</span>"
        + "<p>"+twt.text+"</p>";

    if(this.count>1){
      str+="<span style='absolute; bottom: 0;
          right: 0px; width:80px'>";
```

```
        if(this.crnt!=0) str+="<a href='javascript:TwitterMarker.
aMarkers["+(this.id-1)+"].prev();'>&lt;</a> ";
        str+= (this.crnt+1) + " of " + this.count;
        if(this.crnt<(this.count-1)) str+= "<a
href='javascript:TwitterMarker.aMarkers["+(this.id-1)+"].
next();'>&gt;</a> ";
        str+= "</span>"
      }
    }else{
      str="The 50 Kilometer radius around this point did not message
this value";
    }
    return str;
}
```

6. Let's now add the `next` and `prev` methods.

```
TwitterMarker.prototype.next =function(){
  this.infoWindow.close();
  this.infoWindow.content = this.buildTwitterHTML(this.
aTweets[++this.crnt]);
  this.infoWindow.open(this.map,this);
  return false;
}

TwitterMarker.prototype.prev =function(){
  this.infoWindow.close();
  this.infoWindow.content = this.buildTwitterHTML(this.aTweets[--
this.crnt]);
  this.infoWindow.open(this.map,this);
  return false;
}
```

Load the HTML file, and you should find a working InfoWindow that can accommodate up to 100 tweets per click.

How it works...

Our first change was to change the number of results coming back from the Twitter search API. This change forced us to change the references in our code from referring directly to the first object returned to focus on the full results object and sending it to our `TwitterMarker` constructor. This change created a few smaller changes in the flow of the information within the constructor as well.

Our goals are to create two buttons that will update our InfoWindow. This is an issue as we need a two-way connection between our marker and its InfoWindow. Until now, all our communication with the InfoWindow was one way. The easiest way for us to solve this problem and bypass the Google interface is to create a static array that will store all markers and refer to our static marker when we trigger buttons inside the `InfoWindow` object. All we need to do is add a variable direction to our class name.

```
TwitterMarker.aMarkers= [];
```

By adding our variable directly into the `TwitterMarker` class, we can now refer to it directly at any point and it will not get duplicated in our objects (as it's not part of the prototype). Now that we have an array, it's time for us to go back into our `TwitterMarker` constructor and send a new reference to this array each time we create a new `TwitterMarker` object. Another benefit we get out of doing this is that we automatically get a unique identifier (ID) for each marker as the returned number will always be a unique number for our needs.

```
this.id = TwitterMarker.aMarkers.push(this);
```

In this one line of code, we perform all of the tasks we talked about in the previous paragraph. The array `push` method returns the new length of the array.

Now that we have a way to refer to our marker and have got an identifier, it's time for us to go back into the `buildTwitterHTML` method and add into the rendered HTML two `href` buttons that will trigger the right marker when the next/previous selections are clicked.

Before we delve into that, we want to check and validate that we have more than one Twitter message that came back; if there is none, there is no point in adding the new logic, and we would be introducing a bug if we had next/previous logic for an item that has only one item.

```
if(this.count>1){

}
```

By the following `if` statement, we figure out whether we are currently in the first Twitter message, and if not we shall add the back button:

```
if(this.crnt!=0) str+="<a href='javascript:TwitterMarker.
aMarkers["+(this.id-1)+"].prev();'>&lt;</a> ";
```

This might look like a huge mess but, if we ignore the HTML and focus on the actual JavaScript that will be triggered when the button is pressed, this is what we will get:

```
TwitterMarker.aMarkers["+(this.id-1)+"].prev();
```

The `this.id-1` parameter will be replaced with the actual current number:

As this is rendered into a string to be parsed as HTML, the value that will be integrated into the HTML will be hardcoded. Let's see this in a real case to make it clear. The first array ID would be `0`, and as such the `prev` button would look like this code statement:

```
TwitterMarker.aMarkers[0].prev();
```

Now the logic is starting to reveal itself. By grabbing the marker from the array that is our current element, all that is left for us to do is trigger the `prev` method and let it take over.

The same logic happens for our other end. The only condition is that we are not in the last Twitter result and if not we call the `next` method:

```
if(this.crnt<(this.count-1)) str+= "<a href='javascript:TwitterMarker.
aMarkers["+(this.id-1)+"].next();'>&gt;</a> ";
```

There you have it! The core of our logic is in place.

If we wanted we could have created our InfoWindow by wrapping a `<div>` tag with a unique ID and just called it and made direct updates to our content (try doing that by yourself as that would be a better solution). Instead, we are working with the limitations of the InfoWindow. As we cannot update the full bucket container while it's open, we need to close it to update it and then open it again. Thus our logic in both the `next` and `prev` methods is similar; both have a limitation on the change of the actual value that is being rendered.

```
TwitterMarker.prototype.next =function(){
  this.infoWindow.close();
  this.infoWindow.content = this.buildTwitterHTML(this.aTweets[++this.
crnt]);
  this.infoWindow.open(this.map,this);
  return false;
}

TwitterMarker.prototype.prev =function(){
  this.infoWindow.close();
  this.infoWindow.content = this.buildTwitterHTML(this.aTweets[--this.
crnt]);
  this.infoWindow.open(this.map,this);
  return false;
}
```

All the logic is the same and limited to the highlighted code snippet. If you aren't familiar with this shortcut, the `++` and `--` operators when set before a variable, enable us to add/subtract 1 from it and update it before its value is sent on. Thus in one line, we can both change the number in the variable and send that newly created number to continue its tasks.

In the case of the `next` method, we want to grab the next tweet, while for the `prev` method, we want to grab the previous tweet.

Customizing the look and feel of markers

This will be our last recipe for social mapping. In this recipe, we will revisit our marker itself and give it a facelift. As our marker represents Twitter messages in a clicked area, we will update our marker to look like a Twitter bird (hand made). We will not stop there; after updating our graphic, we will add another graphical layer to shadow our Twitter marker. It will be a shadow, and its opacity will range from zero to full, depending on the number of tweets (a maximum of hundred tweets).

The best way to understand our goal is by checking out the following screenshot:

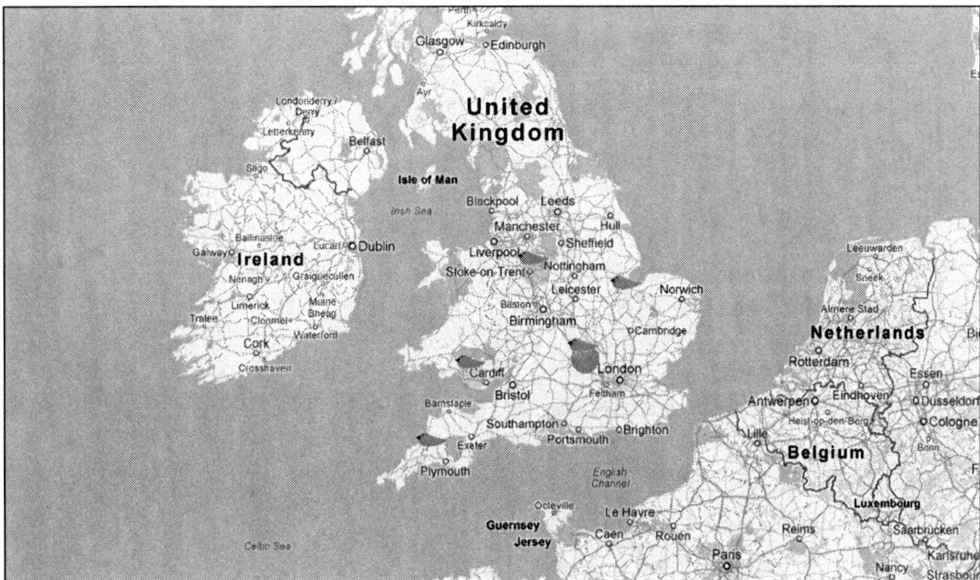

Note how some tweets have no visible circle outline, while others have a very dark one (that is based on how many tweets are there).

Getting ready

To complete this task you need to first complete all the previous recipes in this chapter.

How to do it...

We will jump right into the JavaScript file and continue from where we left off in the previous recipe.

1. Update the `showTweet` function.

```
function showTweet(a,latLng){
      if(!a) a = [{text:'No tweet found in this area for this
topic'}];
      //console.log(obj);

      var marker = new TwitterMarker({
            map: map,
            position: latLng,
            tweet: a,
            title:a[0].text,
            icon:"img/bird.png"     });

  }
```

2. Create an instance of the `MarkerCounter` object in the `TweeterMarker` constructor.

```
function TwitterMarker(opt){
  this.count = opt.tweet.length;
  this.mc = new MarkerCounter(opt);
  this.crnt = 0;
...
```

3. Create the `MarkerCounter` constructor.

```
function MarkerCounter(opt) {
    this.radius = 15;
    this.opacity = (opt.tweet.length) /100;
    this.opt = opt;
    this.setMap(opt.map);
  }
```

4. Create subclass, `MarkerCounter`, for the `google.maps.OverlayView` object.

```
MarkerCounter.prototype = new google.maps.OverlayView();
```

5. Create an `onAdd` method. It will be called automatically when an element is added into the map. In this method, we will finish up all the preparatory work for the drawing but won't draw the elements.

```
MarkerCounter.prototype.onAdd = function() {
  var div = document.createElement('div');
    div.style.border = "none";
    div.style.borderWidth = "0px";
```

```
div.style.position = "absolute";


this.canvas = document.createElement("CANVAS");
  this.canvas.width = this.radius*2;
this.canvas.height = this.radius*2;

  this.context = this.canvas.getContext("2d");
div.appendChild(this.canvas);
this.div_ = div;


  var panes = this.getPanes();
     panes.overlayLayer.appendChild(div);

}
```

6. Last but not least, it's time to override the `draw` method and draw into the new canvas element created in the previous step and position the `div` element.

```
MarkerCounter.prototype.draw = function() {
   var radius = this.radius;
   var context = this.context;
 context.clearRect(0,0,radius*2,radius*2);

 context.fillStyle = "rgba(73,154,219,"+this.opacity+")";
 context.beginPath();
   context.arc(radius,radius, radius, 0, Math.PI*2, true);
 context.closePath();
 context.fill();
 var projection = this.getProjection();
 var point = projection.fromLatLngToDivPixel(this.opt.position);

   this.div_.style.left = (point.x - radius) + 'px';
   this.div_.style.top = (point.y - radius) + 'px';

 };
```

When you run the application, you will find that now our markers look like those of Twitter and the larger the number of tweets that originate from a location, the more opaque the egg under our Twitter bird will be.

How it works...

The first step is to swap the graphic that is the default graphic for the marker. As we are extending the regular marker, we have all of its default features and behaviors. One of these features is the ability to swap the icon. To do that, we pass in one of our object parameters as the icon and its path.

```
var marker = new TwitterMarker({
            map: map,
            position: latLng,
            tweet: a,
            title:a[0].text,
            icon:"img/bird.png"     });
```

You might be wondering how this actually works, as we are not actually doing anything to the icon parameter in our code. It's very simple. If you take a deeper look at the `TwitterMaker` constructor, you will find the following line:

```
this.setValues(opt);
```

Passing the `setValues` method to the `opt` object is our way of letting the marker continue and rendering our marker with the information we just got into our constructor. All the things that can be done in a regular marker can be done in ours as well.

At this stage we have our Twitter bird as our graphic interface for our marker. Unfortunately, this is as far as we can go with customizing our marker; next, we will need to add another visual layer. As we want to create a visual layer that behaves like a marker just visually (as it will be part of the marker), we will need to create a subclass for the `google.maps.OverlayView` object.

Similar to the marker logic, when we are ready to render our element, we want to call the method `setMap` (for the marker it was a different method but the same idea).

```
function MarkerCounter(opt) {
    this.radius = 15;
    this.opacity = (opt.tweet.length) /100;
    this.opt = opt;
    this.setMap(opt.map);
  }

  MarkerCounter.prototype = new google.maps.OverlayView();
```

In our constructor, we are only storing very basic global information, such as our target opacity, radius, and the `options` object. We can store any information we want here. The most important element of information that we will need is the position (latitude and longitude). We will send that information into our marker, and it will be inside our `opt` object.

The `google.maps.OverlayView` object has an `onAdd` method. It's just like a listener, but in addition, we will override this method and add our processing/preparation work when the element is added into the map.

```
MarkerCounter.prototype.onAdd = function() {
  var div = document.createElement('div');
    div.style.border = "none";
    div.style.borderWidth = "0px";
    div.style.position = "absolute";


  this.canvas = document.createElement("CANVAS");
    this.canvas.width = this.radius*2;
  this.canvas.height = this.radius*2;

    this.context = this.canvas.getContext("2d");
  div.appendChild(this.canvas);
  this.div_ = div;
    var panes = this.getPanes();
    panes.overlayLayer.appendChild(div);
  }
```

Most of the logic here should look familiar. We start by creating a new `div` element. We set its CSS attributes to make absolute the position of the `div` element so we can move it around easily. We follow this with creating a canvas element and setting its width and height to be two times the radius of our circle. We add the canvas into our `div` element. Last but not least it's time for us to add our `div` element into the map. We will do that by accessing the `getPanes` method. This method will return all the visual layers this element can contain. In our case, we will go right to our overlay layer and add our `div` element to it. We do this inside the `onAdd` method rather than doing it earlier because the overlay will not be rendered and we will not have access to the last two lines in the previous code.

Just as we overrode the `onAdd` method, we do the same for the `draw` method. This is our last critical step. For the most part, all the work in this method will be very familiar as we have played a lot with canvas in this book. So, let's explore the new steps to find where we want to position our overlay.

```
var projection = this.getProjection();
    var point = projection.fromLatLngToDivPixel(this.opt.position);

     this.div_.style.left = (point.x - radius) + 'px';
     this.div_.style.top = (point.y - radius) + 'px';
```

In the first line in the preceding code, we get the projection. The projection is the relative point of view of our overlay. Through this projection, we can extract the actual point in pixels. We call the `projection.fromLatLngToDivPixel` method, send to it a latitude/longitude object, and get back a point (`x`, `y` values). All that is left is to update the style of our `div` element and position it according to this information (not forgetting to subtract our radius size so our element is exactly in the middle of the actual point that was clicked).

Until now, we have treated our `TwitterMarker` constructor as if there are always tweets somewhere in the world, but the reality is that sometimes there will not be anything, and right now we are creating both a visualization that won't work and a marker that won't visualize it. Let's override our behaviors and put up an alternative marker if there is no result and skip all of our customizations.

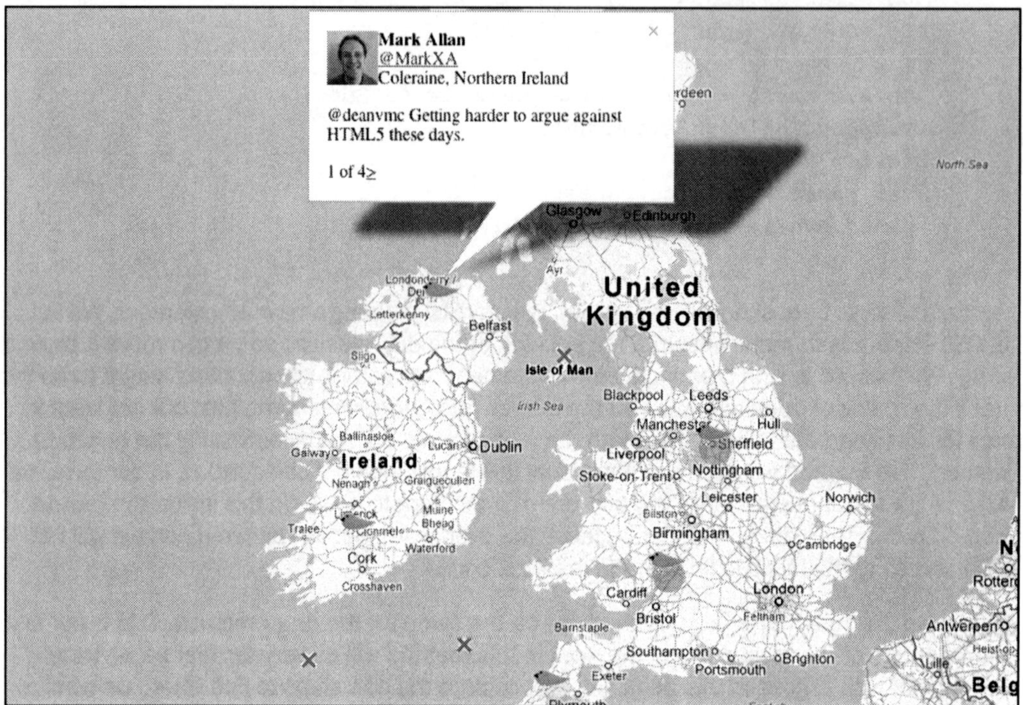

Let's sort it out. We start by removing our original error logic from the `showTweet` method. Instead, we will just update the `text` attribute but will not create a new array.

```
function showTweet(a,latLng){
    var marker = new TwitterMarker({
        map: map,
        position: latLng,
        tweet: a,
```

```
            title:a.length? a[0].text : 'No tweet found in this area
            for this topic' ,
            icon:"img/bird.png"     });

    }
```

In case you are not familiar with the ternary operator, it's a very condensed way of creating an `if...else` statement within code. The core logic of it is as follows:

```
condition?true outcome:false outcome;
```

The outcome is then sent back, and we can capture it right into our variable as we are doing in this case.

The next area we want to change is the `TwitterMarker` constructor.

```
function TwitterMarker(opt){
  if(!opt.tweet || !opt.tweet.length){
    opt.icon = "img/x.png";
  }else{

    this.count = opt.tweet.length;
    this.mc = new MarkerCounter(opt);
    this.crnt = 0;
    this.id = TwitterMarker.aMarkers.push(this);
    this.aTweets = opt.tweet;
    var strTweet = this.buildTwitterHTML(opt.tweet[0])
    this.infoWindow = new google.maps.InfoWindow({
        maxWidth:300,
        content:strTweet
    });

    this.infoWindow.open(this.map,this);
    google.maps.event.addListener(this, 'click', this.onMarkerClick);

  }
  this.setValues(opt);
}
```

The main changes here are that we start our application by first checking if there are any tweets. If no tweets are around, we update the icon graphic to a new **X** icon. If we do have a result, all remains the same. We extracted the `setValues` method to be called out of the `if...else` conditions as we need to call it in any case.

There you go! We've completed our social map. There is much more you can do with this project. A couple of examples could be making it easier to change the search term, and comparing between two search results (that could be very interesting and easy). I would be interested to see around the world the number of times Flash versus HTML5 are mentioned, so if you get to it send me an e-mail.

Final project: building a live itinerary

Although the natural next step from our previous sample would be just to add an extra feature to our already growing social map (which we have built throughout this chapter), we are taking a direction shift.

In our final recipe, we will build an interactive Google map that will animate with the travel information of a close friend of mine in South America while I was working on this book. To build this application, we will animate the map by adding drawings and moving markers; we will integrate with an external feed of travel information and integrate animations and text snippets that will describe the journey. In the following screenshot, you can see a very small snapshot of the plain path:

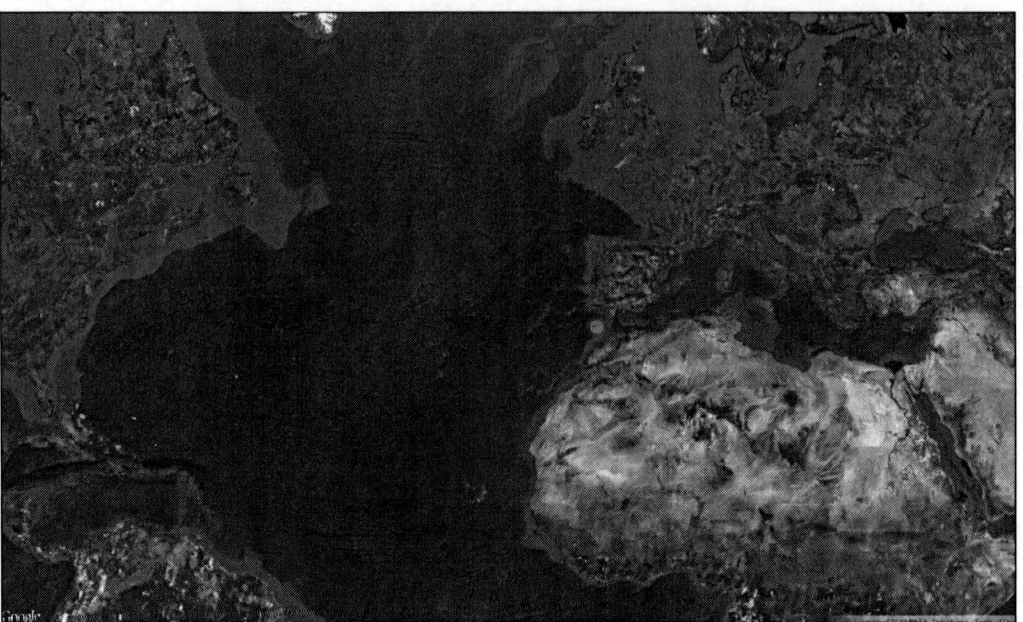

Getting ready

Many of the elements we will be working with in this recipe will be based on work we did throughout all of the chapters. As such, it will not be easy to just jump right in if you haven't gone through the journey together with us. There are no prerequisites. We will start from scratch, but we will not focus on things we have learned already.

As the user "travels" around the world map when there is a message for the user in the data source, the map will fade out and the message will be displayed before the user can continue traveling the world:

How to do it...

In this recipe we will be creating two files: an HTML file and a JavaScript file. Let's look into them, starting with the HTML file:

1. Create the HTML file.

```
<!DOCTYPE html>
<html>
  <head>
    <title>Google Maps Markers and Events</title>
    <meta charset="utf-8" />
    <meta name="viewport" content="initial-scale=1.0, user-
scalable=no" />
    <link href='http://fonts.googleapis.com/css?family=Yellowtail'
rel='stylesheet' type='text/css'>
    <style>
      html { height: 100% }
      body { height: 100%; margin: 0; padding: 0 }
      #map { height: 100%; width:100%; position:absolute; top:0px;
left:0px }

      .overlay {
        background: #000000 scroll;
        height: 100%;
        left: 0;
        opacity: 0;
```

```
        position: absolute;
        top: 0;
        width: 100%;
        z-index: 50;
    }
    .overlayBox {
        left: -9999em;
        opacity: 0;
        position: absolute;
        z-index: 51;
        text-align:center;
        font-size:32px;
        color:#ffffff;
        font-family: 'Yellowtail', cursive;
    }
    </style>
  <script src="http://ajax.googleapis.com/ajax/libs/jquery/1.7.2/
jquery.min.js"></script>
    <script src="http://maps.googleapis.com/maps/api/js?key=AIzaSy
Bp8gVrtxUC2Ynjwqox7I0dxrqjtCYim-8&sensor=false"></script>
    <script src="https://www.google.com/jsapi"></script>

    <script src="./10.05.travel.js"></script>
  </head>
  <body>
    <div id="map"></div>
  </body>
</html>
```

2. Time to move to the JavaScript file, `10.05.travel.js`. We will start by initiating the visualization library and storing a global map variable.

```
 google.load('visualization', '1.0');
google.setOnLoadCallback(init);
```

3. var map; When the `init` function is triggered, the map is loaded and it triggers the loading of a Google spreadsheet in which we will store all of my friend's travel information.

```
function init() {
  var BASE_CENTER = new google.maps.LatL
ng(48.516817734860105,13.005318750000015 );

  map = new google.maps.Map(document.getElementById("map"),{
    center: BASE_CENTER,
    mapTypeId: google.maps.MapTypeId.SATELLITE,
    disableDefaultUI: true,

  });
```

```
  var query = new google.visualization.Query(
      'https://spreadsheets.google.com/tq?key=0Aldzs55s0XbDdERJVlY
yWFJISFN3cjlqU1JnTGpOdHc');
    query.send(onTripDataReady);

}
```

4. When the document is loaded, it will trigger the `onTripDataReady` listener. When that happens, we will want to create a new `GoogleMapTraveler` object (a custom class for managing our experience).

```
function onTripDataReady(response){
  var gmt = new GoogleMapTraveler(response.g.D,map);
}
```

5. The constructor method of the `GoogleMapTraveler` object will prepare our variables, create a new `Animator` object, a `Traveler` object and a new `google.maps.Polyline` object, and will trigger the creation of the first travel point by calling the `nextPathPoint` method.

```
function GoogleMapTraveler(aData,map){
  this.latLong; //will be used to store current location
  this.zoomLevel; //to store current zoom level
  this.currentIndex=0;
  this.data = aData; //locations
  this.map = map;

  //this.setPosition(0,2);
  this.animator = new Animator(30);

  this.pathPoints = [this.getPosition(0,1)]; //start with two
points at same place.

  var lineSymbol = {
        path: 'M 0,-1 0,1',
        strokeOpacity: .6,
        scale: 2
    };

    this.lines = new google.maps.Polyline({
        path: this.pathPoints,
        strokeOpacity: 0,
        strokeColor: "#FF0000",
        icons: [{
          icon: lineSymbol,
          offset: '0',
          repeat: '20px'
```

```
        }],
        map: map
      });

    this.traveler = new Traveler(this.map,this.getPosition(0,1));
    this.nextPathPoint(1);

  }
```

6. The `getPosition` method is a very smart, small method that enables us to create a new `google.maps.LatLng` object each time it's called and to create a point based on an average of points or based on one item.

```
    GoogleMapTraveler.prototype.getPosition = function
  (index,amount){
    var lat=0;
    var lng=0;
    for(var i=0; i<amount; i++){
      lat+= parseFloat(this.data[index+i].c[0].v);
      lng+= parseFloat(this.data[index+i].c[1].v);

    }
    var ll=new google.maps.LatLng(
              lat/amount,
              lng/amount);
    return ll;
  }
```

7. We want to be able to set the position of our traveler, and as such we will want to create a `setPosition` method as well.

```
  GoogleMapTraveler.prototype.setPosition = function(index,amount){
    this.currentFocus = index;

    var lat=0;
    var lng=0;
    for(var i=0; i<amount; i++){
      lat+= parseFloat(this.data[index+i].c[0].v);
      lng+= parseFloat(this.data[index+i].c[1].v);

    }
    var ll=new google.maps.LatLng(
              lat/amount,
              lng/amount);

    if(this.data[index].c[2])this.map.setZoom(this.
  data[index].c[2].v);
    this.map.setCenter(ll);

  }
```

8. In the heart of our application is the ability to automatically move from one step to the next. This logic is applied using our `Animator` object in combination with the `nextPathPoint` method:

```
GoogleMapTraveler.prototype.nextPathPoint = function(index){
  this.setPosition(index-1,2);
  this.pathPoints.push(this.getPosition(index-1,1)); //add last
point again
  var currentPoint = this.pathPoints[this.pathPoints.length-1];
  var point = this.getPosition(index,1);

  //console.log(index,currentPoint,point,this.
getPosition(index,1));
  this.animator.add(currentPoint,"Za",currentPoint.Za,point.Za,1);
  this.animator.add(currentPoint,"Ya",currentPoint.Ya,point.Ya,1);
  this.animator.add(this.traveler.ll,"Za",this.traveler.
ll.Za,point.Za,2,0.75);
  this.animator.add(this.traveler.ll,"Ya",this.traveler.
ll.Ya,point.Ya,2,0.75);

  this.animator.onUpdate = this.bind(this,this.renderLine);
  this.animator.onComplete = this.bind(this,this.
  showOverlayCopy);//show copy after getting to destination
}
```

9. There are two callbacks that are triggered through our `Animator` object (they're highlighted in the preceding code snippet). It is time to create the logic that updates the information on our `onUpdate` callback. Let's take a peek at the `renderLine` method.

```
GoogleMapTraveler.prototype.renderLine = function(){
  this.lines.setPath(this.pathPoints);
  if(this.traveler.isReady)this.traveler.refreshPosition();
}
```

10. In the next step, when the animation is complete, it triggers our overlay logic. The overlay logic is very simple; if there is text in the Google document, in the fifth column, we will darken the screen and type it out. If there is no text, we will skip this step and go right to the next step that is in the `hideOverlayCopy` method that triggers the next travel point (the next line in the spreadsheet).

11. Our previous method of the `GoogleMapTraveler` object is the `bind` method. We already created this `bind` method in the *Moving to an OOP perspective* recipe in *Chapter 6, Bringing Static Things to Life*; as such, we will not elaborate on it further.

```
GoogleMapTraveler.prototype.bind = function(scope, fun){
   return function () {
        fun.apply(scope, arguments);
    };
}
```

12. Create the `Traveler` class. The `Traveler` class will be based on the work we did in the *Customizing the look and feel of markers* recipe in this chapter, only this time it will be an animating marker.

```
function Traveler(map,ll) {
  this.ll = ll;
    this.radius = 15;
    this.innerRadius = 10;
    this.glowDirection = -1;
    this.setMap(map);
    this.isReady = false;

  }

  Traveler.prototype = new google.maps.OverlayView();

  Traveler.prototype.onAdd = function() {
  this.div = document.createElement("DIV");
  this.canvasBG = document.createElement("CANVAS");
    this.canvasBG.width = this.radius*2;
  this.canvasBG.height = this.radius*2;
  this.canvasFG = document.createElement("CANVAS");
    this.canvasFG.width = this.radius*2;
  this.canvasFG.height = this.radius*2;

  this.div.style.border = "none";
  this.div.style.borderWidth = "0px";
  this.div.style.position = "absolute";

  this.canvasBG.style.position = "absolute";
  this.canvasFG.style.position = "absolute";


  this.div.appendChild(this.canvasBG);
  this.div.appendChild(this.canvasFG);


    this.contextBG = this.canvasBG.getContext("2d");
    this.contextFG = this.canvasFG.getContext("2d");

  var panes = this.getPanes();
    panes.overlayLayer.appendChild(this.div);

  }

  Traveler.prototype.draw = function() {
    var radius = this.radius;
```

```
      var context = this.contextBG;

    context.fillStyle = "rgba(73,154,219,.4)";
    context.beginPath();
      context.arc(radius,radius, radius, 0, Math.PI*2, true);
    context.closePath();
    context.fill();

    context = this.contextFG;
    context.fillStyle = "rgb(73,154,219)";
    context.beginPath();
      context.arc(radius,radius, this.innerRadius, 0, Math.PI*2,
  true);
    context.closePath();
    context.fill();

      var projection = this.getProjection();

      this.updatePosition(this.ll);
      this.canvasBG.style.opacity = 1;
      this.glowUpdate(this);
      setInterval(this.glowUpdate,100,this);
      this.isReady = true;

    };

    Traveler.prototype.refreshPosition=function(){
      this.updatePosition(this.ll);
    }

    Traveler.prototype.updatePosition=function(latlng){
      var radius = this.radius;
      var projection = this.getProjection();
    var point = projection.fromLatLngToDivPixel(latlng);
      this.div.style.left = (point.x - radius) + 'px';
      this.div.style.top = (point.y - radius) + 'px';
    }

    Traveler.prototype.glowUpdate=function(scope){ //endless loop
      scope.canvasBG.style.opacity = parseFloat(scope.canvasBG.
  style.opacity) + scope.glowDirection*.04;
      if(scope.glowDirection==1 && scope.canvasBG.style.opacity>=1)
  scope.glowDirection=-1;
      if(scope.glowDirection==-1 && scope.canvasBG.style.
  opacity<=0.1) scope.glowDirection=1;
    }
```

13. We will grab the `Animator` class created in the *Animating independent layers* recipe in *Chapter 6, Bringing Static Things to Life*, and tweak it (changes are highlighted in the code snippet).

```
function Animator(refreshRate){
  this.onUpdate = function(){};
  this.onComplete = function(){};
  this.animQue = [];
  this.refreshRate = refreshRate || 35; //if nothing set 35 FPS
  this.interval = 0;
}

Animator.prototype.add = function(obj,property,
from,to,time,delay){
  obj[property] = from;

  this.animQue.push({obj:obj,
            p:property,
            crt:from,
            to:to,
            stepSize: (to-from)/(time*1000/this.refreshRate),
            delay:delay*1000 || 0});

  if(!this.interval){ //only start interval if not running already
    this.interval = setInterval(this._animate,this.
refreshRate,this);
  }

}


Animator.prototype._animate = function(scope){
  var obj;
  var data;

  for(var i=0; i<scope.animQue.length; i++){
      data = scope.animQue[i];

      if(data.delay>0){
        data.delay-=scope.refreshRate;
      }else{
        obj = data.obj;
     if((data.stepSize>0 && data.crt<data.to) ||
        (data.stepSize<0 && data.crt>data.to)){

          data.crt = data.crt + data.stepSize;
          obj[data.p] = data.crt;
```

```
            }else{
              obj[data.p] = data.to;
              scope.animQue.splice(i,1);
              --i;
            }
          }

      }
    scope.onUpdate();
      if(  scope.animQue.length==0){
        clearInterval(scope.interval);
        scope.interval = 0; //reset interval variable
     scope.onComplete();
      }
    }
```

When you load the HTML file, you will find a fullscreen map that is getting its directions from a spreadsheet. It will animate and show you the paths my friend took as he traveled from Israel to South America and back.

How it works...

There are many components in this example, but we will focus mainly on the new steps that we haven't covered in any other part of this book.

The first new thing we meet is right in our HTML and CSS:

```
<link href='http://fonts.googleapis.com/css?family=Yellowtail'
rel='stylesheet' type='text/css'>
```

We picked a font from the Google font library at `http://www.google.com/webfonts` and integrated it into the text overlays.

```
.overlayBox {
       ...
        font-family: 'Yellowtail', cursive;
    }
```

It is time to travel into our JavaScript file, which we start by loading in the Google Visualization Library. It's the same library we were working with in *Chapter 8, Playing with Google Charts*. Once it's loaded, the `init` function is triggered. The `init` function starts our map up and starts loading in the spreadsheet.

In the *Changing data source to Google spreadsheet* recipe in *Chapter 8, Playing with Google Charts*, we worked with Google spreadsheets for the first time. There you learned all the steps involved with preparing and adding a Google chart into the Google visualization. In our case, we created a chart that contains line by line all the areas through which my friend traveled.

Oren and the South

File Edit View Insert Format Data Tools Help All changes saved

fx sorry to disapoint you, but that was the last one because my flight is tomorrow from a city near by..

	A	B	C	D	E	F	G
1	lat	long	zoom level	name	type	comments	image
2	31.759978	35.217247	10	harakevet, jerusalem,		Call me when you wake up!	
3	32.005453	34.874194	4	TLV ben gurion airport	Shuttle	I was right over your house!!! Thrilling!!! Philadelphia looks interesting from the airport.	
4	39.874589	-75.243842	5	philidelpya AIR PORT	Plane	We had sugar glazed donut and 'small' american coffee. All well branded.	
5	21.155872	-86.799344	6	Cancun Imperial Las Perlas	Plane		
6	20.623367	-87.075192	8	Playa Del Carmen - Hotel Hacienda Del Caribe	Bus	How is it going? Anything new with arrangements of the movings? Now I'm at playa del Carmen. Amazing place.	
7	20.508984	-86.949907		5a Av. Sur 141, Centro, Cozumel, Quintana Roo, Mexico	Ferry	5a Av. Sur 141... This is where I am	
8	20.625414	-87.079286		Playa Del Carmen	Ferry		
9				1a. Poniente Norte (Abasolo) 29, Centro, 29960			

The exception in this case is that we don't want to feed our URL into a Google chart, but instead we want to work with it directly. To do that we will use one of Google's API interfaces, the `google.visualization.Query` object:

```
var query = new google.visualization.Query(
      'https://spreadsheets.google.com/tq?key=0Aldzs55s0XbDdERJVlYyWFJ
ISFN3cjlqU1JnTGpOdHc');
    query.send(onTripDataReady);
```

The next step is to create our `GoogleMapTraveler` object. The Google map traveler is a new way for us to work with Google Maps. It doesn't extend any built-in feature of Google maps but is instead a hub for all the other ideas we created in the past. It is used as a manager hub for the marker, called Traveler, that we will create soon and the `google.maps.Polyline` object that enables us to draw lines on the map.

Instead of having a very static line appearance, let's create a reveal effect for new lines that are added to the Google map. To achieve that, we need a way to update the polyline every few milliseconds to create an animation. From the get go, I know the start point and the destination point as I get that information from the Google spreadsheet created earlier.

The idea is very simple even though in a very complex ecosystem. The idea is to have an array that will store all the latitude/longitude points. This would then be fed into the `this.line` object every time we wanted to update our screen.

The heart of the logic in this application is stored within this line of code:

```
this.nextPathPoint(1);
```

It will start a recursive journey throughout all of the points in our chart.

There's more...

Let's take a deeper look at the logic behind the `GoogleMapTraveler.prototype.nextPathPoint` method. The first thing we do in this function is to set our map view.

```
this.setPosition(index-1,2);
```

The `setPosition` method does a few things that are all related to repositioning our map and our zoom level based on the data in the current index that is sent. It's a bit smarter than that as it takes in a second parameter that enables it to average out two points. As one travels between two points, it would be best if our map is at the center of the two points. That is done by sending in `2` as the second parameter. The internal logic of the `setPosition` method is simple. It will loop through as many items as it needs to, to average out the right location.

Next, we add a new point to our `this.pathPoints` array. We start by duplicating the same point that is already in the array, as we want our new second point to start from the starting point. This way, we can update the last value in our array each time, until it reaches the end goal (of the real next point).

```
this.pathPoints.push(this.getPosition(index-1,1)); //add last point
again
```

We create a few helper variables. One will point to the new object we just created and pushed into our `pathPoints` array. And the second is the point that we want to reach at the end of our animation.

```
var currentPoint = this.pathPoints[this.pathPoints.length-1];
var point = this.getPosition(index,1);
```

The first variable is not a new object but a reference to the last point created, and the second line is a new object.

Our next step will be to start and animate the values of our `currentPoint` until it reaches the values in the `point` object and to update our traveler latitude/longitude information until it reaches its destination as well. We give a delay of 0.75 seconds to our second animation to keep things more interesting.

```
this.animator.add(currentPoint,"Za",currentPoint.Za,point.Za,1);
this.animator.add(currentPoint,"Ya",currentPoint.Ya,point.Ya,1);
this.animator.add(this.traveler.ll,"Za",this.traveler.ll.Za,point.
Za,2,0.75);
this.animator.add(this.traveler.ll,"Ya",this.traveler.ll.Ya,point.
Ya,2,0.75);
```

Before we end this method, we want to actually animate our lines. Right now, we are animating two objects that are not visual. To start animating our visual elements, we will listen to updates till the time we complete the animations.

```
this.animator.onUpdate = this.bind(this,this.renderLine);
  this.animator.onComplete = this.bind(this,this.showOverlayCopy);//
show copy after getting to destination
```

Each time the animation happens, we update the values of our visual elements in the `renderLine` method.

To avoid getting runtime errors, we added to the traveler marker an `isReady` Boolean to indicate to us when our element is ready to be drawn into.

```
this.lines.setPath(this.pathPoints);
if(this.traveler.isReady)this.traveler.refreshPosition();
```

When the animation completes, we move to the `showOverlayCopy` method, where we take over the screen and animate the copy in the same strategy as we've done before. This time around, when we are done with this phase, we will trigger our initial function again and start the cycle all over with an updated index.

```
GoogleMapTraveler.prototype.hideOverlayCopy = function(){
  //update index now that we are done with initial element
  this.currentIndex++;
  ...

  //as long as the slide is not over go to the next.
  if(this.data.length>this.currentIndex+1)this.nextPathPoint(this.
currentIndex+1);
}
```

That covers the heart of our build. It's time for us to talk briefly about the two other classes that will help create this application.

Understanding the Traveler marker

We will not dig deeply into this class, as for the most part, it's based on the work we did in the previous recipe, *Customizing the look and feel of markers*. The biggest difference is that we added internal animation to our element and an `updatePosition` method that enables us to move our marker around whenever we want to move it.

```
Traveler.prototype.updatePosition=function(latlng){
   var radius = this.radius;
   var projection = this.getProjection();
 var point = projection.fromLatLngToDivPixel(latlng);
   this.div.style.left = (point.x - radius) + 'px';
   this.div.style.top = (point.y - radius) + 'px';
 }
```

This method gets a latitude and longitude and updates the marker's position.

As we are animating the actual `ll` object of this object in the main class, we added a second method, `refreshPosition`, which is called each time the animations are updated.

```
Traveler.prototype.refreshPosition=function(){
   this.updatePosition(this.ll);
 }
```

There is more to explore and find in this class, but I'll leave that for you to have some fun.

Updating the Animator object

We made two major updates to our `Animator` class, which was originally created in the *Animating independent layers* recipe in *Chapter 6, Bringing Static Things to Life*. The first change was integrating callback methods. The idea of a callback is very similar to events. Callbacks enable us to call a function when something happens. This way of working enables us to only have one listener at a time. To do this, we start by creating the two following variables that are our callback functions:

```
function Animator(refreshRate){
  this.onUpdate = function(){};
  this.onComplete = function(){};
```

We then trigger both functions in the `Animator` class in their relevant location (on update or on complete). In our `GoogleMapTraveler` object, we override the default functions with functions that are internal to the `GoogleMapTraveler` object.

Our second and last major update to the `Animator` object is that we added smarter, more detailed logic to enable our animator to animate both to positive and negative areas. Our original animation didn't accommodate animating latitude/longitude values, and as such we tweaked the core animation logic.

This covers the major new things we explored in this recipe. This recipe is jam-packed with many other small things we picked up throughout the chapters. I truly hope you've enjoyed this journey with me, as this is the end of our book. Please feel free to share with me your work and insight. You can find me at `http://02geek.com` and my e-mail is `ben@02geek.com`.

Index

Symbols

A

B

C

D

E

F

I

J

L

M

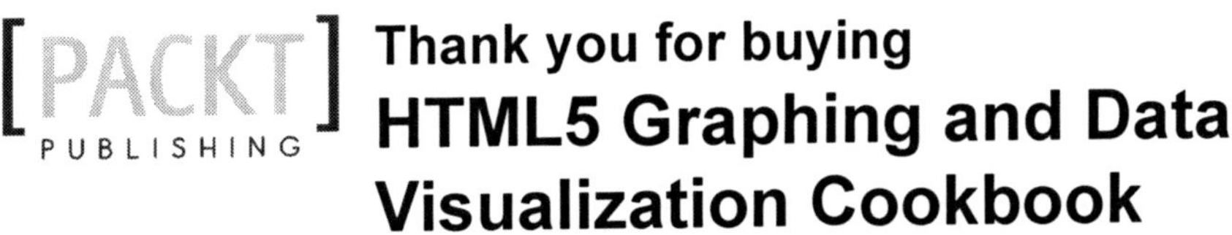

[PACKT] PUBLISHING
Thank you for buying
HTML5 Graphing and Data
Visualization Cookbook

About Packt Publishing

Packt, pronounced 'packed', published its first book "*Mastering phpMyAdmin for Effective MySQL Management*" in April 2004 and subsequently continued to specialize in publishing highly focused books on specific technologies and solutions.

Our books and publications share the experiences of your fellow IT professionals in adapting and customizing today's systems, applications, and frameworks. Our solution based books give you the knowledge and power to customize the software and technologies you're using to get the job done. Packt books are more specific and less general than the IT books you have seen in the past. Our unique business model allows us to bring you more focused information, giving you more of what you need to know, and less of what you don't.

Packt is a modern, yet unique publishing company, which focuses on producing quality, cutting-edge books for communities of developers, administrators, and newbies alike. For more information, please visit our website: `www.packtpub.com`.

Writing for Packt

We welcome all inquiries from people who are interested in authoring. Book proposals should be sent to `author@packtpub.com`. If your book idea is still at an early stage and you would like to discuss it first before writing a formal book proposal, contact us; one of our commissioning editors will get in touch with you.

We're not just looking for published authors; if you have strong technical skills but no writing experience, our experienced editors can help you develop a writing career, or simply get some additional reward for your expertise.

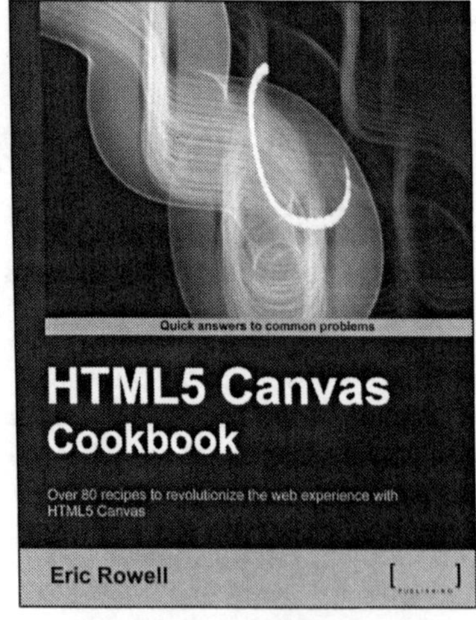

HTML5 Canvas Cookbook

ISBN: 978-1-849691-36-9 Paperback: 348 pages

Over 80 recipes to revolutionize the web experience with HTML5 Canvas

1. The quickest way to get up to speed with HTML5 Canvas application and game development
2. Create stunning 3D visualizations and games without Flash
3. Written in a modern, unobtrusive, and objected oriented JavaScript style so that the code can be reused in your own applications.
4. Part of Packt's Cookbook series: Each recipe is a carefully organized sequence of instructions to complete the task as efficiently as possible

---

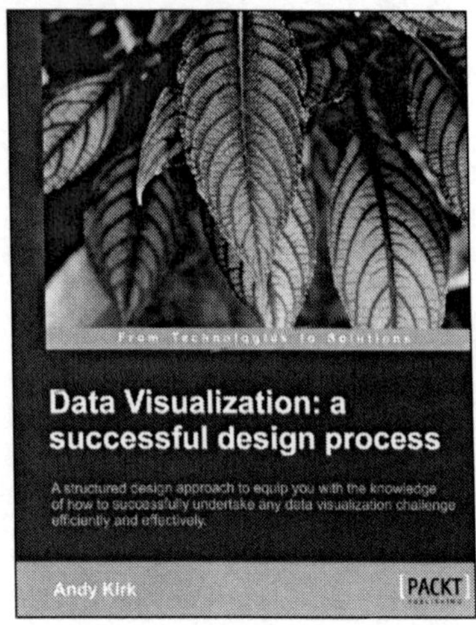

Data Visualization: a successful design process

ISBN: 978-1-849693-46-2 Paperback: 96 pages

A structured design approach to equip you with the knowledge of how to successfully undertake any data visualization challenge efficiently and effectively.

1. A portable, versatile and flexible data visualization design approach that will help you navigate the complex path towards success
2. Explains the many different reasons for creating visualizations and identifies the key parameters which lead to very different design options
3. Thorough explanation of the many visual variables and visualization taxonomy to provide you with a menu of creative options

Please check **www.PacktPub.com** for information on our titles

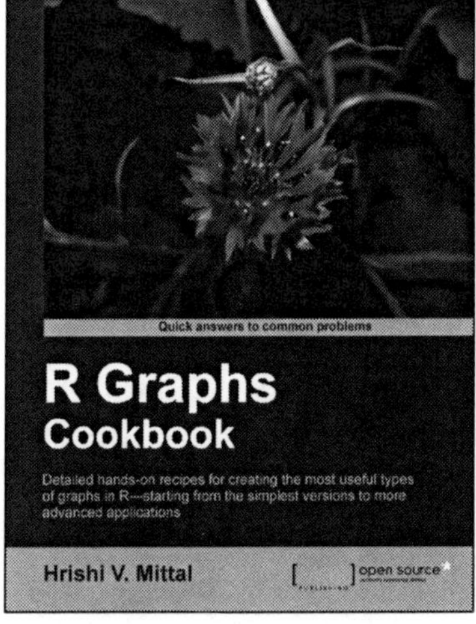

R Graphs Cookbook

ISBN: 978-1-849513-06-7 Paperback: 272 pages

Detailed hands-on recipes for creating the most useful types of graphs in R—starting from the simplest versions to more advanced applications

1. Learn to draw any type of graph or visual data representation in R
2. Filled with practical tips and techniques for creating any type of graph you need; not just theoretical explanations
3. All examples are accompanied with the corresponding graph images, so you know what the results look like

---

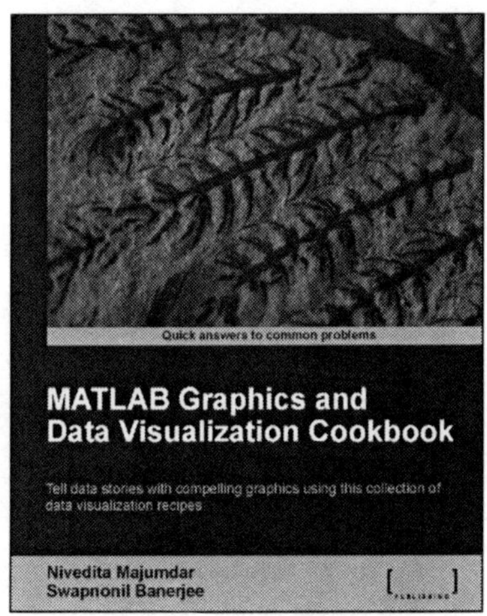

MATLAB Graphics and Data Visualization Cookbook

ISBN: 978-1-849693-16-5 Paperback: 350 pages

Tell data stories with compelling graphics using this collection of data visualization recipes

1. Collection of data visualization recipes with functionalized versions of common tasks for easy integration into your data analysis workflow
2. Recipes cross-referenced with MATLAB product pages and MATLAB Central File Exchange resources for improved coverage
3. Includes hand created indices to find exactly what you need; such as application driven, or functionality driven solutions

Please check **www.PacktPub.com** for information on our titles

Lightning Source UK Ltd.
Milton Keynes UK
UKOW050038250513

211227UK00003B/35/P